# BARBARA B

Dr. Brown maintains a biofeedback laboratory at the Sepulveda Veterans Hospital in California and is associated with the UCLA Medical School. In great demand as a lecturer, she conducts seminars in universities all over the United States. "Nearly every living human being is a potential candidate for biofeedback," she says. "The techniques and goals of biofeedback are to *stay* well as much as to *get* well."

The world-famous authority on stress, Dr. Hans Selye, says of *Stress and the Art of Biofeedback:* "It is a unique and major accomplishment . . . I feel that I have learned a great deal about this promising new field . . . and hope that many other readers will derive a similar benefit from its study."

# STRESS AND THE ART OF BIOFEEDBACK

BARBARA B. BROWN

FOREWORD BY HANS SELYE

BANTAM BOOKS
TORONTO · NEW YORK · LONDON

STRESS AND THE ART OF BIOFEEDBACK
*A Bantam Book*

*PRINTING HISTORY*
*Harper & Row edition published February 1977*
*2nd printing ....................... February 1977*
*Bantam edition / January 1978*

*Bantam Books are published by Bantam Books, Inc. Its trade-
mark, consisting of the words "Bantam Books" and the por-
trayal of a bantam, is registered in the United States Patent
Office and in other countries. Marca Registrada. Bantam
Books, Inc., 666 Fifth Avenue, New York, New York 10019.*

PRINTED IN THE UNITED STATES OF AMERICA

# CONTENTS

clinical EEG biofeedback . . . Alpha biofeedback
in neuroses, psychoses, and behavior problems
. . . Alpha biofeedback and pain . . . Critique of
study as example of current inadequacies in the
art of alpha biofeedback . . . Insomnia . . . Epilepsy . . . Evolving uses for EEG biofeedback:
(1) Shifting dominant EEG activity between the
hemispheres . . . (2) Promoting empathy . . . (3)
As a meditation aid

   *Therapist's tasks for the biofeedback treatment
   sessions:* The introductory session . . . First, or
   first several, biofeedback training sessions . . .
   Subsequent biofeedback training sessions . . .
   Final series
   *Implementing the training sessions:* The introductory session . . . Importance of set and setting
   . . . Patient's record keeping . . . Relaxation
   techniques . . . Home exercises . . . Physiologic
   and psychologic testing . . . The biofeedback
   psychologic interview . . . Record keeping for
   the clinic

# FOREWORD

In the exact sciences such as mathematics, physics, and chemistry important breakthroughs can often be traced to a single creative act of one investigator. Original discoveries are usually due to an unplanned intuitive flash which happens to occur in a prepared mind that can appreciate its potentialities before others are aware of it. Logical planning by Bacon's "scientific method" plays no role here. It is only subsequently that a multitude of highly trained experts are required for the development of the discovery so as to make it generally known, acceptable, and useful.

Even in the less exact science of somatic medicine some important discoveries can be more or less clearly traced to a single source, for example the discovery of the pathogen responsible for a disease, a new drug, or a subcellular particle. However, there are almost always some vague precursors without which the discovery could not have been made. In any event, the original ingenious hunch would never suffice to make a substantial addition to the understanding or cure of disease without the subsequent purely intellectual application of the scientific method, aided by knowledge, laboratory facilities, and patient, often monotonous work on the part of countless individuals who complete the discovery by its development.

In the case of new concepts in philosophy, theology, psychology, sociology, or even the life sciences this historic sequence is comparatively rare. Here, and particularly in the concepts of biofeedback and stress with which this volume is concerned, we may say that almost invariably the sequence of evolution is the reverse. Usually some vague realization of the concept goes back so far in history and its authors are so numerous that by the time it is generally accepted, we can no longer identify the origins of the idea with any degree of precision. It is only the confluence of scattered data—the creative act—that can gather them into a powerful river, a major stream of thought of such proportions that it can act as a receptacle and outlet which gives direction to innumerable additional tributaries.

In such cases, we are tempted to speak of a "critical mass" that must be achieved by someone sometime whom we then justly call the "discoverer," although innumerable predecessors may have seen bits and pieces that were not yet viable in themselves. In other words, here the discoverer is the scientist who discovered the subject not for the first time, but more than anybody else.

Discoveries of this type are by no means the least important. Far from it. The greatest progresses in science come from people who look at things that many people have seen before and make of them a majestic picture that no one has ever seen.

As Dr. Brown is so careful to point out in this book, biofeedback has many precursors going back to Hindu gurus and fakirs, but I think we can say that she, more than anyone else, has discovered it by giving it the "critical mass" required to transform the previously vague concept into a generally accepted approach to psychotherapy. Thanks to her it was sufficiently strengthened by objective scientific data to serve as a self-perpetuating field of research, continuously enlarged by the work of many investigators throughout the world.

*Stress and the Art of Biofeedback* provides us with an authoritative text not only about biofeedback but also about its relationship to what I have called "biologic stress" and many of the stress-induced diseases of adaptation, such as hypertension, muscular dysfunction, gastrointestinal derangements, and various nervous disturbances.

Here we also find precise outlines of related concepts and psychotherapeutic measures such as Autogenic Training, Progressive Relaxation, Transcendental Meditation, operant conditioning, Zen, yoga, and other techniques which elicit a relaxation response so important in combating psychogenic stress. The book is written as much as a guide for the therapist as it is for the patient, who should know as much about the theory and practice of biofeedback as possible in order to derive maximal benefits from it.

Biofeedback is essentially a nonspecific therapy, a technique for the mastery of psychogenic stress by bringing into awareness certain stress indices such as changes in heart rate, a rise in blood pressure, muscular tension, or any combination of these. Thus, we can learn how to control stress itself, to a considerable extent, by becoming aware of its intensity and avoiding the danger of exceeding our natural stress level. I feel that the author admirably achieves her objective of clarifying this process and, hence, the title she chose is most suitable. Little, perhaps, has been said here about stress itself or other means of combating psychogenic stress, for example, through a code of behavior, or the treatment of stress-related diseases by pharmacologic means. For that, however, there are other sources of information which the author quotes at some length among her references.

The volume offers a technique for the symptomatic treatment of one of the most important types of stress in man, who (because of his highly developed central nervous system) tends to respond defensively, but often inappropriately, to all kinds of threats and desires, primarily through his central nervous system. It is a unique and major accomplishment to have succeeded in summarizing a literature on biofeedback which, Dr. Brown tells us, now comprises about 2,000 references in a well-structured single volume; it could hardly be expected that she should do the same for the more than 110,000 references on various other aspects of stress and the diseases of adaptation.

It was a great pleasure to have been invited to write a foreword for *Stress and the Art of Biofeedback*. Despite my long-time association with stress as such, my knowledge of biofeedback was quite rudimentary when I started to read the volume; I feel that I have learned

a great deal about this promising new field and hope
that many other readers will derive a similar benefit
from its study.

*Université de Montréal*                    —HANS SELYE
*1976*

# SPECIAL NOTE TO THE READER

It is often in medicine and psychotherapy that the details of diagnosis or treatment procedures are shared with the patient, or an accounting is made of the intimacies of body or mind changes before, during, and after treatment. There is, however, growing evidence that medical and psychological approaches to the treatment of human ills are changing. More and more it is recognized that human beings possess inherent capabilities both to prevent illness and to restore health when illness occurs.

During the past ten years, medical and psychological insights have converged in the realization that the more understanding and information a person has about his illness or his predispositions toward illness, the more he knows about how his body functions and how to prevent and cure illness, the better he realizes his capabilities to achieve and maintain his own well-being. A large part of this new understanding about relationships between human abilities and their role in health and illness is being formalized in the new therapeutic approach called biofeedback.

Nearly every living human being is a potential candidate for biofeedback. The techniques and goals of biofeedback are to stay well as much as to get well. It is an unsuual process because it is a self-helping "treatment," dependent upon patient, or more properly, person involvement. The benefits of biofeedback depend upon a working relationship between therapist and patient; more precisely, between the person who has knowledge about biofeedback and the person who is learning to work with and control or normalize his own body physiology and emotional reactions. Biofeedback is, moreover, useful also (with supervision) for the individual who wishes to pursue exploring awareness of internal states, much as the yogi does, for better understanding of the self.

These are new concepts for patient and doctor, and for every individual concerned with his physical and mental health. Now that biofeedback is emerging as an important new direction in medicine and psychology, there is a need to provide both nonprofessionals and professionals with information and insights about their new roles in medical therapeutics and psychotherapy. Physicians have had little formal experience in psychological techniques despite a deep awareness of their importance, and further, they have not had available comprehensive information about practical, clinical biofeedback. *Stress and the Art of Biofeedback* is thus intended to provide clinicians not only with a survey of biofeedback uses and techniques, but it is equally intended to describe ways of implementing the changing role of the patient.

There is a great deal of biofeedback that is new also to the psychotherapist and psychiatrist. Because the emphasis of biofeedback is on body responses to emotion and the role of mental processes, in this book I have attempted to synthesize these aspects toward a psychobiological treatment approach useful in these therapeutic disciplines. And finally, because the effectiveness of biofeedback depends so much upon the participation of the individual, *Stress and the Art of Biofeedback* is for interested nonprofessionals as well.

The dramatically new involvements and relationships among health professionals and patients or prospective patients mean that they all need pretty much the same kind of information about biofeedback. I have attempted to provide the justifications, logic, evidence, and guidelines for the clinical practice of biofeedback, while at the same time describing the role and responsibilities of the patient. The general reader, the interested nonprofessional, should not be concerned by the few technical details necessary for the clinician, and should feel free to skip or skim these. The technical material occurs mainly in the first two short sections of

Chapter 3, the short Chapter 4, and in the appendixes, except for Appendix 1, which is for the general reader. Other material about biofeedback for the general reader is available in *New Mind, New Body*,

# WHAT IS BIOFEEDBACK?

The emergence of a new medical perspective . . .
Biofeedback as a new therapeutic model . . .
The nature of biofeedback . . . Changing medical
beliefs . . . Biofeedback and changing doctor-patient
roles . . . Information and the biofeedback learning
process . . . The role of the therapist: his problems
in biofeedback . . . The therapist's functions in biofeedback therapy . . . The patient's role in biofeedback: his problems . . . The patient's functions . . .
The patient learns to control body functions . . . Concepts of biofeedback . . . Why is biofeedback different? What is new in the biofeedback process? . . .
For medicine and psychology: the ethical issues

## The Emergence of a New Medical Perspective

The world of stress is very much with us. Books,
magazines, radio and TV fill the media with reports on
stress. The media are satisfying a need, the need of a
fast-paced society suddenly aware that mind and body
distresses seem somehow connected to the frustrations
and exasperations of social survival. Pop psychology,
with its emphasis on interacting and asserting, is giving
way to a broader realism of understanding the concept
of self and individual accountability. Psychologists are
evolving new ideas and new techniques for self-realiza-
tion, for coping, for exploring one's own consciousness. Eastern religions for knowing the inner being are
being embraced by growing numbers of seekers, and
many philosophical systems of the East are being lit-
eralized toward the more material goals and needs of

the West. Transcendental Meditation, for example, has invested an extraordinary effort in proving the beneficial chemistry of meditation and the usefulness of T.M. as an antidote to the stress of ordinary living.

Biomedical science has changed too. Paralleling the public's interest in mind and consciousness and relief from stress, biomedical and psychological scientists have been exploring the mind-body control systems. For the first time the materially oriented intellect of Western science is being satisfied that mind generated of brain is indeed a powerful controller of the health and illness of man. This new perspective is contained in the new word biofeedback, and in the realization that the mind-brain complex possesses a remedy for the distress of stress that is unique in the history of therapeutics.

Biofeedback is an unexampled process for treating human illnesses because it evokes complex mental processes to regulate and normalize even the most complicated functions of the human body. It is called biofeedback because its effects rest upon making information about biological activities, including those of the brain, available to the mind. And when the mind receives information about itself and its body, information about how it reacts to stress and how it can return to well-being, mental faculties of awareness and understanding and control are aroused to action. By some obscure capacity, cognitive faculties are set in motion to restore the mind and body to a state of balance and relieve the effects of stress.

Biofeedback is an unprecedented therapy. It is both psychological and medical. Its uses cover nearly the entire range of human emotional and physical disorders, and its uniqueness lies in the fact that the therapeutic process takes place in the mind-brain of the patient. It is the patient whose mind-brain does the work; the therapists and machines give him the right information and guide and assist him, but the process itself is a remarkable reversal of the patient-therapist roles. The implications of this role reversal are striking:

The patient is no longer the object of the treatment, he *is* the treatment.

## Biofeedback as a New Therapeutic Model

Even after the severest critical scientific reviews, biofeedback still appears to be the closest thing to a panacea ever discovered. Remarkably, it seems to have happened at the right time and in the right place. It happened at the peak of the social revolution of the '60s, and possibly was caused by it; and it happened in the United States, a country beset by problems of stress, by soaring medical costs, and a growing restlessness with therapeutic inefficiencies. The implications of the biofeedback phenomenon are so vast, there is no question but that it will stand as a landmark in changing attitudes about mind and body, about health and illness and about human consciousness. It has already successfully catalyzed a gamut of new attitudes: new attitudes about medical therapeutics and psychotherapy, new attitudes about mind and consciousness, and new attitudes about human abilities and the potential of the human mind.

Skim through this book and note the number of therapeutic applications of biofeedback. There are more than fifty major medical and psychological problems in which biofeedback has been used with either greater success than conventional treatments or at least with equal benefits. The mind and body ailments that respond to biofeedback treatment span the entire spectrum of illnesses human beings suffer: emotional, psychosomatic, and physical disabilities. This fact alone speaks to its importance as a fundamental phenomenon of man's nature.

Probably no discovery in medicine or psychology compares in breadth of applications or in scope of implications to the biofeedback phenomenon. More important than its multiple uses, more important perhaps than its apparent universality as a cerebral tool of man, is its potential for recasting therapeutics and therapies into new standards of practice in which individual man assumes, or at least shares, responsibility for his own health or illness.

## The Nature of Biofeedback

The field is too young to have developed a precise definition agreed upon by a body of scientists. A tentative definition is that biofeedback is the process or technique for learning voluntary control over automatically, reflexly regulated body functions. The term biofeedback was conceived as a shorthand expression to describe the process of "feeding back" physiological information to the individual generating the information.

The technique is essentially one in which a selected physiologic activity is monitored by an instrument which senses, by electrodes or transducers, signals of physiologic information about such body functions as heart rate, blood pressure, muscle tension, or brain waves. The sensed information is amplified, then used in the instrument to activate a display or signals that monitor, i.e., reflect changes in, the physiologic activity. The process is a bit like feeling the pulse, or taking the blood pressure or temperature, where the physiologic information is "sensed," and is translated into numbers, as beats per minute, or millimeters of mercury of blood pressure or degrees Fahrenheit. Although special instruments are not always necessary, the instruments developed especially for biofeedback are preferred because of their convenience and accuracy. Most of them have been designed so that the individual undergoing biofeedback training can see or hear (or both) the monitor of his selected biological activity more or less continuously. The light or tone monitors change with the normal fluctuations of physiological processes.

Although body temperature changes somewhat slowly, the average person can demonstrate to himself the biofeedback phenomenon by using an ordinary thermometer purchased from the drugstore or hardware store. One six to eight inches long and filled with red fluid is best. He can tape the thermometer bulb to the fat pad of the middle finger with masking tape, making sure of good contact, but no constriction of circulation. After five or so minutes of quiet sitting, preferably with the eyes closed, note the temperature of the finger. Then, while still sitting quietly, repeat a few autosuggestion phrases to yourself, slowly, such as, "I feel relaxed and warm," "My hand feels heavy," "My arm feels heavy," "My hand feels warm." "My hands feel warm and relaxed," "I feel calm and relaxed."[1] Repeat the phrases slowly, allowing the suggestion to take effect, then go on to the next one, and then repeat the series. Every five or ten minutes, take a reading of the finger temperature. Most people will show a rise in finger temperature after ten to twenty minutes, some increasing their finger temperature three to five or even ten degrees, some only a degree. Only a few may not change or may even show a small fall in finger temperature. With repeated practice, everyone can learn to increase finger temperature. By using mental activity.

This home demonstration shows all of the basic elements of biofeedback. There is the monitor of a physiologic function, the thermometer recording body temperature, which provides information about that particular body activity; there is an implicit intention to change body temperature; and, there is an as yet indescribable mental mechanism which exerts an effect on the physiologic activity. The result is voluntary control.

## Changing Medical Beliefs

For decades biomedical authority and psychophysiology have taught the doctrine that neither human beings nor animals could control those internal physiological activities of the body's vital functions. They were functions carried out by automatic control systems and by reflexes, beyond the control of mind.

---

1. See Appendix 1 for other autosuggestion phrases.

There was (and still is to many biomedical scientists) no such thing as mind, only brain, and certainly no such thing as mind over matter. Mind was an illusion about the mysteries of the brain.

The average person has always been more pragmatic than the denizens of ivory towers. The average person could rear his child to the reality of pain by saying "it's not bleeding, so it can't hurt," and it didn't hurt anymore. The average person caught on to sugar pills, and even when he suspected they were a placebo, he felt better, and he had an awareness that his body was benefitting by his beliefs. Or, if he travelled, he watched the Indian yogis control the most vital of their interior beings by slowing the heart beat or controlling breathing in closed boxes or thrusting the gut about and in and out of the body. The average person, revelling in the surprising whimsies of his mental self, has always known there was such a thing as mind, and that the mind could do wondrous things to its body and to itself.

But science is science, and it said, "prove it," and then became so busy with drugs and surgery on its one side and Freud and Jung on its other side, that it had little time to put the mind and body together, or to divine the complexities of mind from the biochemistry and electrical currents of the brain. Yet literally, all science had to do was look in the mirror.

And wink. Winking is such an obvious example of biofeedback, it's surprising that curiosity about it didn't touch off the biofeedback revolution long ago.

Winking is learned by biofeedback. It is the intervention (or more properly, supervention) of voluntary action over a reflex. Blinking is the reflex activity that ensures even distribution of moisture over the eyeball, a reflex performed automatically a thousand times a day, a reflex so vital to eye function that it is difficult *not* to blink. Yet we can also learn to control that reflex. Most people learn how to wink as youngsters, either by working with a mirror or with Mother. They get biofeedback information about what the eyelid is doing and whether it is moving correctly either as visual information from the mirror or auditory information from Mother. Then somehow, in the brain, this information is integrated with information coming in from tension sensors in the eyelid muscles, and sometimes with other information (such as from the sensations when muscles around the eye move), and the result is learning how to wink.

As a matter of fact, much the same process is used in learning how to drive a car or play tennis. Biofeedback, in the form of information about muscle tensions "sensed" (detected) internally by special nerve cells in muscles, is combined with visual information, and is used by processes of the central nervous system to make appropriate adjustment of the muscles to accomplish predetermined goals. This is what voluntary control is: a nebulous process of intentions and decisions to reach a goal of body performance projected in the mind's eye and convincingly recognized by both mind and body once the goal is realized. We *know* when we are performing an activity we projected even though we have never before experienced that particular bodymind state. Voluntary acts are those in which an activity of the mind-brain can change the physiologic activities of the body in a way that is based upon making decisions, establishing goals, and predetermining what the end result *should be*.[2]

Could the same voluntary control work with the more interior body functions, those that make the heart beat, or the blood pressure change, or even those mysterious electrical forces of the brain that reflect the mind? Until biofeedback the Western scientific answer was categorically no. After less than ten years of biofeedback research, the answer is categorically yes.

What has happened to change our medical and psychological thinking?

---

2. The same thing happens in the creative arts, including engineering or any thought activity. The conscious mind knows only that a certain *effect* is desired, but not what will produce that effect nor any idea of what the goal actually is. Yet the conscious mind recognizes exactly which created product fits the projection once it has been created. For example, an artist wishes to express some feeling in design. He works with perhaps hundreds of different designs and combinations, none expressing that vague, inexpressible feeling, then suddenly the designs fit together and he knows that is what he had in mind.

It has been, in fact, two new uses of biological information that have propelled biofeedback into both public and scientific prominence. The first is giving biological information *to* the patient instead of filing it only for the eyes of the physician or therapist. That is what the term biofeedback means: the "feeding back" of information about the body's physiologic activities to the person whose physiologic activity it is. Not unlike recent events with the CIA, biofeedback has declassified medically classified information. Now the patient can watch displays or hear sounds that monitor a selected body function; he can begin to know the actions of the interior being, much as he can watch and feel his body moving in tennis or writing or sewing.

The other use of biological information is the surprising effect of observing the flow of internal, biological events: that the patient, the average person as a patient, almost without knowing it, can use that information to change those biological events by an act of intention or decision.

He can, as hundreds of biofeedback studies have now demonstrated, learn to exert voluntary control over skin temperature, over heart rate, over blood pressure, over muscle tension, over brain waves, or over any internal biological function capable of being monitored. And he can learn how to normalize disturbed body activities.

Let me give an example. For reasons described elsewhere, my laboratory has devoted the past year to a study of what constitutes successful biofeedback treatment or therapy. One patient, referred by an internist friend and professor of medicine, suffered intensely from Raynaud's syndrome. This is a condition of severe constriction of blood vessels of the hand, and during acute attacks the hand becomes extremely painful, very cold and blue. The patient had a sympathectomy some time back,[3] but this had not relieved his condition, nor was any medication helpful.

---

3. The nerves governing the reflex constriction of the small blood vessels had been cut.

Our practice with new patients is first to conduct a full hour's chat about the meaning of biofeedback, what it means in terms of the patient's role, and how we as therapists can be helpful. We also stress that any benefits from the treatment are primarily up to the patient's subconscious use of the various kinds of information we can give him. We explained to this patient that we would use skin temperature feedback, and that the objective of the treatment was for him to learn to increase the temperature of his hand so that he could keep his hand temperature normal and increase it whenever it might fall because of stress or emotion. We emphasized the fact that *trying,* by making an effort, or by consciously attending to the hand, would not help him in the learning, and we told him that we would be standing by to help, to encourage, and to offer strategies.

The following day he was given his first temperature biofeedback treatment session. He knew he was to try, *passively,* to raise the temperature of his hand. He watched the temperature meter, and despite his agonizing desire, the temperature of his hand fell by 9 degrees Fahrenheit, and stayed there. Expectedly, he was dismayed and defeated. But unexpectedly, he returned for another treatment session. This time we casually put thermistors on *both* hands, but ignored the left hand, which was generally less painful. The patient focussed his attention on the right hand and again the temperature began dropping, although this time more slowly, and his hand discomfort increased. After about fifteen minutes we drew his attention to the temperature meter monitoring the temperature of the left hand. It had warmed up a few degrees. The patient began to understand. Despite instructions, despite the biofeedback information, effort made for failure; no-effort made for success. He was echoing his grandchildren when he said, "Oh, I see, you have to let it happen."

In his third biofeedback session he raised the temperature of his painful right hand 10 degrees Fahrenheit. The remainder of his treatment was practice, then finally training without the electronic thermometer to make sure he could control hand temperature at will, at home, under stress.[4]

In its main features, this is a typical case, and similar cases are being encountered by clinicians throughout the country.

Applications of the biofeedback principle seem almost limitless. The list on pages 65–66, for example, gives some of the disorders reported to have been successfully treated by muscle (EMG) biofeedback techniques. The list—for only one kind of biofeedback—reads like a list of uses for patent medicines. Yet the majority of these reports are by researchers or clinical investigators or by serious, even skeptical, general practitioners, or clinical psychologists, and dentists as well. Some reports show a high level of scientific expertise, some do not; some studies have been confirmed, some have not. For the larger picture, it makes little difference, for the science of biofeedback is young, and not all practitioners of the art are expert yet. Its adolescent state of ebullience mixed with inexperience is illustrated by a recent panel of dentists discussing the use of biofeedback in bruxism (grinding of the teeth). Two dental clinics reported excellent results, one even noting that they could not keep new patients out of the study (it was to be a limited number), while the third clinic reported little success because so many patients dropped out of the biofeedback treatment program.

Why? Perhaps because biofeedback is still an art, not yet an exact science. The difference between success and failure may have been due to differences in expertise, or enthusiasm, or even differences in attitudes. Or perhaps because the practice of biofeedback introduces quite new elements in therapy. Our scientific evidence to date indicates that the success of biofeedback treatment depends as much upon the patient as upon the therapist: the practice of biofeedback thus may mean a breaking of the traditional doctor-

---

4. I have omitted some details of the total treatment picture for this example, but a complete procedural prototype is presented in Chapter 9.

patient relationship, and breaking this may be more difficult for the doctor than the patient.

## Biofeedback and Changing Doctor-Patient Roles

Biofeedback is a partnership between patient and therapist. The key is communication, the exchange of information. In its simplest expression the doctor *gives* information and the patient *performs*. Biofeedback is most effective as a treatment when both patient and his doctor or therapist have a solid understanding of the biofeedback process, why it can be effective, what its critical elements are, and possibly most important, that they are working with a quite different human capability than either ever before believed existed. The concept about biofeedback that we Americans find so difficult to believe is that some totally unconscious yet complex, sophisticated mental process might be "supermind," that we may actually possess mental capabilities that can absorb information about internal states and use that information to bring internal functioning up to an optimal level. We find such a concept difficult to believe because our philosophy and our psychology say that to achieve anything, to conquer anything, takes effort, consciously directed hard work. We believe that we can't be productive unless we keep concentrating on our goals, attending, consciously directing our actions. Yet apparently the trick in biofeedback is to get the consciousness out of the picture, let the information pour in, and let whatever mental giant resides in the great unconscious use that information to put our body's activities aright without our conscious interference. It's part of the process Dr. Elmer Green (and Schultz before him) calls passive volition, or the process the free spirits use when they say "let it happen" and put their conscious awareness and direction and interference aside to let the good things happen.

As a therapeutic device, biofeedback entails a radically different doctor-patient relationship than is traditional. The reason for this is obvious: biofeedback therapy is a learning process. The patient must learn how to control his internal biology just as he has learned how to control his muscles to perform purposefully. The nature of the biofeedback learning process requires new perspectives on learning, for in biofeedback the entire learning process is internal and self-actuated. When the physiologic activity of interest is externalized in the form of the biofeedback signal, nothing more than relevant information and mental activity are needed to accomplish learning how to change that physiologic activity. Since the patient has little knowledge of either his internal body processes or of ways to control them, he must rely upon the therapist to provide appropriate information. The task of the doctor-therapist is to have a clear understanding of what kinds of information the patient needs to control internal activities and the circumstances under which the information can be most effectively used.

## Information and the Biofeedback Learning Process

If the biofeedback process is considered from the standpoint of the elements that facilitate learning, and thus positive therapeutic responses to biofeedback training, it can be reduced to a quite simple expression of requirements for successful biofeedback learning.

As I see the biofeedback process, it is solely dependent upon the kinds and quality and accuracy of the information provided. The *kinds* of information are:

1. Biological information, which is the biofeedback signal.
2. Cognitively useful information, which is background information that facilitates use of the biological information, i.e., what the physiologic activity does, how it behaves, how it is measured, what the instrument does, and other relevant information.
3. Strategy information, i.e., clues or directions for changing physiologic activity "by mental means."

4. Psychologically supporting information, which is encouragement and reinforcement of performance that acts to consolidate the learning experience.

5. Experiential information, which is the internally derived information from memories and from associations of the newly perceived information from the biofeedback signal with internally perceived changes in mind and body states.

When these kinds of information are optimally accurate and relevant, biofeedback learning can proceed with considerable efficiency. Thus, in biofeedback learning, and learning to control one's own biological activities, the learner must have access to the relevant information, and the "teacher" must provide the information. This is remarkably different from the traditional doctor-patient relationship, and it entails quite different problems and new functions for both the therapist and for the patient.

## The Role of the Therapist: His Problems in Biofeedback

The first problem that the biofeedback therapist faces is his new responsibility for imparting information to the patient. Traditionally, the therapist provides mainly judgmental information, considered opinions which his experience and education lead him to believe will assist the patient in his recovery.

Most therapists beginning to use biofeedback training quickly realize that the success of the treatment lies mainly with the patient. His next problem is *how* to help the patient in his process. This is a new situation for the therapist, since he cannot intervene in a process that can be accomplished only by the patient's internal, and usually unaware, manipulation of his own physiological activities. Here the therapist is faced with a flood of problems: no consensus has yet been established about most effective procedures; experimental laboratory procedures are often not appropriate to the clinical situation; he has little expertise in the instrumentation; there are several quite different theoretical concepts for the biofeedback process, and the problem is which to choose as a basis to proceed.

Biofeedback has developed so rapidly and from so many inputs that appraisal and consideration, or any cohesive synthesis of how to use it most effectively, have been slow to be communicated. Most would-be practitioners of the biofeedback art must wait for the yearly or semi-yearly meetings or published reports that have a long built-in delay of publication, or they must depend upon word-of-mouth or workshops, often conducted by biofeedbackers who have a particular point of view to sell or with little real background in biofeedback or in any of the multiple scientific disciplines it comprises.

Ideas about biofeedback, its procedures and instruments and concepts have descended upon the clinician like an avalanche. Many practitioners are rightly confused about biofeedback procedures and objectives and the kinds of biological mechanisms that may be involved. What the diversity of opinion and advice from experts, pseudo-experts and laboratory theorists means is confusion, uncertainty, and a number of unavoidable errors when the new practitioner leaps into biofeedback.

One of the most important functions of this book is to provide an analysis of the transition of biofeedback from research laboratory to the clinical setting. There are marked procedural differences between the laboratory and clinical uses of biofeedback which contrast sharply with the systematic transition from research to application found for most other therapeutic tools, and it is essential for the practitioner to understand that the objectives, methods, theories, and even the errors of experimental, laboratory biofeedback are quite different from the objectives, methods, theories, and potential problems of the clinical, therapeutic use of biofeedback. The unique situation also means that the practitioner must understand the process, not solely in terms of physiology or psychology, as is customary for therapists, but he must also understand the biofeedback process in terms of the patient's very individual and subjective participation.

For these reasons *Stress and the Art of Biofeedback* describes the details of clinical procedure and provides a guide to the practice of biofeedback that is based upon surveys of its most successful use. The clinical procedure described in detail in Chapter 9 for the use of muscle (EMG) biofeedback can serve as a model from which more specific procedures using other modalities of biofeedback can be derived.

## The Therapist's Functions in Biofeedback Therapy

Obviously, the therapist does not relinquish his therapeutic responsibilities when he prescribes biofeedback training. He is responsible for knowing whether biofeedback training is indicated, and whether it is the treatment of choice or a supplementary measure. And he is responsible for constantly evaluating effects of the treatment and when to terminate it. The major change in responsibility is in properly and effectively supplying the kinds of information the patient needs to work with to ensure progress in his biofeedback training. I have categorized the kinds of information above (biological information, cognitively useful information, etc.) and they are fully described in the section of the clinical practice of muscle biofeedback in Chapter 9.

The remaining function of the therapist lies in his ability to recognize and act appropriately upon both the psychologic and physiologic results of biofeedback training. It is because these results are new to the therapeutic situation that they are so important to recognize and deal with. First, when the biofeedback learning changes the physiologic activity, whatever concurrent medication has been used to control the activity can become excessive, producing drug side effects.[5]

The psychologic changes are equally important. The associations between subconscious subjective feelings

---

5. Several striking incidents illustrating this crucial potential side effect of biofeedback training in patients on medication occurred in diabetics. Various biofeedback relaxation procedures apparently caused physiologic changes that rendered the insulin dosage excessive, causing undesirable effects of insulin overdosage.

and physiologic changes frequently result in new insights and appraisals of the illness, and these new awarenesses can change the patient's concepts of his illness, his therapist, and his ability to deal with his problems. It is, of course, the therapist's role to determine whether these changes in attitudes and feelings are beneficial or detrimental. If detrimental, this then is a psychologic side effect of biofeedback, and can pose a problem for the medical therapist. Yet this is part of the changing therapeutic picture and underlies the importance of the therapist understanding his total role in the therapeutic process, both medical and psychological. And as with an undesirable effect of any treatment, the problem can be readily traced to the treatment mechanics. In the case of biofeedback, the biofeedback training itself may be inappropriate for some individuals, elements of essential information to the patient may be lacking, therapeutic attitudes may be deficient, or the undesirable attitude may be a part of the recovery process itself.

## The Patient's Role in Biofeedback: His Problems

For the patient, biofeedback is not only a new experience, but his role in the treatment process is quite different from the traditional role of the patient. The patient is no longer an object, a body absorbing the interventions of the therapist. The patient, with some latent capacity of his mental processes, possesses the magical therapeutic power to rid the body of the excesses of inappropriate reactions or misdirected physiology. What the patient needs to activate this inherent normalizing mechanism, this resident physician, is information.

The art of biofeedback is a creation of the patient, once he has the tools, and the tools are varieties of information. So this book is for the patient, who is the critical element in the success of biofeedback. In its most elementary form, biofeedback is simply the providing of information about physiologic activities to the patient along with an instruction to change the physiologic activity in a specific direction. The patient does the rest.

One problem the patient may encounter is his attitude about controlling internal processes of his body. Most people welcome the idea; the problem lies in implementing a change in attitude about control from the learned dogma that it has never been possible and that only medical authority could responsibly intervene in body processes. While the idea of self-control is appealing, the weight of culture and beliefs can often act to confuse the patient. The phenomenon is a bit like cultural shock, where uncertainty about adopting a new lifestyle in a new environment means a struggle between past experience and an unknown future.

## The Patient's Functions

The patient's functions can be summed up as: (1) to learn, (2) to supply experiential information (subjective reports), (3) to become aware, either consciously or simply by performing, that he can perform, and (4) to report his evaluations.

The objective of biofeedback training, regardless of body system, for both the patient and the therapist is for the patient to develop as much control over the selected body system or activity as possible. Generally, significant and usable control also requires some degree of awareness.

The ideas of control and awareness in biofeedback have been confused in the minds of many researchers, and this lack of clarity about the goals of biofeedback training affects what the patient does.

To many researchers, the idea that individuals can learn to control a selected, unfelt internal body activity (such as muscle tension or heart rate) means that the individual can be "conditioned" to react in a specific way to a stimulus, i.e., to a signal containing the biofeedback information. In laboratory experiments and in some clinical applications, this approach to achieving "control" is brought about by giving the biofeedback signal every time the individual's physiologic activity changes in a predetermined way. This is called reinforcement, and the signal is used to reinforce what the individual has learned. When the signal containing the biofeedback information is used in this way, the person attempting biofeedback learning essentially is experimenting with changing his physiology, and when he is successful in performing according to the criterion set for him, he is rewarded by being given the biofeedback information. This tells him that he has performed correctly, and his task then is to try to consolidate whatever elements of his activity led to a correct response and repeat it. In other words, the individual is rewarded for already having completed a performance, that of changing a selected physiologic activity in a desired direction, and his brain mechanisms must now search for relationships between performing correctly and the biofeedback signal that led him to the correct performance. This kind of delayed reinforcement during learning frequently leads to dependence upon the presence of the signal to initiate the "control."

This is quite different from the biofeedback training situation in which the biofeedback monitor is continuously available. Here the biofeedback signal has a twofold role; first, it provides a constant source of information about the physiologic activity that is used cognitively by the patient and incorporated into associations with subjective states, with the associated material then being used as a guide toward the goal of voluntary control; and second, the biofeedback signal contains a constantly reinforcing value. It is a bit like the difference between analogue and digital information where analogue information follows all levels and variations of the physiologic activity, while digital information consists of discrete information about what the activity was. The changes in the continuously available biofeedback signal provide continuous confirmation of the learning process. The process becomes completely internalized, and the control over the physiologic function can be activated by intention, i.e., by voluntary control.

It would seem to me that the only useful result of biofeedback training would be that kind of voluntary control over body activity that can be invoked *at will* and when necessary or appropriate or desirable. Obviously this means that the patient's training should reach a point where he can demonstrate control over the selected physiologic function *without the biofeedback signal*. Occasionally, as in psychoses or severe behavioral disorders, this may not be feasible.

Another problem that stems from the habits of theoretical psychological research is that of defining awareness and consciousness. For some researchers and some clinicians, awareness exists only when it can be expressed, preferably verbally communicated. One of the consequences of biofeedback is that we now have a technique for communicating internal activities and awarenesses by changing biological activity. I have called this biological awareness, and have proposed it as a state of consciousness.[6] Very often in biofeedback training, and particularly when physiological activities with which the patient has had no previous experience, such as brain waves or muscle fiber activity are used, the patient readily learns control over these obscure, unperceived body activities but his ability to perform far exceeds his ability to communicate *how* he performs except by proving his ability to perform upon demand.

## The Patient Learns to Control Body Functions

Biofeedback has starkly isolated the critical elements of much learning: the complex activities of the brain and its mind. The striking aspect of *successful* biofeedback applications is in the effectiveness of the quality and quantity of information provided to the organism. In the early days of biofeedback, when the turned-on generation was, and still is, using alpha biofeedback for a high, it was the *social* aspects that played a large role. Those social aspects were more and more information about what brain waves were, what instruments did, clues how to get a high, clues about feeling state

---

6. "Biological Awareness as a State of Consciousness," *J. Altered States of Consciousness* 2, 1975.

descriptions, and what the socializing did was to supply information that was cognitively useful.

Research studies on the amount and kind of information important to the success of biofeedback learning have duplicated this phenomenon. When volunteer subjects or patients were given varieties of conceptually useful information about the physiology of the system they were trying to control, given information about how the instrument worked, given strategy information about how to change the function by mental manipulations, how to relax, what the consequences were, etc., biofeedback learning was eminently successful. Information is also contained in the attitudes of the people in the environment, in the kind of room and even in incidental decorations.

One of the stumbling blocks to understanding the pervasive role of information in successful biofeedback training is that for the first time both researcher and clinical practitioner are dealing with a mental mechanism whose effect is a change in physiologic activity. It is a learning process that is now taking learning research into areas where there is difficulty in assigning traditional learning variables to the process.

## Concepts of Biofeedback

Inferences about the mechanisms concerned in the biofeedback process tend to center around several concepts of human behavior, learning, and known mechanisms of physiologic activity. It seems likely that each of the concepts contributes in a major way to understanding the biofeedback phenomenon.

When used clinically in therapeutic applications, the differing methodologies and theoretical objectives of research studies espousing the different concepts of biofeedback can account for differences in therapeutic results and differences in therapeutic procedures. The major concepts concerned in the biofeedback process can be summarized briefly as:

*1. Conditioning as biofeedback.* Much of the early biofeedback work developed from operant conditioning theory. Briefly, this concept says that behavior and learning result from appropriate rewarding of innate biological activities for performance. By manipulating temporal and performance relationships to the reward, behavior can be shaped. The biofeedback monitor is used as a reward for correct performance. In the operant conditioning tradition the biofeedback signal is provided when the activity of a particular physiologic activity changes to a previously specified new level; the physiologic activity can then be shaped by changing the performance criterion, making it easier or more difficult to achieve. For example, the individual in a heart rate learning situation is instructed to increase his heart rate; he will receive the reward of the biofeedback signal (information about his heart rate) when he achieves the desired change. During shaping the criterion level may be easy to achieve, and only gradually increased to a level more difficult to achieve.

Several variations of the conditioning procedure that have been used both experimentally and clinically manipulate the shaping procedures. In some studies there have been hierarchies of rewards, beginning with fairly frequent and easily achieved light or tone signals, indicated successes for small changes, then augmented by more emotionally appealing rewards for improving rate of successful performance over longer periods of time.

Another variation is alternating the conditioning of a physiologic response in two opposite directions with the same reinforcing signal, such as increasing and decreasing heart rate or muscle tension until discriminant learning is achieved. Still another variation is augmenting the biological reinforcement signal with verbal reinforcement.

When the reinforcement is given almost continuously or verbal encouragement is added, these variations tend to shift the effects of procedure into less definitive techniques and more ambiguous interpretations.

*2. Stress reduction as biofeedback.* Currently this approach deals largely with the use of biofeedback to reduce tensions and anxiety manifest as increased muscle and visceral tension. The stress-reduction approach is theoretically grounded in the "arousal" or "fight-or-flight" concept based upon the way in which the body systems respond to threats of danger by mobilizing its defenses. The success of the stress-reduction approach lies in the clinical effectiveness of a wide variety of relaxation therapies and research. The basis of the relaxation effect is the development of awareness on the part of the patient of the *feeling* of relaxation, and the discrimination of fine differences between different levels of tension and relaxation. In this approach, the biofeedback information is used by the patient to facilitate his discrimination between tension levels, and procedurally, the technique may employ a variety of biofeedback signals.

*3. Biofeedback as a cognitive mechanism.* In a substantial portion of solid biofeedback research, and certainly in the *successful* applications of biofeedback, there are only two observable, quantifiable events in the biofeedback phenomenon: the conceptual information of the biofeedback procedure, i.e., the instructions, the attitudes, and the physiological biofeedback information, and second, the result, which is learned, voluntary control over the selected physiological function.

Between the information input and the resulting learned physiological control, extraordinarily complex information processing must occur, where appropriate information to the brain is associated, integrated, evaluated, put into memory, and the product of this brain activity is used to activate patterns of neural activity that result in discrete, channelled directions to control the selected physiologic activity.

With few exceptions, studies which have optimized the availability and the accuracy of the information about the process have found remarkable changes in physiologic functioning. The implication seems clear, that there is an internal, presumably a cerebral, information-processing system capable of discriminating productively useful information and activating physiologic mechanisms to achieve specific, directed changes in physiologic activity. Science is now reorganizing the validity of claims and demonstrations by yogis of control over even the most automatic of internal physiology. The element that is common to biofeedback seems to be the development of a keen awareness of internal events; the difficulty in the concept is that such an awareness can be specific to pinpoint accuracy yet inexpressible by conventional means of communications. The communication of the awareness may be solely by the physiologic change, i.e., a biological communication.

The concept of higher mental activity as the controller and normalizer of all physiologic systems can be viewed as an extension and definition of the stress-reduction concept. By postulating a cerebral control system operating specifically to appreciate, to integrate and to direct biological activities, one can account for the influence of the numerous "cognitive" aspects of biofeedback procedures which appear to contribute to the widespread effectiveness of biofeedback in an extraordinary number of human disorders. In successful clinical practice of biofeedback, it is the factors of set and setting, of clinical attitudes, of psychological support, of strategy information in the form of relaxation techniques, imagery, reverie, or meditation exercises, of information about the physiology and mechanics of the process that appear to be almost as important as the biofeedback information signal itself.

The idea that human beings may possess brain or mind systems that can process unfelt physiologic events toward optimal states of functioning has traumatized a few experimental psychologists, neurophysiologists and some academic physicians who feel responsible and protective for the more mechanical views of mind-body relationships. The consensus of the biofeedback practitioners and users is, however, almost unanimous in the impression that biofeedback deals with higher mind processes of awareness, interior concentration, subliminal perception, and complex mental processes.

Possibly the unique feature of *Stress and the Art of Biofeedback* is its emphasis on the cognitive factors involved in the biofeedback learning process. I assume both the possibility for, and the objective of, voluntary control of the body's physiologic activities. There is ample evidence to conclude that biofeedback learning is primarily a cognitive, mental process, albeit a subconscious one, as indeed is any learning. It is time, I feel, that the scientific authority that deals with brain mechanisms acknowledges the concept of mind apart from brain chemistry and physics. I was chided by an occasional neurologist for using the word "mind" in *New Mind, New Body,* and reminded that medical evidence could not support the concept of mind. Since then I have been encouraged by the speaking out of a few eminent brain scientists who are expressing doubts about the adequacy of explaining mental phenomena solely in terms of brain activity. In this book the term mind is used to indicate higher mental processes, either consciously or subconsciously appreciated, although I have used some care to reserve the word mind for only occasional use.

## Why Is Biofeedback Different?
## What Is New in the Biofeedback Process?

Clearly, biofeedback is a remarkable development. In less than seven years, from fewer than ten researchers who developed the field, there are currently more than 2,000 researchers and clinicians actively investigating and applying biofeedback. There has rarely, if ever, been any comparable development that has moved so swiftly in the fields of either medicine or psychology.

What are the ingredients of the biofeedback phenomenon that have made its success in therapy stimulate so much interest in both doctors and patients, in psychology, medicine and forward-looking multidisciplinary academia? A list of its unique characteristics is surprisingly long.

1. In the biofeedback learning process, information about internal (vital) physiological activities is provided to the individual. Rarely in either medical or psychological treatment does the therapist share the information he extracts from the patient's interior, be it physiological or psychological data. Traditionally it has

been the doctor who "knows best." Biofeedback has shown this is not completely true.

2. The subject or patient is given information about his internal physiologic functioning in the form of easily perceived signals, i.e., the tone or light or meter monitor presents biological data in units which are easy to understand. This is in considerable contrast to the usual methods for summarizing information about either the physiologic or psychologic nature of human beings. In medical examinations the body's biochemical or physiological functions are sampled and numbers are related to averages for different functions obtained from hundreds of thousands of normal and pathological conditions, and the numbers have a significance only in the degree of normality or abnormality they indicate. In biofeedback the physiologic information refers exclusively to the individual's own specific range of functioning. In psychological or psychiatric examinations and treatment, information about the individual's emotional and mental state is inferred from what the patient verbalizes and observations of his behavior. In biofeedback psychology and psychiatry, the information about psychic problems can be read via monitors of changes in physiologic activity that accompanies feeling responses, attitudes and even thoughts which have an emotional significance to the patient. The sensitivity of the biofeedback monitoring technique allows for a more direct and accurate appraisal of the patient's emotional state.

3. Moreover, biofeedback information is generally given almost continuously. The information about physiologic state is thus augmented by information about variations in the physiologic activity as contrasted to the sampling techniques used in medicine.

4. The convenient and continuous availability of information about internal activities gives the subject or patient the opportunity to interact with, to experience his own internal states, much as he can interact with and experience external events.

5. Probably the most revolutionary aspect of biofeedback is that it shifts the locus of control of the

self from external to internal dependence. No longer does the patient look to dependence on the therapist or drugs or physical therapy or any external intervention; the control of his physiological functioning can and does come from within; and he learns that he can depend upon his internal control systems.

6. The social significance of shifting the locus of control spells a revolutionary reversal in therapeutic approaches in medicine and psychology. It is the patient who can and must use the biofeedback information; it is the patient who learns to control or normalize his own physiological activities; it is the patient who develops the understanding or rapport with the inscrutable interior.

7. And for the first time in therapeutics, complex mental processes are evoked to change the body's physiologic activities. This leads not only to learned control over "involuntary" functions, but also to changing states of awareness and mental perspective.

8. Equally as important as learning to regulate physiologic activities and its psychophysiologic benefits is the communications function that the learning performs. Since the involuntary physiologic activities mirror emotional, and even attitudinal, states, changes during learning to control these activities comprise a mode of communication between patient and therapist.

## For Medicine and Psychology: the Ethical Issues

The unique characteristics of biofeedback that are of the most immediate concern, and have the greatest immediate implications for practical applications are: (1) biofeedback is useful in both organic illnesses and in psychological problems, and (2) the biofeedback procedures themselves are combinations of medical *and* psychological procedures.

At the present time biofeedback is being widely used in a variety of medical specialties as well as by psychologists in the treatment of emotional problems and in counselling. Moreover, the techniques are being used by educators, by teams of psychologists and social workers, and by a population of unlicensed, uncertified individuals caught up in the promised magic of biofeedback for exploring states of consciousness.

Because the effects of biofeedback span both the physiologic and psychologic functions of human beings, there are growing concerns by professionals in both areas as to what form or structure professional responsibility should take for the well-being of the patient. When biofeedback is a significant treatment in various medical specialties, this is less of an issue than it is for other biofeedback uses. On the other hand, in the use of biofeedback for emotional problems, the effect of biofeedback is a change in biological activity, and this use of biofeedback thus requires consideration of the physiological, and hence, medical consequences.

The extraordinarily diverse applications of the biofeedback phenomenon contain equally diverse questions and problems for implementing the technique on a practical level. There are, for example, questions of appropriate and effective procedures for the different applications, questions about which variety of biofeedback is appropriate for a specific disorder, questions about record keeping and methods for evaluating the effectiveness of the biofeedback treatment, and the serious, ethical questions about responsibility for the well-being of both the medical and psychological aspects of the patient undergoing biofeedback training.

There are many very practical consequences that arise from the traditional separateness of medicine and psychology for the effective practice of biofeedback. At the same time that biofeedback is exciting doctors in both psychology and medicine and their patients, the fact that it is mainly a process of mind capable of normalizing an amazing variety of medical problems is bedeviling the ethics committees of every kind of therapeutic specialty. The ultimate battleground is between the conservative physician and the non- or weakly certified psychotherapist, always a favorite battleground.

The first consequence (which has also been a major concern in the concept of this book) is the question of clinical proprietariness of biofeedback. One of the paradoxes of biofeedback is that, with a few exceptions, biofeedback techniques for clinical applications have stemmed largely from experimental psychology, while the chief applications of biofeedback lie in the area of medical practice. The first question raised by this consequence is the matter of jurisdiction of treatment, and this is the issue for the present volume.

Psychologists generally exploit psychologic therapeutic techniques widely, there being few, if any, restrictions against describing the techniques and mechanics of the procedures for the popular media. On the other hand, there has been an unwritten rule in medicine about divulging medical treatment and treatment programs, and access to most medical treatment is guarded by laws restricting use of drugs and the practice of surgery. The rationale for these restrictions is obvious enough. Democratic societies traditionally legislate against forces destructive to themselves.

Where then do biofeedback procedures and treatment programs fit? They have been derived mainly from psychophysiology, and certainly the underlying process affected appears to be a process traditionally claimed by, or relegated to, psychology, i.e., varieties of mental processes. These processes, however, not only induce changes in physiology conventionally associated with the physiologic mechanisms underlying response to emotion, but in practice the biofeedback process further appears to influence positively those mechanisms of pathology generally believed to be physical or organic changes, and hence the province of medicine. One argument for transferring these pathologies to psychophysiology or psychosomatic medicine would be if higher mental activities can exert a rehabilitating effect on physical process. Under this circumstance the etiology of that pathology may, after all, be a psychologic rather than primarily a physical process.

The opposite view may be equally valid, i.e., the target and effectiveness of biofeedback in illnesses of organic origin may be primarily the concomitant symptomatology of emotional origin. The reported widespread applications of muscle-tension-level biofeedback suggests that more illnesses than originally believed are not only accompanied by overlying emotional symptoms but that the emotional symptoms may intensify the actual physical problem. In this light, one of the benefits of biofeedback therapy may be the discrimination of psychologic from physical components of the illness, if indeed there is a difference.

For illnesses or pathologies responding to biofeedback therapy, there are thus both the functional and organic etiologies as well as mixed etiologies to consider. But because biofeedback generally employs instrumentation, the weight of tradition and law tend to limit the use of biomedical instrumentation to members of the medical profession. Given the recognition that biofeedback instruments are harmless in themselves, the major consideration must be how the *use* or *result* of use of the instrument affects the course of the illness.

To date, no FDA rulings concerning restrictions of biofeedback instruments have been made; however, because the primary responsibility of the FDA is to ensure the safety of therapeutic agents and instruments and the safety of biofeedback has been neither proved nor disproved, it seems likely that the FDA will rule that use of biofeedback instruments must be under medical supervision. At best, the supervision may be extended to qualified professionals in psychology, education and sociology, as uses in these areas become defined.

There are, however, valid reasons why such an FDA ruling would be unreasonably restrictive to readily demonstrated non-medical uses of biofeedback and severely inhibitory to the further development of biofeedback and biofeedback-related techniques for both psychologic and psychosomatic uses. It should be recognized that a large share of the training in biofeedback procedures is occurring under the aegis of psychology whereas little or no medical training in biofeedback has been instituted. Considered analysis of the role of biofeedback in therapeutics and therapy shows it to be a unique problem. The phenomenon of biofeedback clearly implicates a mind-body process, and it is this unitary process that is producing remarkable new gains in the understanding and treatment of illness.

Undue or unwarranted restrictions of the use of biofeedback risks negating the extraordinary value of biofeedback. They would lock the procedures into exclusive medical use and put severe constraints or relevant issues in psychology and psychosomatic medicine. In view of the past and current research in biofeedback demonstrating its range of uses in psychosomatic medicine, psychology, and sociology, as well as medicine; and particularly in view of the evidence that biofeedback treatment both exposes and successfully treats at least the functional aspects of certain organic illnesses, the decision was made to record current information on the techniques and uses of biofeedback for public use.

In face of a great demand for information about biofeedback and the unavailability of organized, structured, comprehensive data on techniques and results of biofeedback treatment, I have undertaken this study. Hopefully a much-needed synthesis and comprehensive discussion of information on techniques and uses of biofeedback can be of value to biofeedback practitioners in their effects to institute self-regulating policies within their separate specialties.

"Biofeedback is the newest, most exciting, and potentially farthest-reaching discovery ever to emerge from the busy basements of biomedical research" is a line written for *New Mind, New Body* nearly four years ago. Now *Stress and the Art of Biofeedback* emphasizes the remarkable breadth and depth of biofeedback, reinforces the information contained in *New Mind, New Body, The Alpha Syllabus* and *The Biofeedback Syllabus,* and tries to stimulate the development of appropriate educational institutions and curricula in the specialty of biofeedback.

# 2

# MUSCLE TENSION AND RELAXATION

The mechanics and psychogenesis of muscle tension
. . . Muscle behavior under stress . . . Mental processes and muscle control . . . Subliminal cognition
and muscle control . . . Cognitive influences in tension
and relaxation . . . Muscle responses to social stress
. . . Relaxation techniques used with EMG biofeedback . . . Progressive Relaxation . . . Hypnotic suggestion and autogenic training . . . Transcendental
Meditation . . . Relaxation is an awareness process

## The Mechanics and Psychogenesis of Muscle Tension

The reality of muscle fibers is that they have a response repertoire of one. All they can do is contract
and this is the response they make to the electrochem-
ical stimulation of impulses carried via the motor
nerves. Relaxation is the removal of this stimulation.

There are at least two, or two sets of, muscles to
maintain the balance or posture or set of any particular
body part. To produce a movement some muscles contract while their opposites stretch. The stretching is
both passive and a result of the action of special
nerve-muscle control systems in which inhibitory impulses are conducted to important junctions where they
act to block excitatory nerve impulses. Thus what muscle fibers do is dependent upon highly complex neural
networks which can, upon direction from the brain that
is making constant adjustments, selectively excite
the fibers to contract or actively prevent (inhibit) the
excitatory impulses from reaching the muscle fibers.

What is known about tension in muscles has been accumulated from studies concerned mainly with movement and contraction, and while tension is the basis of contraction for movement, tension without movement is a normal body reaction to any stressful stimulus. What muscles do (contract, tense) is dependent upon the number of nerve impulses coming down the motor nerves which innervate them, and the number of nerve impulses in turn is dependent upon a large complex of muscle control systems in the brain and spinal cord. What the muscle control systems do in turn is dependent upon the kinds and amounts of sensory information coming inward from sensory receptors throughout the body.

There are at least five sets of internal nerve-muscle sensing systems, two sets of skin sensing systems, along with auditory, visual and vestibular sensing systems, and it is the central (brain) integration of all of this sensed information that is used by the central muscle control systems as the moment-to-moment monitoring of muscle activity and is the reference from which subsequent muscle activity is projected and initiated. Functionally, all of these neural, sensory information channels provide the information input to the internal muscle feedback control systems of the brain and spinal cord. The control systems then integrate the internally derived information with other sensory information about what the muscle should be doing or what it is projected to do, then activate the appropriate mechanisms (the motor nerves) to alter the muscle activity. The cycle acts continuously in this fashion; hence "feedback control system."

Muscle control systems are exceptionally efficient mechanically, and once muscle behavior is learned, they function almost automatically with no specific conscious direction and only a vague, general conscious concept of the objectives of muscle performance. Muscles attract attention only when they become obstinate in a new muscle learning task, or when they are extremely fatigued, or when tension or bruising knots them up and causes aches and pains. These kinds of minor muscle problems are not considered harmful enough to warrant serious biomedical study, yet over time they can be just as destructive to an individual's well-being as hepatitis or a broken leg. But because such problems primarily affect social rather than physical well-being, their impact upon medicine has been greatly neglected. Although teaching muscles new patterns of activity can be frustrating, and fatigued muscles may recover slowly, it is the insidious toll of stress and emotional tension on the well-being of muscles that can aggravate emotional disturbances, that can cause psychosomatic disorders, and that can magnify the distress of all other illnesses.

## Muscle Behavior Under Stress

Exactly how stress, social pressure, and emotional tensions are translated into the tensions of muscles is poorly understood. One reason for this is that it is traditional in medicine and psychology to consider reactions to stressful situations either in terms of the mechanics causing physiologic changes, generally ignoring psychologic causes (as in asthma, colitis, etc.), or in terms of the psychologic mechanics involved in the emotional changes, generally ignoring the contributing physiologic causes. What has *not* been conceptualized about the kind of stress that modern society faces and suffers in response to is that it is not a stress directly affecting the physical organism, but is a cluster of stresses related to social behavior in a social environment. A more detailed discussion of how social stress can cause the whole range of tension reactions from anxiety to ulcers follows this section dealing with the physiologic changes involved in muscle tension.

The most popular current theory of the mechanisms underlying muscle tension posits that the organism is "aroused" or "alerted" by threatening stimuli, and the arousal activates a physiological preparation of the body to take action. It is much the same as the "fight-or-flight" theory formulated more than fifty years ago, and is based upon the observation that when obviously threatening situations occur (you meet a grizzly bear on a narrow mountain path), the body responds by mobilizing its resources. The muscles tense, ready to fight or flee or freeze; the viscera respond in such a way as to ensure emergency functioning, i.e., the heart rate and blood pressure increase to give emergency supplies of oxygen to tissues, the gut stops, the blood pools where it is needed, and so the skin blanches, secretions dry up, etc. All of these physiological responses are dramatic and obvious.

When threatening stimuli are less obvious, such as in socially threatening situations (as competition for jobs, or for affection), many of the same body changes occur. If someone is apprehensive, say about meeting someone new, his heart rate and blood pressure may increase, and his muscles will tense. The physiologic changes can be recorded biomedically although the person himself often may not be aware of the changes.

Most people do respond to social pressure with increased muscle tension. This kind of muscle set is called "bracing," the muscle act of preparing to defend or freeze or to avoid unpleasantness by having the important action muscles ready to move or stand by. Considerable degrees of muscle tension, even "knots," can develop in the muscles. For the most part, such muscle tensing is scarcely recognized consciously, especially during the tension-producing situation or even when recalling it later emotionally. It is only when the conscious attention is not concerned with the emotional situation that the muscle tension becomes significantly appreciated. Even considerable muscle tension may not be felt. This is understandable if we remember that muscles are large masses of muscle fibers, and that an enormous amount of partial tightening of muscle fibers can occur before it is recognized in the form of muscle spasms or knots or as pain.

To understand the consequences of stress on muscle tension, we have to assume either that the social pressure and tension are fairly frequent if not almost constant, or that the responses to it are frequent, if not sustained. Spontaneous relaxation following increased tension occurs very slowly; even sleep is generally not the answer, since subconscious memories can keep the muscles tense during sleep, and dreaming may actually increase the tension further. Since the tension diminishes slowly, it can still be at a high level when the tension-producing situation recurs or a new one comes along. If the situations are frequent, or if the individual continues to think or ruminate and mentally recreate even one such situation, two muscle events occur: muscle tension becomes sustained at higher levels and may continue to increase, and the tightness of the muscles causes them to be hyperreactive. Uptight people usually startle easily and vigorously.

If muscles are not given relief from tension by relaxation or change of activity, the muscle fibers physiologically "adapt" to the states of increased tension. It is as if there were some deficiency in the internal muscle regulating systems. Under normal conditions the special nerve cells in muscle tissue sense when a fiber is contracting, how fast it is tensing, the length of the fiber at any given moment, and other complex aspects of the muscle contraction, sending the information to the central muscle control systems for the appropriate adjustments. But when it comes to sensing *how long* muscle fibers have been tense, the system seems to become inefficient (as if man were not designed to handle so much social stress). With continued stress or rumination about the stress, the muscles have little chance to recover completely from their increased tension, and the tension becomes sustained at higher levels. Even this is not the entire picture since with so much muscle mass being tense, the muscle tension sensors relay an excessive number of tension messages to the brain muscle control areas. These should be enough to attract conscious attention, and sometimes do under acute circumstances, but with conscious attention generally occupied with the emotional situation, tension states are only minimally appreciated in awareness. To account for this relative failure to appreciate increased muscle tension consciously, it has been postulated that cortical inhibitory effects come into play; that is, some active cortical process blocks recognition of the increased tension. At the same time normal muscle control is inhibited, and the cortical effect is to direct the muscles to stay prepared for action, and thus they tend to remain in a tense state until either the tension-provoking situation is removed or until it is recognized and re-evaluated and emotional adjustments made.

## Mental Processes and Muscle Control

One of the curiosities of medicine, especially psychosomatic medicine, and of psychology, particularly the psychology of emotion, is the long-continuing neglect of the obvious role of muscles in illnesses of both mind and body. It is the custom of Western medicine and psychology to focus on the mechanisms of the physical nature of man, even when that nature is heavily influenced by the mind and emotions.

If we were to look at man whole and afresh, undissected by science, we would see man as mainly muscles. Man can, in fact, do nothing without his muscles. All of his behavior, all of his expressions, are implemented by muscles. If his well-being is implemented and expressed by muscles, it would be eminently logical to believe that disorders of his mind and body would also be implemented and expressed by his muscles.

It has taken biofeedback to change the scientific perspective on muscles. No longer can we talk about muscles solely as the vehicles of our desires, as the mechanical devices that move us about, sit us up, make us tired, help us to see and hear and eat and survive. The extraordinary utility of muscle biofeedback in relieving all varieties of human problems is convincing us of the role of muscles as expressors of a great complex of mind and body activity. Even the most subtle of the mind's machinations, even the most sophisticated of the body's nerve electrical actions, have now been demonstrated to be intimately tied to a maelstrom of unfelt, unseen muscle activity.

Precisely because the complexities and intricacies of the mind's and brain's effects on muscles are unfelt and unseen, science has had difficulty in pinning down the relationship between mind and muscle. Physiology and physical medicine have learned a great deal about muscle mechanics and the remarkably complex nature of the brain's control of muscle activity, but although the neural networks of the motor systems of the brain are known in great detail and they form a dominant mass of the brain with widespread connections, virtually nothing is known about how they relate to the higher brain systems that mediate emotion, feeling, mood, attitude, cognition, motivation, curiosity, or desire.

If man can do nothing without his muscles, his muscles can do nothing without the central nervous system and its nerves. People, even medical people, tend to think simplistically about muscles, as if it were the muscles themselves that can be trained to perform fine movements, or that they can be rested by simply not using them. But it is anatomically and physiologically true that the muscles themselves can do very little without the activation and direction and modulation that come from the highest, the most cerebral, of the brain's activities. It is, in fact, the complicated and still obscure operations of higher mental activities that coordinate and direct, plan and project, every muscle movement we make, consciously *and* subconsciously.

The potency of higher mental control becomes clear in biofeedback learning. For example, in most kinds of anxiety the physical expression of anxiety, if not a good share of the anxiety itself, is in the unfelt, unseen muscle tension that braces the body against fearful situations without consciousness being much aware that tension exists, generally not until long after the cause for anxiety has been removed. With the biofeedback signal monitoring the actual muscle tension, and with the desire to relieve that tension, the feedback signal responds to decreasing tension effected by nerve impulses initiated by some indefinable and inexpressible cerebral appreciation of the problem at hand and its ability to set in motion the nerve networks needed to remove the tension.

Studies using various relaxation or meditation techniques to achieve states of tranquillity and relaxation show significant reductions in muscle tension. Here also, as with biofeedback, there are no externally controlled interventions that force muscle activities into other modes, such as drugs, or deep massage or electric shocks; the relaxation and meditation techniques deal with *mental* aspects that intuitively and cognitively, yet passively and subconsciously, affect the cerebral mechanisms that are tied to those that make the muscles respond.

Little is known about the subtleties of such cerebral control, or of the psychophysiological aspects of muscle activity. The problem is further complicated by the fact that neither language nor biologic measures can define the effect of most influences of mental activities, particularly as they relate to their role in changing physiologic activities. It is largely for such reasons that the practice of biofeedback can sometimes remind one of the shotgun approach to therapeutics, or the laying on of hands. As described below, both clinical research and practice surround and supplement biofeedback by many different, but related, techniques, all of which elicit the influence of cerebral control for effects.

Those mental activities which subtly but surely affect muscles are influenced in turn quite specifically by various orders of information which are perceived. These can be illustrated easily in examples from everyday life. Take, for example, driving a car. First, there is the physiological information directly from the muscles about the degree and status of muscle activity that is relayed to the cortical integration areas of the brain. This is chiefly various kinds of information about muscle tension sensed by special nerve cells in the muscles and by pressure sensors in the skin; it gives a measure of how much muscle pressure is on the accelerator. How *much* pressure to put on the accelerator is also guided by other information, visual and auditory. All of this physiological information is directed by and toward the goals of driving, but achieving the goals is implemented by a judicious use of a variety of *other* kinds of information that are used cerebrally: cognitively useful information (some knowledge of the mechanics of the car), strategy information (how and when to get in the right lane), and experiential information (e.g., knowing how to move with the flow of traffic).

In the world of biology and medicine, in psychology and physiology, academic attention has concentrated on the mechanical control of muscles, and by and large our culture has been conditioned to accept the concept that muscles respond to the demands of environment, with relatively minimal or tangential interference by complex cognitive processes. It is the politics of science, quite literally, that has shaped the behavior of our muscles:[1] the physics and chemistry of nerves and muscles account for the nature of muscle activity, but they do not account for the *reasons* muscles do what they do. Nonetheless, despite their inability to account for mental activity, it is the physical sciences which dominate theories about the physiology of the body, and from their position of power, they have ignored volumes of research evidence that implicate, with equal data, the superiority of mental processes over physical ones in the control of the body's physiology. It is a situation similar to the one N. F. Dixon, the famous British authority on subliminal perception, commented on, noting that there are more research papers on subliminal perception than for any other aspect of psychology, yet less space (if any at all) devoted to the subject in any college or graduate text.

## Subliminal Cognition and Muscle Control

So it is little wonder that Westerners, including the biomedical scientists themselves, find the biofeedback process perplexing. It is only when we begin to think through the biofeedback phenomenon that we are forced to face all of those compartments of complex mental activity that have been kept in scientific obscurity. For there are, in truth, only two observable events in the biofeedback process: the intake of information (what the muscle is doing; what should be done about it; perhaps a clue about how to change it),

---

1. For centuries and predominantly even today, we sit bolt upright for hours in badly built chairs (built for the "average" body) expending vast unproductive quantities of muscle and cerebral body control energy while we listen to lectures with the half-mind not occupied by struggling with an unnatural position.

and the result, a specific change in muscle activity compatible with the intention to change it. At the very least one must acknowledge that the information taken in somehow got associated properly, in some way got matched up with intention, and by some exquisitely precise mechanisms, exactly the right physical and chemical processes were activated to produce the desired change.

It is an elegant process, and one that far exceeds the capacity of modern science to dissect and catalogue. If, however, we analyze what may be going on in the mind as we carry out voluntary acts, we can recognize and label distinctive steps in the process, as in the example of driving a car. These steps are perceiving, associating, and integrating perceptual data with experiential memory data, using logic patterns, evaluating the significance of past and present experience, making judgments, etc.

It is likely that much the same thing happens in the biofeedback process. Here most of the physiological information is provided by the feedback monitor. Used alone, without other, supplementary information, the feedback signal information may be enough to allow the patient to change muscle activity, although often it may be a small change. Most experimental work has found that the other categories of information are almost equally important. Paralleling the example of driving a car, there is the cognitively useful information, such as descriptions of what the physiologic process is about, what the instrument does, and what the relationship of these is to therapeutic effectiveness. There is also the strategy information, such as the more formalized relaxation procedures or modifications which emphasize visualization, passive volition, directing attention internally, capturing awareness, etc. And there is the kind of information that provides clues about how the physiologic change may occur, clues both to dissociate conscious effort and to learn how simply to feel or become aware of internal states.

Finally there is experiential, supportive information, the kind of information that is conveyed by concept and attitude and surroundings. Whether this information is conveyed simply by an understanding and pleasant demeanor, or by set and setting, or whether the therapist discusses the biofeedback process in terms of the patient's ultimate ability to control internal states, the significance of the information lies in its capacity to encourage, impart confidence, motivate, and consolidate the biofeedback learning experience.

What the patient experiences during biofeedback training and his awareness of the physiologic changes are chiefly subjectively appreciated events only, and can be referred to and described vaguely at best. Our communications about internal events are solely by agreed upon analogies to experiences which have been previously analogized over the centuries. For example, in temperature feedback training in Raynaud's syndrome, the patient may say, "My hand feels as if it were alive again," or "It feels the way I thought it would feel if my hand were in a basin of warm water, except without the wetness of water."

Such fumbling attempts to describe new sensations typify the difficulties in communicating the biofeedback experience as well as the difficulties involved in guiding the patient toward a goal of self-control of his own biological activities. The idea of control itself also can be communicated only by referring to vague analogies, such as "It's much like the feeling, the knowing, you have when you are hitting a golf ball exactly right, or when you are braking your car for a perfect stop." Even though these kinds of communication are rough and indirect, they supply the information that the patient does indeed have the capability for control and that he is on the right track. The effect of information couched in these terms also contributes to an awareness that the idea in successful biofeedback is to deemphasize the idea of conscious effort.

Because biofeedback learning deals with completely internal processes, it is important for the therapist to recognize that it is indeed a different kind of learning experience, and that it is dependent upon mental activity and not upon external events designed and controlled to elicit responses. What is important is the kind and quality of the information supplied to the mental processes. Given adequate and accurate information, the mental activity can effect quite remarkable changes in the body's physiology. The difficulty in understanding the process is that it takes place without conscious awareness. All learning, in fact, takes place via subconscious mechanisms, a fact that we rarely acknowledge. In biofeedback learning, the role of subconscious mental activity is not only readily apparent, but it can easily be demonstrated that conscious awareness and attention interfere with biofeedback learning.

## Cognitive Influences in Tension and Relaxation

The mind-brain mechanisms that mediate the physical effects of *social stress* have received scant scientific attention, presumably because of the considerable difficulty in documenting the elusive, poorly expressed, and often unaware subjective state for use in correlating subjective changes with physiological changes. Nonetheless, the chain of events occurring between perception of social dynamics and the physiological responses to social stress can be readily deduced.

Social stress becomes distress because of uncertainty about future social relationships. Shifting social relationships are often immediately traumatic, but their persistent effects are sustained to a large degree by mental manipulation of the emotions. Imagery, interpretations, expectations, and assumptions about how future events will be affected by the directly disturbing experience are all used to extrapolate the significance of social events. Other social stress derives from observations and interpretations about one's social environment, colored by inferences, suspicions, hopes and fears, and other mental activities recruited in an apparent attempt to maintain a relatively stable state of emotional well-being. When changes in the social environment and social dynamics become stressful, it is largely because the information needed to adjust or resolve problems is incomplete, and thus mental projections about the social future continue to be uncertain. It is the uncertainty that keeps both the mind and body alerted and prepared to take action against seemingly impending threats to well-being and security and survival. In other words, social stress is not stress until the mind-brain interprets perceptions as indicating stress or disharmony or threats in the social environment and relationships. Only then is the body alerted, and only then does the body react.

There are a number of subjective mechanisms that can be inferred to operate to maintain stress reactions of the body's physiological systems. One is the process of rumination (not necessarily obsessive), that conscious or subconscious activity of recall of social events, mental regurgitation, preoccupations, pondering and speculation about the social stress that amplifies and intensifies the social stress complex. The effect of rumination is to occupy a good deal of the associational mental circuitry with the stress idea, focussing attention on the stress problem and so concomitantly less attention and awareness are available for perceptions *not* related to the stress problem. Equally as important is the fact that rumination is a series of mental images, and the images themselves can and do produce profound effects on the body's physiology (for details, see section on Progressive Relaxation). Second, the process of perceptual modulation tends to become concentrated on the stress because of the persistence and force of rumination, and so the narrowing of perceptual interpretations over time modulates perceptions such that elements in the social environment not originally concerned in the stress projection gradually become encompassed in the mental stress construction and projection. Cultural influences and belief systems also tend to become concentrated toward the social stress problem and intensify the perceptual modulation effect.

Another mechanism which sustains the stress reaction is the internal feedback of information about the status of the physiological systems reacting to the stress. Proprioceptive and visceral afferent information about the uptight muscles and viscera is relayed to the central nervous system where it is available for association with interpretive mechanisms and reinforces both the emotional sensations and the cognitive reactions to stress.

To relieve the effects of social stress one of these mechanisms must be reversed. Aside from drugs, the chief device which can interfere in the mental construction of the stress is to redirect the attention and rupture the fixed, self-reinforcing circular mental activities of perception interpretation, rumination, perceptual modulation, and the effect of these mental activities on physiologic activities. Distracting the attention is effective but transient. More effective devices are to provide information that can rechannel the information-processing activity and intervene in the perceptual-conceptual-physiological information loops that have become fixed in their activities.

There are two major routes by which information can be introduced into the information-processing systems of the mind-brain, which is then used to modify and resolve the imbalances among social realities, the perceptual interpretation of the events in the social environment, and the body's reactions to the interpretations. One technique for introducing remedial information into these systems is to supply conceptually useful information that leads to interpreting the stress situation differently and expands perspectives on stress-coping mechanisms, and this, of course, is psychotherapy and counselling.

The second technique for introducing therapeutic information is by supplying information about the physiologic state, i.e., information about the degree of tension of the muscles and viscera. And this, of course, is biofeedback.

## Muscle Responses to Social Stress

Although the skeletal muscle control system is effective for muscle movements, it is strangely inefficient in handling the effects of social pressure or emotional tensions. Not only do the muscle fibers themselves adapt to higher levels of tension, there is also an effect in the cortex that works to maintain muscle tension and prevents recognizing the tension. The cortical effect suggests that much of the inefficiency in handling tensions occurs within the higher cerebral systems, quite possibly at the interfaces of information input and information output of the mind-brain mechanisms. It is often forgotten that the muscle feedback control systems have multiple information inputs, and very powerful inputs are perceptual, cognitive, and memory. Much like Jacobson's demonstration that imagination activates muscles,[2] it is known that rumination, that insidious process of mentally rehashing an annoying or disturbing incident over and over, also increases and sustains muscle tension, often quite dramatically.

In essence this circular mental activity is part of a closed feedback loop between muscles and the mind, i.e., the mental activity is also a feedback loop, operating between sensory mechanisms subserving perceptions and brain mechanisms concerned with the integration and synthesis of information. Since these cerebral mechanisms also process the information about muscle activity and the cerebral-muscle system can operate automatically as a feedback control system, the integrative brain mechanisms can be viewed as providing two interfaces, interacting on the one side with muscle control activity and on the other side with perceptual recognition processes. Within the integrative brain, information is exchanged between the two feedback loops. Thus, as the cerebral processes are engaged in rumination, there is a stream of emotional stimuli impinging upon the muscle control systems, activating and tensing the muscles. The tense muscles in turn send streams of information about the tension to the cortical appreciation areas which simply continue the stimulation to ruminate about the tension.

On the other hand, because the system consists of a perceptual-cerebral feedback loop and a muscle-cerebral feedback loop which dynamically interact with each other to sustain both the subjective and muscle

---

2. See section on Progressive Relaxation, pages 52–55.

states of tension, the effect of excessive tensions can be relieved by relieving either the muscle or the cerebral tension.

When muscle tension is relieved by relaxation procedures, tension information from the muscles being sent to the central nervous system becomes less and less, and its stimulating effect on the cortex is diminished. There is a good bit of research evidence to indicate that the stimulating effect of increased muscle tension on the cortex activates muscle control mechanisms preventing relaxation. That is, the neural pathways from the cortical muscle control areas to lower brain muscle control areas are activated and the downstream neural message is to maintain the tension. The effect is to prevent relaxation, keeping the muscles uptight and ready to move or defend. As the alerting effect on the cortex is relieved by relaxation training, there is then a relief of the cortical tension-activating effect and the muscles begin to return to normal activity.

This explanation has been derived from neurophysiologic studies which measure effects of muscle contraction (not tension) on the muscle-activating mechanisms of the cortex only. Effects on subjective cerebral activities have not been measured. Nonetheless, psychologic and psychiatric therapeutic techniques are used effectively to induce changes in the mental and emotional (the perceptual-cerebral) feedback loop, decreasing its activity and resulting in less internal cerebral activation of muscle tension.

In light of EMG biofeedback research, which involves the effects of perceptual and cognitive information on muscle activity, it would seem logical to assume that there may be changes in the higher cerebral activities that parallel changes occurring in the more reflex regulation of muscle activity (the muscle-cerebral feedback control system).

Since the cortex reacts to alerting by relaying excitation causing inhibition of other brain neuronal activities, it is likely that the cortical alertness may also inhibit cerebral appreciation of the incoming neuronal messages about the increased muscle tension. That is, since muscle control systems receive information both from peripheral muscles and from higher cerebral activities, tension information from the muscles may communicate as well with those cerebral mechanisms contributing to the subjective appreciation of body activities. The effect would be to inhibit cerebral functions that evaluate the significance of perceptions of social and emotional stimuli and of internal states of tension. When alerting of the cortex decreases, whether from relaxed muscles or diminished cortical tension effected by psychotherapy or drugs, so does this effect of cortical inhibition, and muscle tension levels can then be appreciated, either consciously or subconsciously.

This explanation may account for the differences in correlations between muscle and subjective changes resulting from the different relaxation techniques, including EMG biofeedback-assisted relaxation, when used under different therapeutic conditions. Because the concept seems somewhat involved at first glance, it is restated as follows:

Research and clinical evidence suggest that the central nervous system mechanisms relating to control of muscle activity are comprised of two dynamically interacting aspects: the muscle mechanisms and the cerebral mechanisms. Of these two subsystems, the cerebral system has the more dominant and extensive capabilities. Every purposeful muscle activity, including unfelt muscle tension, is initiated and guided or modulated by integrated cortical or higher cerebral actions and these actions include such complex influences as the meaningfulness of perceptions, consideration of consequences, projection of intention, etc. The fact that muscle activity can quickly become automatic means that the muscle control systems can function automatically with a minimum of cerebral intervention, and thus the system can rely upon feedback control systems. That is, in the oversimplified concept of the muscle feedback control systems, information from the muscle fibers is relayed to central control areas where it is compared to what the control is set for in any given situation of muscle activity, and appropriate adjustments are activated. This is the muscle-cerebral feedback control loop. In this automatic mode of operation, the effect of alerting or stressful stimuli activates primarily the more mechanically involved cortical mechanisms which affect movement and preparation for movement, and this, of course, changes muscle tension levels toward a defense mode.

Obviously, at the same time the alerting or threatening stimuli have activated the perceptual-cerebral mechanisms which judge stimuli to be threatening and set in motion the muscle reactions. At the same time the response of the cortex may parallel the changes going on in the direct muscle control system, i.e., the occupation of the cortex with the emotion-producing stimuli continues to activate its focus on the emotional problem and raises its threshold for recognizing or appreciating the increased muscle tension. This would mean that while the cerebral mechanisms are concerned with the perception (and rumination) of the alerting situation, the stimuli would continue to convey the alerting signals to the muscle control systems, aggravating the tension, increasing or sustaining it, as actually happens. Only when a cerebral or psychologic change occurs to affect the *significance* of the alerting information would the cerebral aspect begin to appreciate and be aware of the increased muscle tension, which would then in turn release the inhibitory effect on the muscles sustaining the tension and restore normal control functioning. This sequence could account for the effectiveness of psychotherapeutic effects in relieving muscle tension.

In parallel fashion, inducing relaxation by focussing awareness on muscle effect (such as Jacobson's tense-relax exercises) results in fewer muscle tension impulses being sent to the central nervous system, and so there are fewer stimuli to affect the cortex, keeping it alerted, and this in turn decreases the cortical action on the lower-brain areas which have been maintaining the muscle tension. At the same time there are fewer stimuli reminding the cortex about the reasons for the tension, and this relieves the inhibition of awareness by the cortex. Continuing in this dual circular fashion, the increased awareness of muscle tension causes a decrease in the cortical action on the muscle control systems, augmenting the peripheral relaxation effect.

In the Jacobson type of learned relaxation, a cognition or awareness of the differences between tension and relaxation is developed, and the cerebral effect is to attend to relaxation, which signals the muscles to relax. As this occurs, fewer tension impulses are sent to the cerebral association areas, and this in turn diminishes the stimulation of perceptual-memory associations related to the tension, diminishing both cortical inhibition of muscle relaxation and the calling forth of emotional significances, hence mental tension diminishes as well.

The concept of a perceptual-cerebral system at least equipotent with the more mechanical muscle control system fits well with the research findings of Hefferline. From his studies, Hefferline concluded that people learn to block the recognition of muscle tension at the brain level, a process he called conditioned inhibition. Part of the evidence for this conclusion was that when people could learn to become aware of their muscle tensions, they would recover the memories of what had caused them to tense their muscles in the first place. This has been reported in biofeedback-assisted relaxation, and it seems possible that as relaxation proceeds, and awareness of tension occurs, the cerebral associations of the need to defend would lead to recovery of memories of why there was a need to defend, and so both muscle and mental tension are relieved.

The same series of events occurs without any "conditioning" at all. The following anecdote illustrates the significance of the two factors, muscle and cerebral, that are concerned in developing and relieving muscle patterns of tension or action. I became aware that I was having difficulties remembering friends' telephone numbers during times I was in my office. I then recalled that the office phone is a dial phone whereas my home phone is a touch-tone telephone. I often ring up my friends from home and rarely do so from the office, and when I do, I find that my fingers hover over the dial uncertain of the numbers to dial, and the actual numbers refuse to jump into consciousness. On the other hand, at home the fingers touch the right numbers without any conscious thought at all of the number I am calling. The numbers have become muscle action patterns, much like Jacobson's muscle tension-image patterns, to be used just as the action-image patterns for my leg muscles can be called upon for walking action patterns.

The concept of a perceptual-cerebral muscle control system at least equipotent with the more mechanical muscle-cerebral control system has important implications for the way in which biofeedback therapy is implemented. If reversing a physiologic change that has caused both physical and emotional symptoms, and only the medical aspect is considered, then the usefulness of the treatment may suffer. Consideration of the importance of the cerebral aspects can contribute both to optimizing the therapeutic procedures and to capitalizing on the effects produced by relaxation. The former is discussed under the heading of strategy information such as the use of visualization, inwardly directed attention, distinguishing passive from active concentration, and other subjective factors. As biofeedback training continues and awareness of internal states develops, the changing awarenesses bring forth associated memories, changing perspectives on the status of internal activities, and the significance of external stimuli on the body's reactions. These new insights then can be understood and used to maintain the improvement.

## Relaxation Techniques Used with EMG Biofeedback

The use of learned relaxation for the treatment of emotional and psychosomatic disorders is not new. Two quite different techniques, Autogenic Training and Progressive Relaxation, have been used successfully as medical therapeutic techniques for more than fifty years. The former is popular in Europe and in various medical centers around the world; Progressive Relaxation is practiced mainly in the United States. Both entail months, sometimes years, of relaxation practice.

The popularity of EMG biofeedback-assisted relaxation seems to be the result of its adding efficiency to proven therapeutic procedures. While EMG biofeedback improves the efficiency and effectiveness of demonstrated relaxation procedures, in actual clinical practice, EMG biofeedback relaxation is almost invariably combined with elements of the other relaxation techniques. The following discussion reviews the concepts and principles of those techniques most commonly used with EMG biofeedback.

Autogenic training (A.T.) was borrowed from hypnotic techniques, and is a combination of self-suggestion about relaxation and more advanced self-suggestion phrases for learning to control consciousness, as in meditation. The emphasis is on the subjective aspects of relaxation or non-tension, and experimental evidence suggests that there is not always a correlation between muscle relaxation and relief from mental tension. Progressive Relaxation (P.R.) relies largely upon sensations of muscle activity, using the differences between the feelings of muscle contraction and relaxation to develop an understanding and awareness of deep relaxation. In P.R. relative muscle relaxation is first induced, and is compared to muscle tension to develop the feeling of relaxation. Both A.T. and P.R. are selective in that only those patients with considerable persistence follow the training procedures long enough to enjoy their benefits. Both techniques also have the same disadvantage: the lack of specific information about the level of existing muscle tension. Learning to control muscle activity depends on a variety of sensory information, including visual information from watching muscle activity and pressure information from the skin when muscle masses move, as well as upon the internal information about muscle tension sensed by special nerve endings that send the information to the central nervous system. During relaxation training, only the latter is available.

The obvious and critical new element that biofeedback brings to relaxation training is the technology to detect and provide precise information about muscle activity that is otherwise unfelt. In a sense, it replaces much of the internally derived information people usually use to learn to control muscles, and precisely because it does supply direct and accurate information EMG biofeedback should be, and is, extremely efficient in achieving the goals of relaxation procedures. The goal of relaxation procedures is not simply relaxation; the goal is the voluntary control of the tension-relaxation dimension of muscles, and the inexpressible but subjectively known awareness that gives one the ability for control.

## Progressive Relaxation

The prime expert, perhaps the sole expert, in the psychosomatic specialty of muscles has been Edmund Jacobson, who, since 1908 through the present, has supplied both the fundamental and applied researches of mind-muscle relationships to medicine. Through some delightfully creative research, Jacobson has forged decisive, convincing evidence for the mutual interdependency of mind and muscles upon each other for their well-being. While other medical researchers have accumulated evidence to support one or another psychophysiologic theory of emotion, particularly arousal theory, by studying reactions of the autonomic nervous system, Jacobson has systematically documented the powerful effects on muscles of such higher mental activities as imagination, attention, and awareness.

In the medical world of therapeutics, Jacobson's contribution rests upon his major thesis that anxiety and relaxation are mutually exclusive. That is, anxiety does not, cannot, exist when the muscles are truly relaxed. And while the physiologic details to support this idea have not been worked out with the precision that particulate neurophysiology demands, the clinical successes of Jacobson's relaxation techniques give the concept a good bit of merit.

Jacobson's Progressive Relaxation is based upon the

very simple procedure of comparing tension against relaxation. Since a person generally has very little awareness of the *sensation* of relaxation, he is asked first to tense a set of muscles as hard as he can until he can feel real tension, even tenderness and pain in the muscles. Then he allows those muscles to relax, and tries to become aware of, to feel internally, the difference between tension and relaxation. For example, in some of the first exercises in Progressive Relaxation the patient is asked to hyperextend the wrist, i.e., to bend the hand so the back of the hand is aiming toward the top of the forearm. The muscles contracting the hand backward are tensed as much as the patient can, and are held until he feels the sensations of tension and even tenderness in the muscles of the upper side and about the middle of the forearm. Then the hand is flopped down to a loose, relaxed position. As a single exercise, this alternation between tensing and relaxing is practiced no more than about three times in a fifteen-minute period. A good share of the time is spent in trying to discriminate the feelings of tension and relaxation, i.e., the absence of tension. As practicing continues, the patient begins to discriminate more and more finely different degrees of tension and relaxation. The procedure is not hurried; each exercise with *each* set of muscles is practiced for perhaps two weeks, and only then does work begin with another set of muscles. Since the procedure goes progressively through all of the muscles in the body (hence its name), to accomplish the entire procedure requires considerable time, let alone persistence.

As used first in desensitization techniques and then in conjunction with biofeedback training, Jacobson's relaxation technique has been modified. In current practice all time periods for the different exercises have been shortened, and some practitioners run through the entire progression within an hour or even less time.

Jacobson's work has contributed much more to understanding the effect of tension and anxiety on the health of human beings than just the development of a relaxation technique. He demonstrated, for example, that learned relaxation of the muscles can generalize to smooth (involuntary) muscles and can cause relaxation of muscles of the gastrointestinal and cardiovascular systems.

A major contribution stems from his work with imagination. Jacobson conducted a number of fascinating experiments which recorded the physiologic effects of imagination. For example, when people were asked to pretend they were operating an old-fashioned telegraph key with a middle finger, but not to move a muscle, as they imagined pressing the key there were bursts of muscle activity only in those muscles involved in moving that middle finger to tap a key. From such kinds of experiments, Jacobson was able to demonstrate that there is an energy expenditure during imagination. Actually, the objective of the experiments was to identify various influences on the awareness of internal states. Jacobson incorporated the concept of energy waste in his Progressive Relaxation therapy, particularly in the treatment of anxiety and tension.

Jacobson pointed out that while most people believe anxiety and tension are caused by the existence of a problem, that is, by external influences, his experimental and clinical evidence indicates that anxiety is caused by the effort-tension to solve problems, and that anxiety is really *muscle tension-image patterns*. In other words, the mental review of tension-producing situations, even the subconscious image or sensation of the experience, sets the muscles into particular patterns of tension, such as bracing for a blow. Since many of these tension-image muscle patterns are lost to memory, Jacobson conceded that imagery could be used to elicit an accurate identification of the muscle tension-image pattern. After one could relate the image causing the tension to the muscle tension, the idea would then be to practice relaxation and gradually eliminate the image which in itself caused tension.

In clinical practice, Jacobson's technique, combining psychologic with physiologic awareness, constitutes a psychobiologic therapeutic procedure for the treatment of anxiety and stress-related problems. The procedure consists of three stages: (1) identification of the difficulties, i.e., the situations which cause tension; (2) identification of the muscle tension-image patterns (e.g., the businessman in a conference must concentrate on listening, analyzing information, etc., and so tenses the face, around the eyes, even the ears, tenses the shoulders, etc.), then (3) practicing the relaxation procedures. Identifying the tension-image patterns is similar to visualizing or recreating the feelings accompanying the difficult events that cause tension, as for example, the businessman imagining the tension-producing situation of the conference can become aware of the eye tension, and this activates the muscles making them tense. Once the tension-image is identified, the patient is asked to relax that image, or as Jacobson directs, "go negative," and repeat this exercise along with the relaxation exercises until the tension-images no longer produce muscle tension.[3] This aspect of the technique is similar to desensitization, where the procedure is to imagine as vividly as possible anxiety-producing situations while learning how to maintain low muscle tension.

It should be pointed out that Jacobson consistently documented the reductions in muscle activity that occurred as a result of following his relaxation procedure, and his results are supported by the consistent reduction currently being reported in studies comparing Progressive Relaxation with other relaxation techniques.

## Hypnotic Suggestion and Autogenic Training

Research and clinical application of biofeedback-assisted relaxation has also brought three other relaxation techniques into prominence: Schultz's Autogenic Training, meditation, and hypnotic suggestion.

Like Jacobson's technique, these techniques are also exclusively concerned with manipulations of the still mysterious activities of the human mind that continue to elude definition by the physical biomedical sciences.

Hypnotic suggestion is not used extensively in either

---

3. Jacobson's procedure is the forerunner of Wolpe's systematic desensitization (see pages 91–92).

medical or psychological therapy for the purpose of inducing and sustaining relaxation although it is used occasionally in a form of systematic desensitization and in research studies.

Autogenic training did, however, develop directly from the therapeutic practice of hypnosis for relaxation as a countermeasure for anxiety and related problems. The complete training program is divided into three categories of exercises: autosuggestion about relaxation, single-focus mental concentration (as in yogic meditation), and finally meditation on abstract qualities of universal consciousness, much as in yogic or Zen meditation. It is principally the first series of exercises, and only occasionally the second, that are used practically in medical or psychologic treatment.

The first series of exercises used with EMG biofeedback are simple self-suggestion phrases designed to mimic the hypnotically induced relaxed state. The phrases range from "my arm is heavy," "my arm is warm," through all parts of the body. In the original, the phrases began with the concept of heaviness, which was serially applied first to the whole body, then to each of the major parts. The sequence was then repeated using the idea of warmth, going on to the concept of deep relaxation. Allowing sufficient time for the autosuggestions to take effect in the mind and in the muscles required somewhat excessively long periods of time, both for each practice session and for the entire course. In modern practice the amount of time has been considerably shortened, so that a whole "round" can be practiced in an hour's time.[4]

As used with biofeedback muscle signals, the autogenic training phrases are focussed primarily on the physiologic aspect (muscle tension or skin temperature) used in the training, interspersed with general suggestions for relaxation. Each phrase is said slowly, allowing time for the patient to begin to feel some awareness of the effect of the suggestion. Often the therapist, at the beginning of treatment, speaks the

---

4. Additional information about A.T. and the phrases are given in Appendix 1.

phrases at the proper pacing and in a soothing voice, similar to hypnotic induction. Some therapists further encourage the use of imagery of situations or memories accompanying states of heaviness, warmth and relaxation.

## Transcendental Meditation

Almost concurrently with the development of biofeedback, certain philosophies of the Maharishi Mahesh Yogi became popular in the United States. His simplified formula for meditation, called Transcendental Meditation, has been studied extensively in psychophysiology laboratories and it is claimed that the procedure, calling for two 15-minute meditation periods a day, produces profound physiologic changes characteristic of tranquillity, when practiced faithfully.

The use of Transcendental Meditation to normalize body functions may be more a matter of changing lifestyle than its having any specific effects on physiology. It occupies a peculiar position in the new categories of psychophilosophic healing arts, being a meditation practice adapted to Western concepts and philosophic backgrounds. T.M. consists of two essentials: the twice-daily meditation practice, each of 15 minutes duration, in which no particular direction of thought may or may not be attempted, but instead, a mantra is constantly repeated to oneself, and second, belief that the practice will bring order to the mind and body.

Research studies demonstrating the dramatic changes in physiologic activity occurring with T.M. practice have been widely advertised by rather professional promotional techniques, with the result that the general population at least has been impressed by the scientific data.

Most serious psychophysiologic and biomedical researchers, however, point out the failure of all research on the physiologic effects of T.M. to date to compare to the effectiveness of simple rest. Their criticism suggests that similar, possibly identical, physiological changes may occur if individuals would simply rest quietly twice daily for fifteen minutes at a time. It is unfortunate that no one has taken the time to gather the data to support this criticism; nevertheless, it is a crucial issue, and most medical professionals hesitate to accept the available data.

The criticism does not, however, deny the usefulness of T.M. practice as an adjunct to therapeutic relaxation techniques, including EMG biofeedback. Nonetheless, as I often remark, practicing Transcendental Meditation twice daily is the first time Americans have ever sat still and focussed on their minds, and one easily could expect to see physiologic changes resulting from this voluntary regime of inactivity. Most responsible people try to meet the fast pace of today's world, and siestas, naps or simply sitting quietly are not part of the average American's routine. There is also the element of belief in T.M. practice that is common to the practice of any other therapeutic exercise. Westerners believe in medical authority by and large, and it is often this belief that produces the beneficial results along with the actual effect of the relaxation exercises or tranquillizers or psychotherapy or even biofeedback.

Of the very few research studies conducted by researchers not within the T.M. fold are two studies, confirming each other, which provide physiologic data indicating that transcendental meditators spend most of their meditation time in sleep stages 1, 2, 3, or 4. One investigator suggests, somewhat catishly, that T.M. teaches people how to cat-nap; the other researcher interprets his data as failing to support the concept of T.M. researchers that meditation produces a single, unique state of consciousness, refuting Wallace's claim.

A third study compared effects of T.M. practice in experienced T.M. meditators with the effects of subjects simply being instructed to relax. Measurements of heart rate, muscle tension, and brain wave alpha activity revealed that the only significant changes occurred in the relaxed, not the T.M. subjects.

It may seem unconscionable for investigators to quibble over a T.M. conclusion that cannot be completely confirmed by present-day psychophysiologic techniques or data analyses. The psychophysiologist who desires to deny the therapeutic significance of learning to control states of consciousness that (1) resemble certain sleep stages electroencephalographically but cannot be proved to be exclusively those sleep stages, and (2) give rise to consensus of subjective reporting of improved physical and mental health, would seem to be more interested in quibbling than in the true objectives of research. It certainly is an important step if T.M. can teach people how to cat-nap, a technique universally agreed upon as a helpful preventive medical procedure, regardless of whether the context of the control is religious, philosophic, mystical, or medical.

## Relaxation Is an Awareness Process

It is a particularly interesting observation to note that three of the four major relaxation techniques used in combination with EMG biofeedback stem directly from Hindu yogic meditation. I have not mentioned yogic exercises which are used by Patel and by Datey and by biofeedback researchers in India since these are discussed in the sections on biofeedback and essential hypertension. Information on yogic exercises is readily available and there is no need to discuss them here except to note that both Patel and Datey use Hatha yoga exercises which require both physical manipulation and concentration on awareness of the body activities.

All of the relaxation procedures described above have been used in conjunction with biofeedback; in fact it is rare that one reads a scientific report on EMG biofeedback without their reported use as supplementary procedures. Although the use of combined techniques for relaxation has been justified on a scientific level, there are interesting social reasons why the combinations are so successful. In addition to the direct accessibility of important information, as noted above, most Westerners have been educated and reconciled to the scientific dictum that what one cannot see or feel about the body cannot be controlled voluntarily. All supplementary relaxation techniques focus upon awareness of internal states, i.e., attention is directed inwardly instead of the usual outwardly directed attention. This change in the normal person's perspective entails a learning process, and the aids supplied by autosuggestive phrases, comparing relaxation with tensing, and sitting quietly becoming aware of the self, act as self-teaching devices to explore personal territory that has been so long screened from awareness.

# 3
## CLINICAL USES OF
## EMG BIOFEEDBACK RELAXATION

## The Technology

Muscle biofeedback is currently concerned chiefly with learning to decrease muscle tension, as in relaxation, or learning to increase muscle activity to recover muscle function, as in the rehabilitation from partial muscle paralysis. The two directions of learning control over muscle activity involve different directions of muscle function and relate to quite different muscle disorders. The significance, methods, and applications of biofeedback-assisted muscle relaxation techniques are described below, while the use of EMG biofeedback as a muscle rehabilitation technique is described in Chapter 4.

Biofeedback of muscle activity is usually referred to as EMG biofeedback, from the acronym for electromyogram, the recorded pattern of muscle electrical activity. Instruments used for EMG biofeedback to reduce muscle tension levels as a relaxation technique are fairly straightforward. Sensors are placed on the skin over an appropriate muscle and at a convenient distance from each other, with a third electrode—serving as the electrical reference—placed on a relatively neutral electrical tissue such as over bone. The electrical signals from the underlying muscle are led to the biofeedback instrument where they are amplified and summed over a convenient time period and then used to activate an auditory or visual signal. The EMG signal is generally used as an integrated value that represents the sum of the electrical activity under the sensors, and the biofeedback signal thus indicates the amount of muscle activity for that time period. The biological information fed back to the individual can be easily perceived in the changing intensity of the light signal, the number of light signals activated, or in the changing pitch of the auditory signal, or, in some cases, by the changing values of numbers of a counter.

It is assumed that muscle tension, particularly that found in emotional and psychosomatic problems, is a function of the number of muscle fibers which are active, more being active during tension states and fewer to none being active during relaxation.[1] The relative accuracy of EMG biofeedback thus depends upon us-

1. Muscle fibers are actually active only as motor units, i.e., families of muscle fibers related because they are all innervated by the same final motor nerve fibril. Strictly speaking, the amplitude or voltage of muscle activity indicates only whether or not some motor units under the electrodes are active. Since in most EMG biofeedback instruments the voltages of motor unit activity are summed, the integrated voltage-frequency value does not indicate whether large- or small-amplitude motor units become active or inactive, i.e., the integrated value does not give any information about *which* motor units are active at different levels of tension. While this deficiency may be less important with small muscles, variations in active and inactive motor units do occur in large muscles; moreover, these variations can be considerable among different muscles, and particularly if positions of the electrodes are varied from training session to session. Since healthy motor units become active according to the all-or-none law, summing motor unit activity as an integrated value may sometimes be misleading since it may give undue weight to conditions of high muscle tension when many units are active, and proportionately less weight to conditions of relaxation.

ing standard electrode placements for specific muscles to ensure reliability of muscle electrical activity with respect to the distance (depth) of active muscle fibers from the receiving electrodes and with respect to differences in amplitude and rate of muscle electrical activity in different muscles. Practitioners of EMG biofeedback should be aware that such factors are important when different muscle groups are used and can be important to the success or failure of EMG biofeedback training.

## Preview Summary of EMG Clinical Applications

EMG biofeedback is probably the most useful of all the biofeedback techniques, having an extraordinary range of applications. In the present state of the art, it is also one of the easiest forms of biofeedback to instrument and one of the easiest for the patient to learn.

The psychological and medical disorders that have been reported to respond to EMG biofeedback listed on pages 65–66 read like a tour of therapeutic fantasyland, yet they all derive from only two root causes: (1) emotional tension reflected in body tension and (2) injury or pathology of nerves supplying the muscles. The former are treated with EMG biofeedback relaxation techniques and the latter are treated with EMG biofeedback to increase muscle activity.

Emotional problems such as anxiety, neuroses, behavioral problems, drug abuse, alcoholism, psychotic behavior, or other forms of disturbed behavior have in common increased muscle tension which apparently results directly from the emotions of anxiety and kindred emotional states of apprehension, insecurity, frustration, or inadequacy. These are all emotions which evoke defensive behavior, particularly the activation of muscles in preparation to defend against threats to one's well-being. Continued stress and emotional pressure maintain the muscle tension, and over time the muscles adapt to higher and higher levels of tension. One theory suggests that such muscle tensions are sustained because of a learned central (brain) inhibition which blocks recognition of the increased tension and no corrective information from the brain is activated to reduce muscle tension. This is discussed more fully in other sections of the book.

If the increased muscle tension is due to an emotional difficulty rather than to a muscle difficulty, why can relaxation relieve the emotional problem? Edmund Jacobson proposed that anxiety is incompatible with relaxation, and he demonstrated that effective and controllable relaxation was sufficient to provide relief from anxiety. Schultz and Luthe, from clinical work with autogenic training, suggested that primary muscle relaxation relieves emotional problems by decreasing muscle tension impulses to the cortex, in turn decreasing the cortical influence on lower muscle control centers keeping muscles tense in the defense posture. Many emotional problems, however, are complex, and in such cases the objective of EMG biofeedback as used to decrease muscle tension is to afford enough physical relaxation to allow for decreased mental tension by removing the distracting muscle tension impulses going to the central nervous system. This in turn appears to allow the patient's attention to shift to more productive memories, insights, and control which he and the therapist can use for the resolution of the emotional problem.

Although it is generally believed that emotional problems are the source of psychosomatic problems, because psychosomatic disorders have a specific focus of physiologic dysfunction, they have a different order of complexity. If the physical changes, such as in asthma, ulcer, colitis, etc., have not progressed too far, then it appears that relaxation procedures diminish body tensions sufficiently to allow for recovery, and the mechanism is similar to that for emotional problems. The major difficulty is that in some cases the visceral tension (that causing the pathology) may be greater than the muscle tension. In these instances it has been found that recovery could occur if EMG biofeedback training were continued until a transfer of the relaxation effect to smooth muscles took place.

The physical problems responsive to EMG biofeedback consist of two principal categories: (1) disorders directly involving the innervation to the muscles, such as muscle paralysis, spasticity, tremors, etc., and (2) organic illnesses with either emotional problems arising because of illness or in which emotional distress may play a major contributing, but not causative role. In the first category, where nerve injury is the primary disorder, EMG biofeedback training is used to increase tension levels, which leads to overactivity of the remaining innervated muscle fibers, in turn leading to budding of the injured nerve terminals and re-innervation of the muscle fibers. In the second category it is well known that all illness is accompanied by emotional distress, and in some physical illnesses emotional factors may be major contributing elements. The emotional tension causes a body tension overload which can aggravate the primary condition quite remarkably, and thus tension relief, through stress-reduction biofeedback relaxation procedures, materially assists in recovery from many physical illnesses.

## Disorders Reported to Respond to EMG Biofeedback

### Primarily Emotional Problems

1. Anxiety
2. Phobias
3. Tension headache
4. Chronic headache
5. Social problems . . . unemployment
6. Learning problems, hyperactive children
7. Stage fright
8. Subvocalization
9. Insomnia
10. Alcoholism
11. Drug abuse
12. Depression with anxiety

### Primarily Psychosomatic Problems

1. Asthma

2. Essential hypertension
3. Bruxism
4. Intestinal disorders (ulcer, colitis, spasms of smooth muscles and sphincters)
5. Menstrual distress

*Primarily Physical Problems*
1. Muscle spasms with pain
2. Nerve-muscle injuries . . . stroke, paralysis
3. Hyperkinesias, dyskinesias
4. Spasticity
5. Cerebral palsy
6. Spasmodic torticollis
7. Tinnitus with anxiety
8. Migraine headache
9. Dystonias
10. Dysphonia

The exact reasons for the success of EMG biofeedback in emotional, psychosomatic, or stress-related illnesses is not yet clear, however, for a number of reasons. Surprisingly, even in basic research studies, the effect of EMG biofeedback has been independently evaluated in few studies, and when used clinically, EMG biofeedback is invariably supplemented by other therapeutic techniques. When EMG biofeedback has been used independently, results tended to be equivocal, with no correlation between changes in muscle tension and changes in subjective relief from tension.[2] Nonetheless, combining other clinical relaxation procedures with EMG biofeedback produces strikingly effective results, strongly suggesting an important interplay between a range of relevant information sources with EMG information.

The extensive utility of EMG biofeedback appears to relate quite specifically to the function of muscles as the implementors of reaction and to the inherent ability for voluntary control over muscles. Human beings can

2. Reasons for equivocal results may be inappropriate instrument design, faulty equipment, inexperience with equipment, investigator bias, nonrelevance of muscles used to the perception of muscle tension in the presenting ailment, errors in electrodal distance, etc.

develop extraordinary degrees of voluntary control over muscle activities, and the ease of biofeedback learning to control very low levels of muscle activity would seem to indicate that the ability to control muscle movement is simply extended when information about low-level nonmovement muscle activity is made available, as in the form of muscle biofeedback signals. The lights or tones of the biofeedback signal provide an approximate indicator of muscle activity that is consciously unfelt, as when muscles are at rest or are partially paralyzed. The EMG biofeedback information corresponds to muscle information normally sensed internally and used to control muscles voluntarily; the biofeedback technique simply detects lower levels of muscle activity. The interesting difference in the biofeedback from the non-biofeedback situation is that in biofeedback the information about muscle activity is detected electronically and is "sensed" auditorily or visually. The effect apparently is the same; the integrative brain systems use the additional, low-level activity information to control muscle activity to achieve a cerebral identification of different levels of muscle tension that previously made no impression upon awareness. The auditory or visual feedback information about the muscle activity is then used in the same manner as the normal flow of internal muscle information to accomplish the voluntary physiologic control of muscle tension. The EMG biofeedback instrument thus acts as (1) an extended muscle sense, and (2) a simple converter of information about muscle electrical activity into visual or auditory sensory information.

## Headache

As many as half the world's population may be headache sufferers. We know, for example, that somewhere between 10 and 20 percent of the world's population suffer migraine headaches, and while this is the most commonly occurring kind of headache, there are at least eight other types of headache, ranging from the tension headache to headaches triggered by different food chemicals to the cluster headache and the chronic headache of mixed origins.

The head area, the noble headland of evolutionary progress, is endowed with enormous complexity that not only gives it its advantages but burdens it with properties that make it most vulnerable to environmental assaults on the body. Because of its great labyrinthine internal expanses, it contains the most sensitive nerve endings in the body and it also has the greatest vascular networks to guarantee its proper blood supply and drainage. There seems to be an almost innumerable array of elements which can affect both the nerve endings and vascular beds of the head adversely and cause the pain of headache. There are at least three fundamental causes of headache: (1) muscle tension: as in simple tension headache, the scalp muscle contraction headache, that caused by muscle injury, and the headache syndrome which stems from emotional causes; (2) the vascular headache in which the vascular system of the head area is attacked by food chemicals, pollens, barometric changes, drugs, or other specific elements; and (3) the vascular headache in which the vascular system reacts to unknown events or causes. Whatever the ultimate origin of the headache, clinical evidence suggests that the headache pain arises from alterations in blood supply of the head.

Regardless of the kind of headache, one consequence of headache pain is tension in the muscles of the head and shoulders. In the case of vascular headaches, this generally seems to be a protective device, as if guarding against events which can aggravate the pain, such as sudden movement. Unfortunately, the increased muscle tension nearly always increases the severity of the headache pain.

The muscular and vascular causes of headache pain suggest that biofeedback techniques can play major therapeutic roles in the treatment of headache, and at least three biofeedback techniques have been used with success. Two are concerned with vascular regulation: learning to control hand temperature, presumably as a relaxation technique, and biofeedback of temporal artery pulse pressure (amplitude) for learning to control the vasomotor activity of the extracranial blood vessels of the head. These are discussed in Chapter 5.

EMG biofeedback relaxation is an appropriate treatment for all headache pain, but is the biofeedback treatment of choice particularly for muscle contraction, psychogenic, and muscle injury headaches. It can, however, also be used effectively as an adjunctive treatment to relieve the added effect of the reflex muscle tension that occurs in vascular headaches.

In the following summary the reader should be aware of several circumstances pertinent to a critical assessment of the utility of EMG biofeedback in headache. First, because of the high rate of success of the original experimental work, the relative simplicity of the technique, combined with the relatively uncomplicated nature of tension headache, EMG biofeedback treatment for tension headache has been incorporated into many clinical practices much as a new drug would be, with the result that little formally validated effectiveness of the technique has been published. For example, I personally know at least six biofeedback treatment programs using EMG biofeedback in clinical practice successfully whose results will not be summarized for scientific publication.

Second, the scientific reports summarized below are of the kind which generally appear to support or disprove an original treatment program and, except for the original, such studies are designed to examine the relative importance of different aspects of the technique. The practitioner therefore must weigh projected therapeutic importance from the standpoint of results rather from the standpoint of the research interests.

Third, EMG biofeedback as an independent treatment modality for tension headache is not generally used; successful treatments additionally use a considerable variety of supporting, supplementary techniques.

And fourth, that while it can readily be projected that EMG and vascular biofeedback could be successfully combined for the treatment of the vascular headache, this has not yet been explored.

## Tension Headache

Much of the research and clinical interest in EMG biofeedback-assisted relaxation has stemmed from the original work of Budzynski and colleagues developing the technique for use in tension headaches. A report published in 1973 summarizes the application of their techniques to this tension disorder. Details of a more generalized, clinical version of the technique are given on pages 115–119.

Following a newspaper advertisement, volunteer subjects were screened intensively for tension headache, also known as the muscle contraction headache, and were treated by being given approximately 20-minute

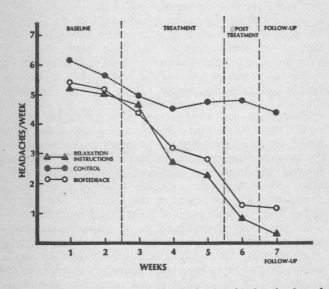

*Fig. 1.* Mean headache rate (headaches/week) for the 2-week pretreatment phase, the week following treatment, and at follow-up as a function of intervention procedure (from Haynes, Griffin, Mooney, and Parise, *Behavior Therapy,* 1975, *6* 672–678).

frontalis[3] EMG biofeedback sessions, twice weekly over a 16-week period. Muscle tension levels decreased from a mean of 10 μV peak-to-peak to about 3.5 μV, and hourly headache activity, derived from self-reports on intensity, decreased from an average value of about 5 to 2, with the most dramatic effect occurring during a three-month follow-up period when headache activity fell to a value of about one and remained there. Two control groups revealed that muscle tension levels were only minimally affected by pseudo-feedback or no-feedback.

A careful analysis of the procedure reveals several psychotherapeutic ploys that were not separately evaluated for their degree of contribution to the success of the treatment. The new elements were specifically: (1) hourly charting of headache activity by the patient, (2) explaining headache and how biofeedback works, (3) offering clues and strategy for reducing muscle tension, (4) regular, twice-daily home practice using a relaxation technique similar to Transcendental Meditation. Aside from these, the procedure, moreover, represents quite a different way of dealing with suffering patients, the new elements of the treatment regime either putting the responsibility onto the patient or giving him information about the process and how to work with it.

A neat replication study of EMG biofeedback as a primary treatment for tension headache has been reported by Hutchings and Reinking. The effect of frontalis muscle EMG biofeedback was evaluated in 18 individuals with severe tension headaches during 10 training sessions of about 30 minutes each. The treatment was augmented by instructions about the concept of passive volition, to use the feedback passively, and also to practice relaxation at home at least twice a day. This procedure was compared to two other procedures, one, using the Jacobson-Wolpe-autogenic relaxation instructions and the other combining the two procedures.

---

3. The frontalis muscles are small muscles located directly above the eyebrows.

From well-established (28-day) baseline data, treatment results showed a composite reduction in headache scores (indicating incidence and severity) from about 10 or 13 to 3 or 4 for both the EMG biofeedback treatment and the combined treatment, whereas the scores for patients receiving the verbal relaxation instructions decreased only from about 14 to approximately 12. Average values for muscle tension showed a marked reduction of muscle tension in all treatment groups although the verbal instruction group responded more slowly and its effect seemed less sustained than for either the EMG biofeedback treatment group or the combined treatment group.

Two studies by Wickramasekera have yielded similar successful results; in one study, using either forearm

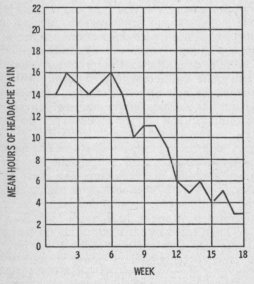

*Fig. 2.* Effect of EMG biofeedback on tension headache as average number of hours of headache pain per week. Weeks 0–3 were pretreatment, weeks 3–6 were sessions with nonrelevant feedback, and weeks 6–18 were biofeedback sessions (from Wickramasekera, *Am. J. Clin. Hypn.,* 1972, *15,* 83–85).

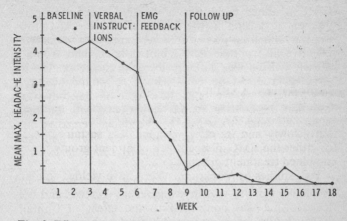

*Fig. 3*. Effect of EMG biofeedback on tension headache as the average of maximum estimated intensity of headache pain. Weeks 0–3 were pretreatment control observations, weeks 3–6 used the verbal relaxation instructions of Wolpe and Lazarus, weeks 6–9 used EMG biofeedback. Results are averages for five female patients (from Wickramasekera, *Headache*, 1973, *13*, 74–76).

extensor muscle or frontalis muscle feedback, five neurologically diagnosed tension headache patients showed a reduction in mean hours of headache activity from about 15 to 3; in a second study, the pretreatment headache activity of five patients averaging 4.25 was reduced to 3.75 by a three-week course in the Wolpe and Lazarus brief relaxation procedure, and was further reduced to 0.5 following three weeks of EMG biofeedback, remaining at this low level during a nine-week follow-up period. It is not clear *why* initial scores of headache activity were so different in the two studies, but it is clear that EMG biofeedback was remarkably more effective than verbal instructions in relaxation.

On the other hand, Cox and colleagues compared the effects of frontalis EMG biofeedback with the effects of practicing an abbreviated form of Progressive Relaxation and breathing exercises in tension headache patients and found no differences in effects with respect to either reduction of headache activity or reduction of tension in the frontalis muscles. At follow-up, the relaxation procedure was found to be equally as effective as frontalis EMG biofeedback, and frontalis muscle tension was actually lower in the relaxation instructed group of patients. The Cox group noted two other interesting events in the course of the study. One was that the control headache patients, without treatment, continued to search for headache remedies during the study while the treatment groups did not. And second, both treated groups showed a shift in locus of control scores toward internality.

The effect of autogenic training alone on tension headache activity was investigated by Haynes and colleagues and was compared to the effect of frontalis EMG biofeedback training. Using eight patients in each treatment group, they found both procedures to be almost equally effective, with improvement maintained over a six-month follow-up period.

In a second study, Haynes and colleagues compared

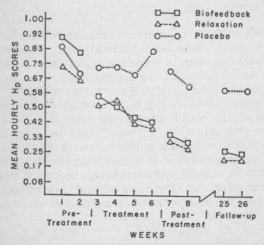

*Fig. 4.* Weekly $H_D$ scores (from Cox, Freundlich, and Meyer, *J. Consult. & Clin. Psych.*, 1975, *43*, 892–898).

CLINICAL USES OF EMG BIOFEEDBACK RELAXATION 75

the effects of EMG biofeedback with the effects of simple instructions to relax in tension headache patients. In this study (totalling 21 patients), the relaxation instructions alone reduced headache activity (measured by an index of incidence, duration and severity) by nearly 80 percent, while reduction following EMG biofeedback training was approximately 60 percent. The control patients, without treatment, actually showed an increase in headache activity. At follow-up, some five to seven months after training, the relaxation instructed group were found to be virtually headache free, and the EMG biofeedback trained group showed roughly only 20 percent of their pretreatment headache activity. The no-treatment group was somewhat below their original headache activity at follow-up.

These results prompted Haynes et al. to analyze their combined data more extensively, and they found many instances in tension headache patients in which there was no relationship between frontalis EMG tension levels and headache activity. For example, some subjects with an extremely high frontalis EMG tension level had few or no headaches while others with relatively low tension levels reported frequent headaches.[4]

Diamond has reported enthusiastically on the success of using EMG and temperature biofeedback concurrently in a variety of types of headaches, principally those with a vascular component. It is noteworthy that he found no difference in effectiveness between an "intensive" treatment regime of two such combination sessions per day for twelve working days and the "routine" treatment regime of twice-weekly sessions for four weeks. He reports a 50 percent improvement in patients with headaches of mixed vascular and psychogenic etiology and an 82 percent success rate in straight vascular headaches. Diamond does note, however, that a major problem of his biofeedback therapy was the

---

4. Problems relating to correlations between muscle tension levels, subjective activity, and symptoms of anxiety, tension and headache are discussed further on p. 86.

failure of patients to practice relaxation after being weaned from working with the biofeedback devices.

Probably the most humorous, but enlightening, report on biofeedback and headaches was presented at the Biofeedback Research Society meetings of 1975. Dr. Leon Otis summarized a series of puzzling research events of the previous year or so. He had earlier, in 1974, reported a quite significant reduction in headache activity following a two-week course with EMG biofeedback in which the basic procedure consisted of 10 trials (sets) of Jacobsonian tense-relax exercises, specifically, one-minute raise, rest, and then lower muscle tension commands with the feedback signal used to reinforce the tension levels. It had been assumed that the patients' headache relief occurred because they had developed varying degrees of voluntary control over muscle tension and the success was related to a developing awareness of relaxation (Jacobson's concept) that was (behaviorally) reinforced by the feedback signal. It was subsequently found, however, that owing to a computer error, the neatly automated experiment had activated a feedback signal *only* when muscle tension was *increased*. Nonetheless, 9 of 11 patients had shown a significant *decrease* in headache activity after the second week of training and 7 of the 11 were *headache free*. In casting about to explain why it was that a signal presumably reinforcing the tensing phases of the exercise and not reinforcement of the relaxation phase had produced the effect, Otis and his colleagues decided that the experimental paradigm was much like that of Progressive Relaxation paradigm (which it is), and thus the feedback signal triggered by the muscle tensing actually reinforced the subsequent relief from that tension.

Other than being crossed up by getting the right result with the wrong procedure, the Otis group made some interesting additional observations about the learning process. First, in comparing the EMG biofeedback technique (basically Jacobson's technique set to music) to the unadorned Jacobson's tense-relax exercises, they found the exercises alone to be just as effective as the frontalis EMG biofeedback training for relief of headache and, in fact, took less training time.[5] They also observed that subjects either learn to relax quickly or not at all. It was further noted that the offending trapezius muscles of the shoulders had about the same tension levels whether a headache was present or not; moreover, while a learned reduction in tension of one of the muscle groups of the head did tend to generalize the relaxation effect to other muscles of the cephalic region, there was *not* a generalization of relaxation to the arms and legs. Finally, they found that Rotter's Internal-External scale successfully predicted 11 out of 13 who stayed in or dropped out of the study.

Either Otis is unconsciously heavily biased about biofeedback, or he leads a charmed scientific life on the side of ultimate probabilities, for he reports two other experiences (not experiments) in his pursuit of biofeedback and headache research. First, in a pilot study comparing Jacobson's tense-relax exercises to EMG biofeedback, 3 of 4 of the exercise subjects showed a significant reduction in headache activity, while only 2 of 6 of the biofeedback subjects found headache relief.

And second, as a result of extraordinary punctiliousness, one study aborted itself. Attempting to adhere to rigid scientific standards for a crucial study, control or "baseline" physiologic data was to be obtained during both headache and headache-free periods. As part of the control procedure, the patients were instructed to keep logs of their headache activity every two hours, and were given timers for this purpose. The baseline data was obtained for all patients for their headache-free periods, but almost no one called to come in for a control session during a headache. Then it was discovered that after six weeks most of the subjects were

---

5. I have always insisted that many so-called biofeedback signals, when used as conditioning reinforcers, may also act as alerting stimuli and therefore may be inhibitory to learning. This is easily demonstrated by comparing procedures, as in this case. These results are, moreover, in sharp contrast to those of other similar studies.

becoming headache free, apparently simply as a result of keeping logs of the headache activity.[6]

Whatever works to produce such out-of-the-way results for Otis, it certainly is not EMG biofeedback. The fact that his EMG biofeedback experiment was successful while it was feeding back information to the patients the reverse of what was intended; his studies finding Progressive Relaxation therapeutically superior to EMG relaxation; the curing of headache before the treatment starts . . . all these events suggest the old familiar scientific cop-outs to avoid or explain "psychic" (psychologic) influences, such as placebo effect, experimenter bias, suggestibility, demand characteristics, etc., to explain effects that are difficult to account for. That the beneficial effects might depend upon complex mental activity is beyond the pale for many traditional researchers. Fortunately, however, there are psychologists and others who are studying the effects of cognitive activity on various human functions.

From Reeves comes an interesting exposition of the cognitive skills training approach and its application to EMG biofeedback reduction of tension headache. Although he deals with a single patient, and quite successfully, the relevance of this approach to biofeedback is made clear in both the experimental design and discussion. Reeves notes that there is a scientific literature showing "that stress reactions can vary as a function of cognitive variables, although the nature of the threatening events remains constant," and that "cognitive reappraisal, in the form of self-statements, can be clinically employed to reduce stress reaction." He notes that "Janis (1971) has posited that providing information regarding a stressful event increases stress tolerance," that is, cognitive "rehearsal allows the individual to develop realistic self-delivered reassurances, and these minimize the emotional impact of the stressor when it is encountered."

---

6. Otis's luck is still holding. He has just reported that a replication of this experiment failed. He explains the success of the first experiment with the timer technique as due to a chance selection of subjects susceptible to the timer technique.

Applying this technique to his headache patient, Reeves found that no changes in EMG or headache activity occurred when the patient was engaged in "cognitive rehearsal"; it was not until the patient was *specifically instructed* to alter his cognitive appraisal, or self-statements, of stress situations that reductions in self-reports of headache activity occurred, and these were *not* accompanied by comparable decreases in frontalis EMG tension level.

In a second stage of treatment, Reeves instituted EMG biofeedback and "stress management" (desensitization procedures), which resulted in markedly decreased headache activity, and with these procedures relief *was* accompanied by substantial immediate reduction in frontalis EMG levels. An evaluation six months later showed maintenance of the same degree of reduction of both headache and EMG activity.

## Other Relaxation Techniques for Headache

Although a number of health professionals do use Progressive Relaxation as a therapeutic device in the treatment of muscle contraction headache, scientific studies of the degree of effectiveness, length of treatment required, duration of effect, details of procedure, and quantification of its effect are scarce. Along with biofeedback, a good deal of interest in Progressive Relaxation has been revived in explorations of its value in techniques of systematic desensitization such as that developed by Wolpe. One recent report by Tasto and Hinkle indicates success in six patients with tension headache.

Curiously, other documented studies using relaxation techniques in the treatment of headache have been for cases of migraine. In two instances Progressive Relaxation was either integral to, or combined with, a desensitization procedure. A part of the rationale for the combination approach was the idea that the migraine patient is characterized by an inability to express hostility in social situations, thus assertive therapy was also included, and that migraine is a symptom of much larger behavioral problems and so cannot be treated by means of single procedures. It was reported that greater relief was provided using the combination treatment than when muscle relaxation techniques alone were used.

On the other hand, Benson has reported on the use of Transcendental Meditation, a procedure which elicits what he now refers to as the relaxation response, in migraine patients. He has cited as the rationale for using Transcendental Meditation the concept that T.M. acts by decreasing general sympathetic nervous system activity. It has been pointed out, however, by Bakal, there is no research which suggests that high levels of sympathetic nervous system activity characterize migraine patients. Nonetheless, Benson reports that trend analysis of his results shows 6 of 17 migraine patients were improved by practicing T.M. although only three showed marked improvement, and the average number of "headache units" per month changed only from 39 to 33 following weeks of T.M. practice.

Lutker used Progressive Relaxation as a "conditioning stimulus" in treating a migraine patient. Beginning with instructions of Wolpe's modification of Jacobson's tense-relax exercises, the patient was instructed in transferring the relaxation feeling to the times of "pressure build-up" just preceding the headache, first by actively practicing relaxation, then simply by thinking being relaxed briefly. Even as the transfer process was being learned, headache activity pain was completely relieved, and eventually the pressure build-up disappeared.

## Other Biofeedback Techniques for Headache

Uses of temperature, alpha, and temporal artery pressure control for the treatment of headache are discussed in the sections on temperature, EEG, and cardiovascular biofeedback.

## Anxiety and Tension

There is an abundance of scientific literature that supports, at least in part, Jacobson's concept that anxiety and relaxation are mutually exclusive. It is also generally inferred that many emotional problems and the majority of psychosomatic disorders contain a large component of anxiety, although anxiety may often be obscured by somatic symptoms or by various emotional compensatory mechanisms. It is a curious dichotomy of therapeutics that when anxiety is the major presenting symptom the therapy is more medication than psychotherapy, while the somatic symptomatology of anxiety tends to be treated mainly medically. The pervasiveness of anxiety and stress responses throughout our society not only constitutes a large area of distress, but implies the relatively unsuccessful nature of available treatments. If biofeedback is to be an important therapy, by virtue of its potential for developing self-control over stress responses, studies which evaluate its effectiveness and efficiency in anxiety and other disorders of tension are of the utmost importance.

The problems for the clinical investigator in isolating the crucial aspects of any new therapy are tedious, and for biofeedback the problem is considerably more complex. The biofeedback requirement that the individual patient must contribute the performing, effective thrust and mechanism of the treatment is the same kind of tough scientific nut to crack as other, internally generated psychologic events that contribute significantly to normalizing any disorder, such as the placebo effect, faith, motivation, etc. There is, moreover, the question of ethics, the inadvisability and thus the unethical process of denying the patient any aspect of a therapy which affords relief of the problem. In the case of anxiety and many other emotional problems and in psychosomatic disturbances, psychologic interventions are critical elements. On the other hand, biofeedback is equated with medical intervention, and largely because of the past significance or importance of physical, medical intervention, many of the supporting psychologic measures are minimized or even neglected. It will take some time to isolate the specific therapeutic effects of biofeedback from the array of new philosophic and psychologic elements which generally accompany its present use.

Because of the therapeutic problems, and because of the unique therapeutic approach employed in biofeedback procedures, it is important not to give undue emphasis to the role of biofeedback, despite its apparent obvious contribution, and to be aware of the supporting "psychologic" measures. For this reason, this section on EMG biofeedback as a relaxation procedure is followed by a section summarizing some of the relevant basic research that has attempted to characterize the contributing role of elements in the biofeedback procedure, and to compare these to related, non-biofeedback procedures.

The specific difficulty in evaluating the effectiveness of biodfeedback for anxiety and tension states is the problem of unraveling the relative involvement of muscles, the autonomic nervous system and the subjective aspects. While one school of researchers concludes that tension of the skeletal muscle system follows emotional tension one-to-one and actually acts to aggravate anxiety, another school of psychologists feels that the experimental evidence implicates a primary overactivity of the autonomic nervous system, while yet another school of psychologists and psychoanalysts emphasizes the primary role of subconscious mental activities, with mental tension not necessarily always evoking muscle or autonomic nervous system activity.

The review of the following studies on EMG biofeedback in anxiety and tension should assist in identifying the relative contributions of the various body systems to the symptomatology and treatment of anxiety and tension.

A thorough study of EMG biofeedback in chronic anxiety was reported in 1973 by Raskin and colleagues. Ten well-documented chronic anxiety patients, with an average age of 27, were administered a biofeedback procedure virtually identical to that described above used by Budzynski for tension headaches. The procedure incorporated some brief instructions about relaxation, symptom chart keeping, imagery strategy, and home practice. In addition, the patients continued to see their therapist regularly, and those patients taking medication continued to do so during the treatment period, i.e., the six also suffering insomnia and the four troubled by tension headaches. The anxiety symptoms were assessed both subjectively and by the regular therapist, and subjective assessments of relaxation were also made following each session.

The high degree of reliability of this study is contained in the criteria established for quantifying the learned relaxation. The authors state: "We considered that the patient was able to maintain deep muscle relaxation when his EMG activity averaged less than 25 μV peak-to-peak per trial for 25 minutes. At this level of relaxation almost no motor unit firing was detectable on an oscilloscope. Once the patient could remain deeply relaxed for 25 minutes, training sessions without feedback were interspersed every two or three days. As soon as some progress in relaxing in the laboratory was evident, the patients were instructed to practice relaxation at home."

Considering the chronicity of the ailment and refractoriness to treatment of the patients involved, the biofeedback procedures produced encouraging results. While four patients were improved and six were not with respect to anxiety, the accompanying insomnia and tension headaches were relieved in all but one patient. Moreover, three patients learned to control situational anxiety.

Raskin cites the comparatively transient nature of the EMG bio-feedback-assisted relaxation effect,[7] pointing out that the reported efficiency of Progressive Relaxation and autogenic training techniques may provide for a more efficient carry-over to everyday-life stress situations. The theoretical issue involved is believed by many to involve the phenomenon of adapta-

7. The training program may well have not been long enough.

tion or habituation, that is, any of the following types of adaptation behavior: learning to maintain either a less responsive state, a less reactive physiologic state, or essentially learning to attenuate specifically physiological responses to stressful stimuli, or to recover more quickly following a response to stress. While this concept is supported in laboratory studies where strong stressful stimuli are used, it is still not clear that the physiologic changes involved when stress reactions build up continuously over time are similar to single responses to strong stress, and the role of habituation in recovery processes is still hotly debated.

The practical point for clinical practice is the choosing between attacking the problem from a physical standpoint versus a cognitive one, or combining the approaches. The physical approach would require either prolonged training of muscle relaxation at the muscle level, invoking a kind of conditioning of the relaxed state (as Lutker used in his migraine patient), while the cognitive approach involves concepts such as used by Reeves, described above, which schools the patient in cognitive skills needed to deal with the cerebral aspects of the problem. The physical approach is typified by the Jacobson technique or desensitization therapy, and requires a moderately long period of training. The cognitive approach appears to facilitate more rapid learning and greater control of reactivity.

The Raskin study also brings out the puzzling general lack of correlation between degree of muscle relaxation and degree of subjective or symptomatic change achieved. Their study revealed a low-level correlation between muscle tension scores and subjective anxiety ratings in the individual patients. A similar clinical finding was reported by Breeden et al. in comparing EMG biofeedback with Progressive Relaxation. Although their patients achieved greater reduction of muscle tension with the biofeedback technique, Progressive Relaxation afforded greater relief from anxiety.

Two laboratory research studies using normal volunteers have also measured the relationship between muscl tension and subjective feeling states. One report by Mehearg et al. using a single EMG biofeedback training session found a significant reduction in muscle tension levels, but no correlation with subjective changes. In fact, subjective measures of tension either remained the same or actually increased. A more conclusive study by Alexander et al. used five 20-minute training sessions, and found no reliable correlation between subjective changes and levels of frontalis muscle tension.

Three additional clinical studies on the effect of EMG biofeedback in anxiety are available for comparison. A well-controlled study was reported in 1974 by Le Boeuf in which effects were compared between patients whose anxiety was accompanied by mainly muscular symptoms, as determined by the Fenz-Epstein Modified Anxiety scale, and those whose symptoms were mainly visceral. After a three-month baseline monitoring period, the patients received three months of EMG biofeedback at least three times a week, and were also given relaxation instructions for home use. Results of the treatment showed a fairly clear-cut difference between the patient groups: those with predominantly muscle symptoms were improved significantly in both symptoms and generalized anxiety, whereas the patients with predominantly autonomic (visceral) symptoms were not, despite the fact that there was a correlation between muscle tension and heart rate changes during the treatment sessions.

Townsend and Addario reported a study of 10 chronic anxiety patients using a two-week period of EMG relaxation training followed by two weeks of self-practice. Changes in muscle tension, mood, and anxiety level were compared to those in a matched group receiving group psychotherapy. Results showed the EMG biofeedback treatment group to have significantly lower EMG levels, improved mood, and relief from anxiety not found in the matched control group.

Kondo and his associates conducted a pilot study comparing EMG biofeedback to Progressive Relaxation in patients suffering depression with chronic anxiety. All patients received an average of 18 sessions, each session being 20 minutes in duration. Comparing EMG levels for the first and last days of the treatments between the two treatment groups showed that both EMG biofeedback and Progressive Relaxation produced similar changes in muscle tension. In contrast, subjective evaluations indicated symptom relief in all patients of the Progressive Relaxation groups but relief in only 50 percent of the EMG biofeedback group.

## Factors Influencing EMG Biofeedback Relaxation in Anxiety, Tension and Headache

A review of factors concerned in the effective use of muscle (EMG) biofeedback for anxiety, and in fact probably for most tension or stress-related disorders, is important in view of the ponderous course that systematic research must take. Because EMG biofeedback does generally appear to be of value, it may be helpful for the practitioner to consider the influence of these factors in order to apply feedback techniques optimally.

The question of just how effective EMG biofeedback is in stress-related disorders cannot be tackled before evaluating certain of the procedural details of the various clinical research studies. Probably the first consideration is the target muscle, i.e., the muscle from which the feedback signal of muscle tension level is obtained.

In evaluating which muscle group might best serve the purpose of learning relaxation of the muscles involved in tension headache, Budzynski and Stoyva selected the frontalis muscles of the forehead. The selection of the frontalis over the trapezius or neck muscles was made on the basis of electromyographic studies indicating a relative difficulty of this muscle to relax. It was felt that learned muscle relaxation of a muscle more difficult to relax would ensure greater generalization to other muscle groups of the head. Although the original report indicated that such generalization of relaxation did occur, other studies suggest that the relaxation effect may not generalize. Among more than ten basic research reports, in which EMG tension of the frontalis was measured for biofeedback effects, and ten studies comparing EMG frontalis biofeedback with other relaxation techniques for effects on muscle tension, only one has been a systematic study designed to measure generalization of relaxation. Using feedback of the frontalis muscle tension level, Alexander found that muscle tension of the forearm actually increased and there was no change in tension in leg muscles.

A more recent report by Freedman generally confirmed the failure of frontalis relaxation to generalize to body muscles, but did find that frontalis EMG relaxation training did result in some relaxation of the masseter muscles of the jaws.

A count of reports that give data about correlations between frontalis muscle tension and subjective feelings with EMG biofeedback or with Progressive Relaxation reveals more often than not a lack of correlation for frontalis EMG biofeedback but a 1:1 correlation for Progressive Relaxation.

There are important questions still open, such as questions about the degree of tension reduction actually attained with the frontalis biofeedback technique, and the question about whether a reduction of muscle tension correlates with subjective changes in the feeling or sensations of reduced tension or awareness of muscle tension. There are further questions as well; whether achieving a relaxed state also affects muscle responsivity to stress, or whether changes of tension achieved by EMG biofeedback training generalize to other manifestations of stress reactions, such as symptoms arising from altered reactivity of the autonomic nervous system, or the subjective emotional disturbances themselves.

The fundamental question is, of course: does EMG biofeedback actually produce a significant reduction of frontalis muscle tension? The clinical aspect of this question has been discussed in the section on headache. A review of the biofeedback literature reveals further surprising and dismaying concepts, studies, and results.

One basic and puzzling observation of muscle tension reduction is that the normal *variability* of muscle tension is markedly decreased by EMG biofeedback. Indeed, this effect can be easily seen in nearly every chart published on the EMG biofeedback technique.

The reduction of variation of muscle tension was found to be the major contributing effect of EMG frontalis biofeedback in a study by Coursey. The study compared frontalis EMG biofeedback training with a control subject group simply asked to relax and also to a "cognitive" group of subjects who were instructed on *how* to relax. Although after training muscle tension was found to be lowest in the EMG biofeedback group and only second lowest in the cognitive group, the decreased muscle tension in the EMG biofeedback group was determined to be due primarily to a change in muscle tension variation. The decreased variability is reminiscent of the one cycle per second slowing that occurs at the moment of beginning EEG alpha feedback, and which I have repeatedly commented on as a curious and important event in the biofeedback process, and which may relate to EEG "driving" or "following" responses. It may be troubling for some neurophysiologists to recognize that often EMG potentials reflect a basic rhythmic pattern frequently resembling EEG alpha activity, and which apparently are due to techniques of electrode placement, electrolytes used, interelectrodal distance, and faulty electrical referencing.

Since the usual EMG biofeedback signal is an integrated value over time, it may be possible that this artificial derivative may modify actual muscle activity patterns, thus affecting true muscle tension levels with the result that they are modulated by the power of this interference, a voltage signal which has considerable amplitude and considerable duration. It certainly seems that proper EMG biofeedback should be accompanied by recording facilities which allow for the display or recording of a wide range of frequencies. Actually, it is improper to speak of frequency range in reference to EMG work, since muscle fibers or motor units have the specific characteristic of firing asynchronously, not synchronously.

One methodologic problem, basic to any evaluation

of biofeedback effects, is the tendency of many investigators to use *single* training sessions, and relatively brief sessions at that. Four of ten studies used a single EMG training session of 20 minutes' duration to evaluate effects of muscle biofeedback on muscle tension levels; three of these used the frontalis muscle. One study found no effect of the biofeedback, a second reported some muscle tension reduction but no correlation with subjective reports, while the third compared relaxation effects in personality structures labelled "internal" and "external." The latter study employed a second session a week later to confirm results from the first session, and reported that people classified as "internals"[8] showed decreased muscle tension following both EMG frontalis biofeedback and Progressive Relaxation training (single sessions), that subjective changes occurred mainly in these "internals" while "externals" responded only to the Progressive Relaxation procedure. On the other hand, one of Elmer Green's early reports showed that subjects were able to learn to reduce tension levels of the *forearm* literally to zero within a single training session.

It should be remembered that these research studies were carried out in normal subjects and electromyographic studies consistently demonstrate higher muscle tension levels in individuals with stress-related disorders.

Such differences do not, however, account for the *relative* effectiveness of EMG biofeedback-assisted relaxation as compared to other relaxation techniques in normal subjects. There are some eleven studies which have compared the relaxation effects of the various techniques, such as Progressive Relaxation, autogenic training, hypnotic suggestion, yogic breathing, and cognitively useful instructions *about* relaxation.

The results of the comparative studies are about equally divided as to effectiveness of the various relaxation procedures in *normal* subjects. About one-third report superiority of EMG biofeedback, one-

---

8. A recent study using biofeedback to learn control of heart rate showed the difference in biofeedback learning between "internals" and "externals" disappeared with continued training.

third report the superiority of either Progressive Relaxation or autogenic training to EMG biofeedback, and one-third report no differences among the techniques. The general failure to find differences among these three relaxation procedures has been noted in the section above on tension headache.

In contrast, studies comparing relaxation procedures in *anxiety and tension* problems suggest that correlations among the variables of muscle tension, autonomic level, autonomic reactivity and subjective feelings of anxiety and tension are still weaker than when normal subjects are used.

Research into the question of effectiveness of EMG biofeedback in relief of anxiety with chiefly autonomic symptomatology has not yet been conducted. Because there is a general resemblance of effects of EMG biofeedback-assisted relaxation to those of the Jacobsonian type of Progressive Relaxation, results of a study on the effects of brief relaxation training on autonomic responses to anxiety-evoking stimuli are worth noting. Connor found that while the procedure did not affect autonomic function levels, it did significantly reduce autonomic reactivity in anxiety situations. He interprets his results as *not* supporting the concept that relaxation affects autonomic arousal levels, but that relaxation training can affect autonomic *reactivity* with instructions and minimal training, and that this change in reactivity does not need to be accompanied by subjective change or alteration of autonomic nervous system (ANS) function. He feels that the relaxation effect is essentially a cognitive effect which is manifest in a change in autonomic reactivity, and hence the primary effect of relaxation training is *not* primarily a muscle effect.

This conclusion is not unlike that reached by Coursey in his 1974 study comparing EMG frontalis biofeedback with a cognitive technique for instructing individuals on relaxation, and as also compared to changes in control participants who were simply asked to relax. This study is particularly valuable since it utilized a series of 8 one-hour practice sessions. Although EMG frontalis biofeedback showed some superiority in degree of muscle relaxation achieved, subjective reports of awareness of tension differed little among the groups.

These kinds of results are both interesting and puzzling when other reports on the effect of relaxation on anxiety are compared. A number of clinical trials with various relaxation procedures indicate that state-anxiety is changed considerably, although one report found EMG tension levels to be significantly decreased while another found that autogenic training actually caused an increase in muscle tension levels.

## Systematic Desensitization

Systematic desensitization is a psychotherapeutic procedure in which the patient is confronted with or recreates in imagination situations which cause him anxiety, with the objective of learning to become less reactive to the stress. Some theorists interpret the process as a deconditioning of the psychodynamic aspects while others argue for psychophysiologic reduction of tension as the underlying mechanism. Although Paul continues to report experiments which demonstrate systematic desensitization to be a counter-conditioning procedure, other investigators in this area report that muscle relaxation plays an important, although perhaps not a primary, role. Lader and Mathews conclude desensitization to be nothing more than habituation, although this seems to be nit-picking about clinically ambiguous terminology. In other reports Mathews describes studies using Jacobson's technique, albeit in abbreviated form, in which the relaxation procedure resulted in decreased muscle tension and skin electrical activity, but no changes in autonomic activity levels. He concluded that the emphasis on muscle relaxation in desensitization simply induces a state of calm and reduced physiologic arousal and that its role is mainly to reduce autonomic responses to stressful stimuli during desensitization or possibly to assist the patient in reinterpreting the stimuli as the subjective state is changed to a calmer one.

These findings are not in agreement with those of other studies, particularly those of Rachman, of Agras, and or others whose experimental evidence suggests that muscle relaxation does contribute materially to the clinical success of desensitization.

Only two clinical reports have appeared on incorporating EMG biofeedback to facilitate the muscle relaxation aspect of desensitization. Wickramasekera reported on the apparently successful treatment of one case of "examination phobia" by a desensitization technique using verbal relaxation instructions and EMG biofeedback training. Similarly, Reeves and Mealiea successfully treated three individuals with an extreme fear of flying (non-Jongian). These authors included an interesting innovation in their technique, that of the cue-controlled variation in which, after the relaxed state is achieved, it is repeatedly associated with either an externally or an internally produced cue. The cue-controlled technique has shown promise in desensitization procedures, for example as reported by Brady using tones to achieve generalization of the laboratory relaxation into the natural environment. The Reeves and Mealiea procedure used an internally generated cue— verbalizing the word "relax" at the time when marked relaxation had occurred.

## Insomnia

It is generally considered that "self-defined" insomniacs are characterized by high levels of anxiety and physiological arousal, conditions already demonstrated to be affected by EMG biofeedback. Montgomery and Besner reported a study of 7 self-reporting insomniacs using twice-weekly thirty-minute periods of EMG biofeedback for a period of 16 weeks. All patients showed marked improvement in ease of falling asleep, stabilization of sleep onset, increase in total sleep time and fewer night awakenings. Similar results were found by Freedman and Papsdorf in four subjects. These investigators compared EMG biofeedback to a comparable training in Progressive Relaxation, with similar results. The chief difference between treatments appeared to be that EMG biofeedback subjects showed a greater percentage of sleep time and a corresponding greater percentage of REM sleep.

In contrast, Hauri and colleagues have reported that frontalis EMG biofeedback training was ineffective as a treatment for insomnia. Measurements of frontalis muscle tension before and during sleep did not correlate with sleep latency. They concluded that neither waking nor sleeping frontalis EMG tension levels distinguished insomniacs from good sleepers, nor did learning to lower frontalis EMG tension improve sleep latency in insomniacs although they claimed they slept better and felt better after the training.

On the other hand, positive results were obtained by Haynes, who compared the effectiveness of frontalis EMG biofeedback with autogenic training in insomniacs. He found no differences in effectiveness between treatments, much as he found no differences between the two treatments in tension headache.

Such results are not unexpected. Berkovec and Fowles successfully treated insomniacs by a variety of methods: Progressive Relaxation, hypnotic suggestion and desensitization while Kahn et al. were successful with a two-week course in autogenic training, finding 11 of 16 patients improved, with the improvement persisting for at least one year.

## Essential Hypertension

The use of biofeedback-assisted relaxation in the treatment of at least some cases of essential hypertension should be an obvious application of biofeedback. The rationale for applying muscle-relaxation techniques is clear, particularly in the light of new concepts of the possible etiology of essential hypertension. This disorder of blood pressure is currently being considered as largely a psychosocial disease, and this attitude is widely discussed in the popular media. Curiously, there is relatively little direct scientific evidence for this conclusion; the thrust of the new attitude seems to derive mainly from a common-sense interpretation of a massive amount of anecdotal material. The status of medical opinion on the causes and treatment of essential hypertension is rather completely described in my book *New Mind, New Body*. At the time of reviewing scientific materials for the chapter on blood pressure and biofeedback for that book, the idea of labelling essential hypertension as a psychosocial disorder was an idea not generally supported by authoritative medical (and, I should add, mainly research) opinion, yet today its psychosocial nature is as accepted as if it had always been acknowledged as a major factor in its development.

Briefly, considerable evidence exists to indicate that essential hypertension occurs first because of a normal

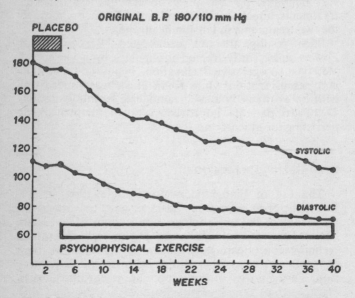

*Fig. 5.* Typical response of a patient with essential hypertension to "shavasan" (yogic exercise). Patient had not previously been on antihypertensive drugs (from Datey, Deshmukh, Dalvi, and Vinekar, *Angiology*, 1969, *20*, 325–333).

aging process in which arteries and arterioles lose their elasticity, with the resulting rigidity sustaining the pressure of the circulating blood. For unknown reasons, aging processes occur more quickly in some people than in others. The second factor appears to be a complex cardiovascular response to stress and social tension. Greater than normal arterial rigidity has been amply correlated with the frequency or severity of stress situations, such as unemployment, social failure, or being black, and with varieties of emotional disorders, including schizophrenia.

If additional rationale is needed to explore relaxation procedures, it can be found in the many reports on the therapeutic use of Jacobson's Progressive Relaxation or Schultz's Autogenic Training that have been reported to allow significant reductions of diastolic blood pressure in hypertensives.

Supporting this notion are the studies using yogic or meditation techniques to effect reductions in blood pressure. A fairly extensive and detailed study by Datey and colleagues evaluated the effect of one specific yogic exercise called "shavasan" in three groups of hypertensives, most of which were of the essential type. One group was not on medication, one group was well controlled by drugs, and the third was only poorly controlled by antihypertensive drug treatment. The "shavasan" exercise is one which concentrates chiefly on controlled respiration, relaxation, and a turning of attention inwardly. It was performed for 30 minutes under supervision, and required about three weeks for the patients to learn. Thereafter it was expected to be a lifetime, daily practice.

A comparison of the blood pressure changes in the three experimental patient groups is interesting. Both the previously untreated group and the drug-controlled group had an average mean blood pressure of about 135 mm Hg; with "shavasan" practice, the previously untreated group fell to a mean blood pressure level of 107, and the drug-controlled group (which had a pre-drug-treatment mean blood pressure of 137 and a mean blood pressure of 102 after drug treatment at the time of beginning the "shavasan" exercise) showed no

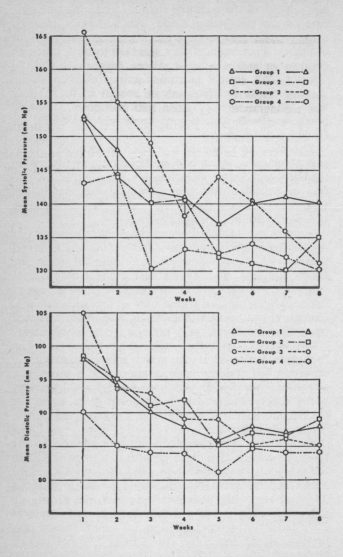

further change resulting from "shavasan" practice. Sixty percent of these patients, however, could reduce their blood pressure drug maintenance dose by 30 percent. The group of patients who were poorly controlled by medication had an average mean blood pressure of 120 as a result of their medication; with "shavasan" practice this value decreased to 110, and 40 percent of this group was able to reduce their medication by approximately 30 percent.

Fifty-two percent of the patients who began the study were benefitted. Of the 22 who failed to respond by a decrease in blood pressure, 10 either could not or would not perform the exercises correctly. Dr. Datey supplies a graph of one patient using "shavasan" only, illustrating the continuing downward movement of both systolic and diastolic blood pressure levels. The patient's blood pressure illustrated in Figure 5 fell from an original level of 180/110 to values of approximately 110/70 at the 38th to 40th week of practice.

Other studies which have used yogic exercises in the treatment of essential hypertension have combined the yogic techniques with biofeedback of skin electrical changes and other modalities. Summaries of these studies are found in the section on cardiovascular biofeedback.

As with the clinical evaluation of tension headache, insomnia, and anxiety, the use of EMG biofeedback in essential hypertension has been combined with use of other relaxation procedures. In a series of "working pa-

---

*Fig. 6.* Changes in systolic (above) and diastolic (below) blood pressure levels during relaxation training (from Weston, A. A.; Love, W. A., Jr.; and Montgomery, D. D.: Working Paper III, unpublished manuscript, Nova University, Fort Lauderdale).

Group 1 received EMG biofeedback for 3½ weeks, then direct blood pressure biofeedback for 3½ weeks with home practice of relaxation tapes throughout the treatment period.

Group 2 received same as Group 1 but with no home practice of relaxation tape.

Group 3 received alternating EMG and blood pressure biofeedback for 14 sessions.

Group 4 received blood pressure biofeedback only for the 14 twice-weekly sessions.

pers" distributed by Love, Montgomery and colleagues, reference is made to a study by Moeller in an unpublished Ph.D. dissertation, citing positive results for the use of EMG biofeedback in essential hypertension.

The combination treatment, i.e., EMG biofeedback and relaxation exercises, was employed by Love and colleagues. Twenty-seven, a fairly large number of patients, participated in the study. The treatment consisted of 16 weeks of half-hour biofeedback-relaxation sessions once or twice weekly, along with taped series of relaxation exercises to be practiced at home. As compared to a control group who sat in the laboratory but received no feedback, the experimental treatment group showed an average reduction of 12.7 mm Hg of systolic pressure and 9.8 mm Hg diastolic pressure. A subsequent report dealing with continued statistical analysis suggested that the highest correlation between actual reduction in muscle tension of the frontalis muscle and reductions in blood pressure levels occurred some two weeks after maximal relaxation occurred. That is, these investigators seem to be saying that the blood pressure effect lags the muscle tension reduction effect.

These same investigators have conducted a number of other studies employing biofeedback in the treatment of essential hypertension, and discussion of this series of "working papers" is continued in Chapter 5, since the majority of emphasis is on direct feedback of blood pressure values.

## Dental Uses (Bruxism)

Many years ago the gentle dental art of pulling teeth was believed to be the panacea for a surprising number of human ills, and to be seriously involved in problems of arthritis, sinusitis, headache, back pain and others. The image of dentistry changed to the concept of prophylaxis and correcting tooth problems before decay or malocclusion or other strictly mouth disorders occurred. But over the past several decades there has been a growing dental awareness of the pervasive problems that can be caused by malfunctioning of the temporo-mandibular joint—the jaw joint—and, by some seemingly preordained direction or research, a significant part of the problem was recognized as abnormal functioning of the muscles of the jaw joint almost at the same time that biofeedback was recognized as an important and efficient technique for relaxing muscles.

Malfunction of the temporomandibular joint occurs chiefly because of muscle tension or malocclusion (a bad "bite"), and often the occlusion problem is a direct result of the excessive muscle tension of the jaw muscles, particularly the masseter muscle. Of all of the dental ways of coping with jaw joint problems, which include splinting and bracing and grinding, none has been found to be satisfactory. Naturally, opinion among dentists is divided as to whether a mechanical or psychotherapeutic approach may be more effective, but at the moment dentists are becoming enthusiastic about the use of EMG biofeedback as an efficient means to relax the masseter muscles and bring relief from the host of discomforts and real physiologic disturbances that arise from problems of the temporomandibular joint. There is a fair amount of evidence from dental research that indicates individuals with TMJ syndrome are people with tensions, people who apparently live with pressure and tension, and who express that tension by misusing the jaw joint. The common misuse is bruxism—the grinding of the teeth.

The phenomenon of grinding the teeth carries with it some striking implications for understanding problems of stress. Significant correlations have been found between the bruxism habit and the levels of anxiety, or amount of job pressure or ability to cope with job pressure, or individual modes of responding to stress. What it all amounts to is that some people express their reactions to stress and tension by grinding the teeth, but the expression is generally successfully inhibited during the waking hours, presumably because we have such frequent reminders to be aware of events in the mouth and around the face. Grinding of the teeth strikes mainly at night, during sleep, and can be recorded to climax powerfully during dream times. It has been reported that some people can "clench" their teeth during dreaming, powerfully, and at a rate of up to twice a second. Clenching the muscles of the jaw can develop tremendous power, and combined with its forerunner, grinding the teeth, the eroding effect even on the hardened enamel is inevitable, as is the overpowering effect of the jaw muscle contraction on nearby and related muscles. It can really pull one's mouth out of shape.

Early on in biofeedback research Budzynski and Stoyva tackled the question of whether EMG biofeedback could produce an effective relaxation of the masseter muscle, hoping to lay the base for a dental use of EMG biofeedback. Electrodes were placed on the masseter muscle, and the biofeedback instrument was used in an operant conditioning mode, i.e., a visual signal was given when the experimental subject achieved a reduction in muscle tension predetermined (individually) by the operators. A second group received an analogue auditory signal which provided moment-to-moment biofeedback information as well. A *single* training session of twenty minutes duration resulted in significant reductions in masseter muscle tension for both of the feedback experimental groups as compared to a control group receiving no feedback and a second control group which was given an irrelevant steady tone instead of any biofeedback signals.

At the 1974 Biofeedback Research Society meetings, Rugh and Solberg reported on their particularly well-designed approach to treatment of the TMJ syndrome. Patients were supplied with portable EMG biofeedback devices. Their first objective was to monitor and identify situations which correlated with their teeth clenching, situations such as freeway driving or encounters with employers. After four to seven days, all patients were able to identify relationships between stress and grinding the teeth. They were then instructed to learn alternative responses to stressful situations or to avoid them. The EMG biofeedback device gave them immediate feedback about the effectiveness of their attempts to alter their behavior. It was reported that this technique was successful in 10 of 15 patients studied.

While no written scientific reports on the effectiveness of EMG biofeedback in bruxism have appeared at the time of this writing, a number of symposia and panel discussions by dental practitioners of biofeedback have occurred, with the majority reporting enthusiastically on the successful use of EMG biofeedback in bruxism. There are numerous dental offices and clinics in California practicing biofeedback for bruxism, and the implication is that these are at least as successful as previous therapeutic techniques or the procedure would be discontinued.

One scientific report has appeared, but in abstract form, and this dealt with attempting to treat bruxism while the patient was sleeping. Interestingly enough, an auditory signal of masseter muscle activity during sleep was effective in reducing the tension levels developed in the masseter; however, when the signal was discontinued, muscle tension promptly rose again.

This is in contrast to the anecdotal reports of dentists in panel discussions who claim that daytime, awake training to relax the masseter carries over to nighttime activity and nighttime recordings apparently have shown that the sleep and dream bruxing can be considerably reduced through EMG biofeedback procedures.

The utility of EMG biofeedback in the multiple problems arising from bruxism has some far-reaching implications for the practice of dentistry. Since many dental authorities consider disorders of the temporomandibular joint to be psychosomatic in origin, the treatment logically should combine elements of dental and psychotherapeutic practice. The dental problems in these instances stem from tension and anxiety, yet traditionally the dentist does not use any systematic psychotherapy. If biofeedback continues to be the effective tool that the initial work suggests it is, it seems likely that dental practice will extend into areas of at least one form of psychotherapy. That may uncover a feedback cycle in itself, i.e., attention to the psychologic tension factors may either uncover other aspects of dentistry in which psychologic activities are the causes and cures of problems, or at the very least, that psychotherapy can lighten the distress of undergoing dental work.[9]

## Hyperactive Children

Braud and colleagues have summarized an interesting and sound systematic series of studies using relaxation techniques in hyperactive children. In a pilot study, 12 EMG biofeedback (frontalis) sessions were given to an extremely hyperactive 6-year-old boy as a way of teaching the child to reduce activity and tension. The child was not receiving medication. "Dramatic improvement was seen in behavior, psychological test scores, achievement tests at school, improvement in self-concept and self-esteem, and a reduction in 'psychosomatic symptomatology' (headaches, allergies, asthma and running nose)." Seven months later the child still had control over his tension and activity levels on command, although the child's behavior was still erratic. It was felt that the erratic behavior continued because the parents and teachers did not establish use of the technique in everyday living situations.

These investigators then studied the effectiveness of relaxation training for both children and parents. The program consisted of six tapes for the parents for learning relaxation and how to deal with their children's behavior in a more positive and effective manner, and six tapes for the children to practice relaxation exercises and to relax during visual imagery "trip" tapes. Thirteen pairs of hyperactive boys and parents were studied and all showed significant improvement as evaluated by a variety of records, behavioral ratings, and classroom observations.

A third study compared the effectiveness of EMG

---

9. A recent report by Miller et al. indicates that EMG biofeedback relaxation is a useful treatment adjunct to relieve the stress of dental patients.

biofeedback relaxation with the relaxation technique. Both treatment groups, of 5 children each, were given 12 training sessions at a rate of two a week. Both treatment groups showed decreased muscle tension; however, the relaxation group showed greater improvement in behavior than did the EMG biofeedback treatment group. It was pointed out by the authors that the EMG biofeedback group received relaxation training for the frontalis muscle only, whereas relaxation training programs essentially work to train *all* body muscles to relax.

Haight and associates compared frontalis EMG biofeedback training in 4 hyperkinetic boys and compared the effects to similar measurements made in 4 hyperkinetic boys receiving no treatment. The study started with a preliminary instruction session on the use of Progressive Relaxation, and was followed by 10 biofeedback sessions of EMG training only. Although the baseline levels of muscle tension were not high and no significant changes in muscle tension were found, all of the treated boys showed improvement as measured by tests for hyperactivity.

A related program, but aimed particularly toward relieving the stress of the school learning situation and only incidentally toward hyperactive children is being conducted by Engelhardt. The program is designed to be available to a large school district on a voluntary basis. The program began by providing the program to school staff members and parents who received EMG and temperature biofeedback training along with relaxation exercises for six weeks, three times a week, each session lasting 30 minutes. Significant improvement was found in both physiologic and personality and subjective state measures of stress reactions. A pilot program with 9 volunteer youngsters was then conducted with preliminary results encouraging enough to expand the program.

## Childbirth

One of the more interesting applications of EMG biofeedback-assisted relaxation is its use as a method of natural childbirth. Gregg, Frazier and Nesbit have presented results of a study in which the effects of biofeedback relaxation training on the discomfort and pain of childbirth were extensively documented. Thirty patients were studied in each of the experimental and control groups, and with 96 percent of all of the patients having previously received Lamaze childbirth education courses at a local community hospital. The experimental group received two modalities of biofeedback. Following comprehensive orientation and instructions, the patients divided themselves into groups of threes, each group being provided with a portable instrument for home use. The small-group concept favored the patients assisting each other during home practice and also reduced the cost of leasing the biofeedback instrument. The usual practice course was four to six weeks, and about 90 percent of the patients used the instrumentation during labor. The two biofeedback modalities were used consecutively; first EMG biofeedback was applied to various major muscle groups of the body, and when consistent relaxation was achieved, the patients then worked with GSR (skin electrical activity) during interviews with the therapist to develop a degree of emotional control.

All important indices of labor were measured, including times and subjective attitudes during the several stages of labor, degree of cervical dilation, rate of fetal descent, medications required, etc. Results showed highly significant differences between the biofeedback-treated and control groups in all measures, and equally important, postpartum attitudes appeared consistently improved.

## Stress-related Behavior Problems (Drug Abuse, Marijuana, Unemployment)

Although numerous research studies using varieties of biofeedback as experimental treatments in stress-related behavior problems have been underway for some time, few using EMG biofeedback have been reported, and even these are all of the pilot variety.

Nonetheless, because of the similarity of the underlying behavioral problems, and also because of the general concept that many behavioral difficulties are stress related, the currently available data are reviewed here.

The common behavioral difficulties in drug abuse, chronic unemployment, and other manifestations of inappropriate social behavior are generally judged to be underlying anxiety, insecurity, and feelings of inadequacy. From manipulation of individuals with social behavior problems primarily by drugs, incarceration or isolation, social attitudes in the past decade have begun to focus on concepts of psychologic support to help the individual in his own rehabilitation. The efficacy of such programs has been largely equivocal, possibly because of the diffusion of effort that occurs during transitions in therapeutic, rehabilitative approaches. One of the basic difficulties that contributes both to the behavioral problem and its yielding to therapy, but that is rarely acknowledged, and is virtually impossible to control, is the concurrent changes in economic and political climate. The powerful impact of social dynamics on the lives of individuals is the inciting agent for social responses, and when either the information level or capacities of the individual are not appropriate to the changing social environment, deficiencies in behavioral coping occur. The deficiencies in coping behavior cause stress and anxiety, reinforcing feelings of inadequacy and insecurity.

The massive socially and psychologically supporting methods which have been applied to social behavior problems during the past ten or more years have concentrated largely on neutralizing the gap between the social environment and the individual. Although psychosocial techniques in general have resulted in some relief in the great area of social behavior problems, such remedies have proved exasperatingly ineffective in relationship to the massive amounts of effort, energy, and money that have gone into them. One of the major problems that remains is the failure of the individual with a social behavior problem to become self-generating with respect to his continued change when the supporting psychosocial measures diminish or weaken. It is to this aspect that biofeedback procedures may apply.

In effect, the rationale for using biofeedback in social behavior problems is twofold. The first is based upon the idea that individuals may learn to become aware of their potential for self-control. Although the impact of this awareness has not been quantified directly in the form of establishing a relationship between degree of awareness of self-control and subsequent behavior, there is a considerable fund of indirect evidence, as in learning the *prevention* or amelioration of headache or vasodilation or attacks of asthma. It seems inescapable that the effect of awareness of actually exerting control to prevent or ameliorate distress augments self-generating processes, i.e., motivation, persistence, etc. The relief from distress liberates a significant portion of cerebral activity for more socially productive behavior.

The second rationale for using biofeedback techniques in social behavior problems is the Jacobsonian concept that relaxation and anxiety are mutually incompatible. As described earlier, learned relaxation has the effect of decreasing the number of muscle tension stimuli conducted to central muscle control systems where, as part of the normal signalling process, reticular activating impulses are excited to alert the cortex. This amounts to the increased muscle tension putting an extra "load" on the cerebral circuitry concerned with monitoring the status of muscle tension. Although this increased central (brain; mind) attention to the peripheral muscles rarely is appreciated consciously, it does constitute a significant diversion of attentional circuitry toward muscles which could be otherwise directed toward other cerebral or mental activities. The effect, however, does not end there; as described earlier, the anxiety-stress reaction arises from a dual feedback mechanism, i.e., the proprioceptive, muscle control system interacting with the cerebral systems which subserve sensations and subconscious appreciation of the condition of readiness of the muscles. As the number of alerting impulses decreases, the cortical-reticular involvement decreases, and the sum of this dual inter-acting change is both relaxation and a lessening of cerebral activities that give rise to the feelings of stress and anxiety.

The Program for Alcoholism, Addictions, Stress and Anxiety (PAASA) under the direction of Kotzen, Schaeffer, Baron and Peiffer has operated for several years in a hospital setting (Houston International Hospital) and illustrates the usefulness of this ap-proach. PAASA is based upon a holistic approach to the treatment of addictions viewed as primarily stress-related problems and includes all of the major ele-ments of psychotherapy, such as videotape training, family therapy, occupational and attitudinal therapy, group and individual counselling, and strict activity, physical, and dietary regimes. Prior to the inclusion of EMG biofeedback in the program, the success rate of the treatment hovered around 40 percent, a fairly healthy figure for drug abusers.

In the past year EMG biofeedback with supplement-ary Progressive Relaxation and autogenic training was added to the program on a four-day-a-week basis. The treatment success rate has risen to nearly 75 percent. More specifically, of 136 young adults, the majority of whose addictions were chiefly amphetamines, LSD, marijuana, 101 were improved or much improved; of 103 young adults whose addictions were chiefly heroin or speed, 71 were improved or much improved; and of 88 adults, whose addictions were mainly alcohol or poly-drug, 68 were improved or much improved. The responsible clinicians feel that the addition of bio-feedback training to the treatment program has rep-resented a tying mechanism for all of the other therap-ies used.

An excellent and provocative pilot study on the use of EMG biofeedback in the treatment of chronic al-coholics has been reported by Steffen. A group of 4 chronic alcoholics was used in a cross-over treatment-placebo experimental design. Treatment was extensive, consisting of 14 one-hour sessions of Progressive Re-laxation exercises combined with frontalis biofeedback training. As a control comparison technique, the idea of "contemplation" was used as an attention placebo treatment. The test for the effectiveness of the treatments was free access to bourbon whiskey over a four-day period, and all data was gathered during this free drinking period. Results were clear-cut and intriguing. Although the Progressive Relaxation–biofeedback treatment group showed significantly lower frontalis muscle tension levels and reported subjective sensations of being less disturbed following the experimental treatment, the experimental and control groups *did not differ* in the number of drinks ordered (from a mock bar) but did differ significantly in their blood alcohol levels, those of the Progressive Relaxation–biofeedback group being lower than than those of the control subjects.

It is tempting to speculate on these results in spite of the small number of patients involved, even though the tight controls used enhance the significance of the results considerably. The discrepancy (or paradox, as the case may be) between number of drinks ordered and blood levels might be attributed to an effect of the relaxation procedures or the compulsion to drink, and even though the usual number of drinks may have been ordered, the patients may simply not have felt like consuming all of each drink as might be usual. The straightforward relationship between intake of alcohol and blood levels restrains any interpretation suggestive of a relaxation effect on the actual metabolism of alcohol, although this cannot be ruled out at this stage. On the other hand, the averaging-out effect of adding additional numbers of patients to the study frequently also normalizes the differences seen using small numbers.

The precision of experimental details needed for scientific conclusions about mechanisms, however, does not necessarily diminish the significance of these results with respect to the practical application of the techniques, not only for alcoholism but for related stress-induced behavioral problems.

The case in point is a study on the effect of EMG biofeedback training on personality factors in marijuana users made by Jacobs and Smith. They provided twice-weekly EMG biofeedback training sessions, for five weeks, to a group of 27 users, and the treatment program was augmented only by minimal counselling. Most of the users were able to achieve criterion relaxation, and these individuals also showed significant reductions in the scoring patterns of the MMPI relating to anxiety and antisocial behavior. Subjective reports revealed a significant reduction in the use of marijuana.

The third related study was designed to determine whether biofeedback relaxation training might influence the tension levels of individuals who averaged two years of unemployment. Other studies (see *New Mind, New Body*) have established that individuals subject to prolonged periods of unemployment do exhibit signs of both increased anxiety and physiologic evidence of stress and tension. In the biofeedback study by Austad, the subjects received EMG biofeedback training ad lib., i.e., they were encouraged to report for training as often as possible. The EMG relaxation training was utilized in a Wolpe desensitization program. The author reported that dramatic progress in learning to control tension had occurred by the fifth training session, and that by the end of the study (time unspecified), all but one of the sixteen individuals in the study had found employment. Considering the study took place during the period of high unemployment in 1974–75, these would appear to be not only remarkable results, but evidence for an effective approach to a part of the unemployment problem.

## Other Stress-related Disorders

For the most part, the successful treatment of the various other stress-related problems listed on pages 65–66 was achieved using procedures similar to those described above for tension headache, insomnia, and anxiety. An example of the effect of EMG biofeedback in asthma is illustrated in Figure 7.

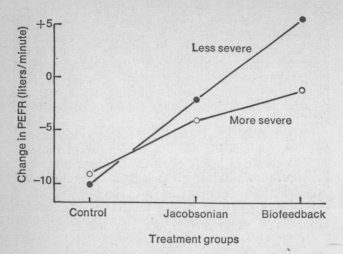

Fig. 7. A comparison of the treatment effects of Jacobson's relaxation exercises and EMG biofeedback in asthmatic children classified as more and less severe cases (from Davis, Saunders, Creer, and Chai, *J. Psychosomat. Res.*, 1973, *17*, 121–128).

## EMG Biofeedback Relaxation and Stress Management

With more than forty reports on EMG and other relaxation procedures in anxiety describing muscle tension levels and subjective changes, and numerous studies on biofeedback in stress-related problems, the reality of biofeedback is well established. There seems to be little question but that relaxation procedures have the potential to benefit psychologic and psychosomatic disturbances positively, and often dramatically.

Little attention, however, has been directed toward maximizing the efficiency and therapeutic potency of biofeedback techniques. At the present state of the biofeedback art, a universally applicable procedure has not evolved for many reasons. Scientific studies have perforce dealt mainly with providing proof for the effectiveness of biofeedback and the experimental methods used have been appropriate to research rather than to practice. There are also problems in reaching a consensus about therapeutic approaches because of the great versatility of biofeedback, the inadequacies of instrumentation and measurement, varieties of supplementary techniques used, differing conceptual approaches, the multidisciplinary nature of biofeedback, etc.

On the other hand, there are ample evidence and direction contained in the burgeoning use of biofeedback to construct highly effective treatment programs. In cooperation with various colleagues in medicine and psychotherapy, I have spent considerable time evaluating the various aspects of biofeedback practice conducive to optimizing its success. The remainder of this chapter and Chapter 9 are devoted to discussing expanded treatment programs for the management of stress and stress-related illnesses.

Before detailing the procedural prototypes, attention is drawn to some critical points not generally covered in discussions of biofeedback practice. In order to keep the potential biofeedback practitioner aware of the problems, the following list of influences on success or failure of EMG biofeedback in stress-related problems may serve as a useful guide.

1. The muscle or muscle groups used are not always equivalent or effective to the desired result. The major question should be, "Is the muscle group relevant to the disorder?"

2. Even for psychologic problems, definition of symptoms with a greater specificity is helpful in deciding the proper biofeedback approach (e.g., muscle versus cardiovascular versus temperature, etc., biofeedback), particularly with respect to dominance of muscle or autonomic or mental tension.

3. Personality structure appears to play a significant role in the success of EMG (and possibly all other) biofeedback.

4. The type of biofeedback signal may be more important than generally believed. While much EMG biofeedback is auditory, certain visual feedback in-

formation is used. It has been demonstrated by Alexander that visual feedback of frontalis activity poses certain problems and is generally ineffective. Moreover, when used with the frontalis, there is the possibility that the instrumentation senses extraocular muscle activity that may be related more to EEG activity than to tension levels of the forehead or other head muscle activity. As noted earlier, present instrumentation may also be faulty by artificially weighting the influence of high tension versus low muscle tension.

5. Since both the patient and the clinician are interested in relief of symptomatology often before tackling underlying causes, the biofeedback practitioner should keep in mind the research reports on those relaxation procedures that are being used as adjunctive techniques with EMG biofeedback. There is some reason to believe that these may even be superior for certain patients, or under different conditions (perhaps one reason being the still young state of the biofeedback art). In any event, not only are these supporting techniques valuable in producing beneficial results, most clinical studies agree that combinations of one or another of these with EMG biofeedback are the most successful.

6. One practice which is becoming common in EMG biofeedback work, and which is utilized extensively by Budzynski, is the use of tape-recorded relaxation instructions. On the market today are a wide variety of such tapes, from reasonably faithful reproductions of Jacobson's technique and the autogenic techniques to innumerable modifications of these for clinical practice.

A study reported by Paul and Trimble in 1970 sheds some interesting light on this practice. These investigators compared the effectiveness on arousal and preventing stress responses of recorded versus "live" relaxation training instructions and hypnotic suggestion. The specific techniques compared were an abbreviated Progressive Relaxation, a hypnotic induction technique which emphasized direct suggestions of relaxation, heaviness, warmth, etc. (much like Autogenic Training), and a self-relaxation procedure as control. These

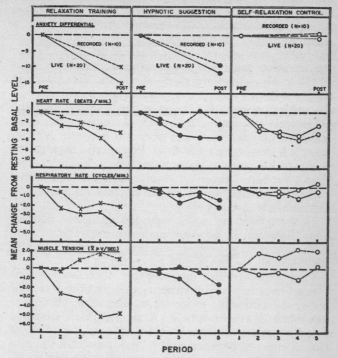

*Fig. 8.* Effects of "live" versus tape-recorded instructions using two relaxation techniques and a control procedure (the self-relaxation control) in which the subjects were instructed to try to relax but were not given any further verbal instructions. The relaxation training consisted of the abbreviated Progressive Relaxation training technique of Paul, and hypnotic suggestion consisted of a hypnotic induction procedure "emphasizing direct suggestions of heaviness, drowsiness, and relaxation, first describing an eye-fixation induction directed to the subject's image of herself" (from Paul and Trimble, *Behavior Therapy*, 1970, *1*, 285–302).

procedures were conducted twice, one week apart. The study measured subjective tension, physiological arousal (heart rate, respiration, tonic muscle tension, and GSR), and also responses to stressful imagery, as in desensitization.

Results of the study are summarized in Figure 8. The self-relaxation control group showed little change in subjective anxiety, no change in respiration, a slight reduction in heart rate response, and although the "live" instructions had no effect on EMG levels, the recorded self-made instructions actually *increased* EMG levels. There were no significant differences in effects of live or recorded hypnotic suggestion, although the subjective effects were relatively greater than the physiologic changes.

The intriguing differences occurred between live and recorded instructions for brief Progressive Relaxation training. Relaxation instructions given by a person, "live," produced excellent results, with subjects showing marked reduction in all parameters measured, including subjective anxiety.

In sharp contrast, while recorded relaxation instructions did result in good to moderate reductions in the subjective and autonomic visceral parameters, EMG tension levels were markedly *increased*.

Paul and Trimble interpret the increased muscle arousal with recorded instructions as possibly a lack of response-contingent progression, i.e., the accumulative effect of reinforcement. A similar result obtained by another researcher was interpreted as the effect or lack of effect of interpersonal relationships. On the other hand, where one might expect interpersonal effects to be mandatory, tape-recorded messages were reported to be highly successful. McGlynn et al. reported that 10 subjects with snake phobia were successfully desensitized by using a taped procedure.

7. The question of the effect of tape-recorded relaxation instructions leads into the related question of the advisability of instrumentation for home practice. No studies have yet been reported which compare effects of home practice with instruments to home practice without instruments and with either self-developed or instructed relaxation procedures. For the clinician-theorist who is persuaded that biofeedback assists in the development of self-control over physiologic functions, the degrees of dependence upon the therapists *and* the instrument are important considerations. There

is already a literature on the advantages of the "weaning" procedures in biofeedback treatment, in which the patient is gradually weaned away from both the instrument and the therapist, and is taught to rely upon his learned awarenesses and control along with other self-generating aids. Since this appears to be an effective procedure for the persistence of benefits from the biofeedback training, it follows that the practice of providing instruments for home relaxation practice should be considered on an individual patient basis. It would seem logical that the patient who improves in the clinical setting is a good prospect for achieving a high degree of self-control, and perhaps in these cases, home instruments should not be used. On the other hand, for the patient who, for some reason, cannot cope with or grasp the self-control concept, the home instrument practice may be a necessary element in his treatment.

## Clinical Procedure Prototype

The treatment paradigm for all of the emotional or psychosomatic problems is similar, except for occasional differences as to the specific muscle or muscle groups used, length of treatment period, criteria for control, or use of supporting measures. The general treatment procedure described by Budzynski for the treatment of tension headache tends to incorporate many of the elements used by the majority of practitioners, and provides a model that can easily be altered either to fit individual patients or as one or another of the supporting elements is shown to take on the greater or lesser significance. A similar approach has been developed under my direction and has been expanded to include as many procedural details as are currently relevant. This is described in Chapter 9. Both Budzynski's and my procedures illustrate the therapeutic approach that shifts the major responsibility for improvement to the patient in developing a critical awareness of differences between the irregularities and the well-being of muscle tension activity. These devices have been noted earlier under the categories of strategy information, cognitively useful information and experientially and psychologically supporting information.

The following treatment program summarizes Budzynski's 1973 procedure:

1. Prior to the beginning treatment, the patient is asked to chart his headache activity and medication hourly for two weeks, or daily, if a migraine patient.

2. For the first two or three training sessions, the patient is instructed in and practices a brief Jacobson's relaxation training procedure, the "tense-relax" exercises, and forearm and frontalis muscle tension levels are measured both before and after the session.

3. The patient is instructed in home practice and is given a tape recording to assist with the tense-relax exercises. He is asked to practice those twice daily and to rate the degree of relaxation achieved on a scale of 0 to 5. Budzynski reports that patients perform the home practice better with the aid of the tape; however, patients frequently forget the practice. To circumvent this, the therapist attempts to determine the times of day the patient is most likely to relax and practice, and as a further reinforcement, some kind of timer can be used. The therapist also asks the patient to make a number of checks of muscle tension a day, as many as possible, and rate the degree of tension or relaxation by his subjective evaluation scale.

4. EMG biofeedback training starts in the third or fourth training session, using the EMG activity from the forearm extensor muscle, along with instruction on the use of and practicing autogenic training phrases. The patient is then given a tape recording of autogenic training phrases for home practice.

5. When the patient can maintain forearm tension below a critical level, and can report feeling the heaviness and warmth in his limbs, the biofeedback training is transferred to using the frontalis muscle. The patient is also given a third tape for home practice.

6. The final phase of the treatment is "stress management," actually, a desensitization process. That is,

while the patient is receiving EMG biofeedback, he visualizes, as vividly as possible, a variety of stressful situations while attempting to maintain the relaxed muscle tension, or at least to be able to recover quickly from an increased tension resulting from the visual image. The patient at this time is encouraged to transfer his tension control learning to real-life stressors, and to try to relax after stressful situations.

7. In the case of migraine patients, the EMG biofeedback training is followed by temperature training (see Green-Sargent technique, Chapter 5), the desensitization procedure is then administered, and at the same time encouraging the patient to wean himself from his medication.

The astute therapist can recognize the several psychologic techniques used that surround the actual biofeedback training: the emphasis on charting, use of both Jacobson's technique and autogenic training, home practice, the substitution of tape recordings for medication, and the desensitization procedure.

The use of such supporting measures and the success of this shotgun type of technique raises many interesting questions both about the role of traditional therapy for stress-related problems and about biofeedback as well. While there is a tendency for researchers to dissect out the relative importance or unimportance of the diverse factors of the procedure, it should be pointed out that by itself (as used alone) biofeedback is a completely new experience for which most individuals have little background and even less insight; in fact, our scientific cultural heritage has mitigated against self (mental) control, and this undoubtedly has an inhibitory effect, particularly in the early stages of learning. The various supporting measures appear to be quite necessary elements in the understanding by the patient both of his abilities and that he is part of a changing attitude about the role of the patient.

Budzynski's comments on the process of this therapeutic approach also give some insight into the need for the supporting procedures. He writes about voluntary control that, "gradually, through a process of trial and error and hypothesis testing, the patient evolves strategies for controlling the feedback and thus the response. As he becomes more successful, he learns to associate certain thoughts, as well as proprioceptive and interoceptive sensations, however subtle, with changes in the feedback." He notes that "the patient may develop some degree of control before he is able to verbalize what it is that he is doing or not doing. With continued training, he is able to express what he is *not* doing, and finally, what he *is* doing, e.g., producing sensations of floating, or heaviness or warmth in his limbs, and excluding certain thoughts." Budzynski feels that "the ability to verbalize control strategies enhances transfer from clinic to real life, therefore, the patient should be encouraged in training to describe his sensations as well as his successful or unsuccessful strategies. Often the patient will use a phrase or a series of phrases that will become conditioned to the desired physiologic pattern."

The goals for the biofeedback training listed by Budzynski are for the patient to develop an awareness of internal physiologic activities or events, to establish control over these functions and to transfer or generalize that control to life situations. It is the objective of achieving control over a physiologic function that tends to be rather imprecisely documented in most biofeedback therapy or training. Control is generally documented on the basis of subjective reports by the patients and by using a criterion for the change in physiologic activity, here reduced muscle tension, which, after training, can be quickly achieved and then maintained in the training session.

It seems likely that biofeedback standards of the future will require a more precise physiological documentation. For EMG biofeedback relaxation, this can be similar to the criterion for control used by Raskin, who required patients to produce, consistently upon demand, a reduced muscle tension of marked relaxation for a 25-minute period *in the absence of the biofeedback signal*. Or, the test for control might be the kind used by Brown, in which the patient guesses which of several signals represents the feedback signal, or is tested by comparing subjective ratings of voluntary relaxation against the monitor, also in the absence of the feedback signal.

# 4

## NEUROMUSCULAR RE-EDUCATION: RETRAINING MUSCLES TOWARD NORMAL FUNCTION

The neuromuscular mechanisms . . . Clinical approaches . . . Severe muscle problems (paralysis) . . . Relatively uncomplicated muscle problems

The success of EMG biofeedback has been no surprise to electromyographers. They have been re-educating disordered muscles since the 1950s by biofeedback techniques. In fact, electromyographers should feel some pique over the ingeniousness of psychophysiologists in their rush to exploit EMG biofeedback. They can, moreover, be rightly critical about errors of instrumentation I have noted earlier and will discuss more fully below. On the other hand, the therapist can rightly chide electromyographers for sustaining a short-sighted perspective on the potential range of applications of their electromyographic retraining techniques.

It is common, if not routine, practice in many clinics specializing in muscle rehabilitation to use audio-visual displays as crucial biofeedback information in the retraining of disturbed muscle function. The process is remarkably simple: using needle electrodes inserted in the disturbed muscle areas (surface electrodes may sometimes do as well), muscle activity is amplified and displayed on an oscilloscope, and for many years the muscle activity has been used to activate an auditory signal simultaneously with the visual display on the

NEUROMUSCULAR RE-EDUCATION

oscilloscope. While the therapist demonstrates the type of muscle activity to be achieved by forcing or asking for a muscle contraction (say in a partially paralyzed muscle), the patient sees and hears signals of the actual muscle activity itself. Various types of movement aids can be used, such as massage or pushing to induce tension, or weak electric shocks in severe paralysis, but the critical part of the rehabilitation process is the use by the patient of the auditory/visual signals as a guide to the direction and degree of his voluntary effort on the impaired muscle activity.

It is important to understand the differences in instrumental designs and displays currently distinguishing the two kinds of muscle biofeedback: the integrated biofeedback signal that *sums* the electrical activity of the muscle is used to achieve relaxation effects as contrasted to the signal indicators of continuous ongoing firing of motor units, the basic units of muscle activity used in muscle rehabilitation. Occasionally in more recent times, the latter technique has been modified by integrating the motor unit firings over very brief intervals of time; however, an oscilloscope or oscillograph display is almost invariably used, in sharp contrast to the EMG biofeedback-assisted relaxation technique in which individual motor unit (muscle cell) firing is obscured by the summing process of the instrument.

What this instrumental difference amounts to is a difference in the amount of sensory information available and directness of the relationship between the biofeedback signals and the voluntary effort being applied. The continuous stream of motor unit activity provides a *pattern,* a very special kind of information. Testimony to the importance of these differences is the consistent evidence that there is a fairly constant one-to-one relationship between muscle activity, subjective effects, and development of voluntary control in muscle rehabilitation biofeedback procedures, while with EMG relaxation using integrated signals such correlations are infrequent. The increased precision may account for the relative greater general success of biofeedback in muscle rehabilitation and the achievement of a greater specificity of effect, although the latter also depends upon the type of muscle disorder.

The objective of muscle rehabilitation is, of course, to restore muscle function; the crucial factor, however, is that the restored muscle function must have the capability of being purposeful, i.e., of being under *voluntary* control. Incredible as it may seem, the ultimate expression of intentional control is found in the control of motor unit activity as it arises from the activation of single anterior horn motor neurons in the spinal cord.

## The Neuromuscular Mechanisms

Motor units are groups or families of muscle fibers (cells) which are all innervated by the same terminal nerve fibril of the motor nerve to the muscle. Each final fibril may innervate 3 to perhaps 300 or more individual muscle fibers; the neural activation of each motor unit can be traced, electrophysiologically, to a single motor-neuron (motoneuron) in the spinal cord. It is the anatomical and physiological separation of these cells that ensures the sequential and coordinated activation of muscle cells resulting in smooth contractions of muscles for movement. Motor units (families of muscle fibers) do not become active (fire) simultaneously, but are activated at intervals of microseconds from each other. Motor units fire only when sufficient numbers of nerve impulses arrive from the motoneuron, and the number of impulses depends upon the type of muscle-nerve fiber it is and upon many other neural controlling influences. Thus, the activation of the motoneuron is dependent upon the number of excitatory or inhibitory nerve impulses it receives from a variety of neuronal influences from the higher nerve centers, from relays in the spinal cord, and from interneuronal systems between the cord and the muscle.

Motor unit activity can be recorded on an oscilloscope or an ink-writing EMG recording device, the number of units recorded being dependent upon the speed of the recorder as well as upon the distance between electrodes and other mechanical factors. Because each family of muscle fibers (motor units) is composed of a different number of fibers, and because even closely related motor units do not fire simultaneously, when muscle activity is displayed on an oscilloscope, each motor unit writes a distinctive electrical signature. Used in this way in biofeedback training, the biofeedback signal (the oscilloscope tracing) contains information about both individual motor unit activity and patterns of related muscle activity.

Under normal circumstances of activity, motor units are activated asynchronously, that is, in effective sequences of microsecond intervals, to ensure smooth muscle movements. This means that the voluntary control of muscles also includes the ability to recruit motor units *as desired for different projected purposes,* and this in turn implies a voluntary capability to alter, to some degree, *sequences* of activating related motor units. Thus the complexity of voluntary control is enormous and clearly defines the vital role of cerebral activity in the control of muscles. The actual nerves and muscle fibers are largely the mechanical implementors of cortical action.

It is the involvement of cortical activity and the associated mental processes that provide the logic for using biofeedback and the reason for its success as a muscle rehabilitation technique. It should be remembered that electromyographers have been using the biofeedback principle for some time without defining it as such, and that what is new about biofeedback in muscle rehabilitation is its extended use and a change in some of the instrumentation. The principle has been defined as an augmented or atlernate sensory feedback process by J. Brudny since the essential factor of the procedure is substituting visual or auditory information about muscle activity that cannot be appreciated by means of the usual internally derived (proprioceptive) sensory information.

Muscles are activated by impulses from the central nervous system conducted along motor nerves to the muscles. Contained in the same nerve bundles are nerves conducting information about muscle states *to* the central nervous system. Thus most deficits of muscle function are caused by injury or pathology of the primary sensory-motor pathways or nerves, leaving most of the other avenues of sensory information input intact, such as receptors in the skin, joints, vestibular and visual systems. Since this information is still available and operational despite the failure of the muscle to express its influence, the major difficulty in most muscle disorders is the loss of the primary source of information, that is, the proprioceptive information, or the loss of the primary mode of indicating the result of voluntary control of movement, i.e., muscle contraction, or both.

Remarkably, these two deficiencies can be at least partially restored, one by biofeedback techniques, and the other by a neuromuscular compensatory mechanism. When the primary source of information about muscle activity is lacking, i.e., when the information arising from the internal sensors in muscle fibers is cut off from the central nervous system by injury or pathology, in the context of the total amount and kinds of information used by brain systems for voluntary control, the loss is only fractional. Since the other sensory mechanisms are still intact, what the brain control systems need is information about the *muscle* activity, and this can be rather easily simulated by providing the information about muscle activity as biofeedback signals. Using electrodes and electronic devices to sense and display internal muscle activity is possibly nothing more than simply changing the route of getting the muscle information to the brain systems. Instead of impulses coursing upward through muscle sensory nerves, the same information is picked up by the biofeedback device and is available for the visual or auditory sensory systems. Since the auditory and visual systems are already strongly associated centrally with the total pattern of neural activity that promotes voluntary control, the auditory and visual information can fairly readily substitute for the primary proprioceptive information, or when it is not entirely lost, can augment the primary muscle information.

It seems reasonable to assume that the substitute information readily moves into the vast integrating neuronal networks because it already carries with it certain related associations; thus patterns of cortical motor activity can be re-established. The situation is probably not unlike that described by Bach-y-Rita in "Tactile Vision Substitution System" in which critical aspects of the visual system can be substituted for by the tactile sensory system, and blind people can use tactile impressions of objects to "see." The relative rapidity with which patients use the alternate sensory information in EMG muscle rehabilitation supports the concept of that kind of "plasticity" of the central nervous system to use sensory information appropriately, regardless of its source.

The most dramatic confirming evidence occurs in motor unit biofeedback work such as that extensively reported by Basmajian. When the individual's task is to learn voluntary control over motor units, if he has an audio-visual display of the activation of these muscle cells, he can very quickly learn to control them in a surprisingly complex manner. Individuals can, in a matter of minutes, learn to control a single family of muscle cells, then learn to control up to a dozen or so, or learn to control specific sequences of activating motor units, or make them fire on time to an externally paced rhythm. In these situations, there is no known conscious awareness of the internal sensory information about the activity of muscle cells (and in fact it may not even be needed, as the neurophysiologic studies of Taub have indicated), yet soon after the information is made available in auditory or visual form, the individual quickly realizes control, quite specific control, over these fragments of muscle. Such learning is truly amazing, since it has been amply demonstrated that the learning involves selective (but unconscious) manipulation of motoneurons (cells) in the spinal cord.

The biofeedback signal thus restores the first deficit in nerve-muscle disorders, that is, the loss of internal information about muscle fiber activity. The second deficit, that of transmission of the motor nerve impulse to the muscle fibers so that muscle activity can be restored, is accomplished by a natural biological compensatory mechanism of re-innervation.

When remaining functional muscle fibers of a muscle mass whose nerve supply has been disrupted by injury or pathology, as in paralysis, are exercised and overworked, a miraculous response of the affected nerve occurs. When activity is continued in the nonparalyzed portion of the injured muscle, the injured nerve responds by a process called budding or sprouting. Buds or sprouts of the nerve appear and grow outward to reinnervate the muscle fibers which have lost their nerve supply. Depending upon the extent and type of injury or pathology, various proportions of recovery of muscle function can be achieved. With the development of biofeedback, "overworking" muscle fibers, especially in paralyzed or injured muscles where no evidence of muscle fiber activity can be observed, can now be accomplished by working with the biofeedback signal to learn to increase the activation rate of the remaining healthy fibers.

Restoring the physical, anatomical connection between nerve supply and the muscle fibers does not, however, ensure *appropriate* muscle activity. More often than not, muscle cells which have been re-innervated by the budding or sprouting process do not easily come under voluntary control. This is somewhat surprising, since the nerve cells from which the new innervation comes are at the least closely related to the original nerve supply, if not the same. It is curious that the re-innervated muscle fibers must be re-educated to central control, that is, to voluntary control. This fact strongly suggests a higher degree of specificity of cortical control than do direct cortical stimulation experiments (or at least as much). While there are as yet no explicitly stated conclusions that biofeedback directly assists in bringing these newly innervated motor units under voluntary control, the degree of biofeedback-assisted recovery and the rate at which it occurs indirectly indicate the role of biofeedback.

## Clinical Approaches

Any interruption of the transmission of motor nerve impulses from the central nervous system (or within it) to the muscle results in the failure of muscle function. The interruption can be temporary or permanent, functional or real, partial or complete, central or peripheral. The nerve may be injured or inflamed, damaged from pressure or suffer a lesion; the results are similar; only the degree of muscle function impairment differs.

Whether it is a modest loss of muscle function or severe paralysis, recovery of muscle activity is a dramatic example of the learning to control the activation and selective direction of nerve cells, literally a learning to control the coordinated activities of the anterior horn spinal cord motoneurons (cells). If the injury or pathology is severe, it may take some searching, by changing position of the electrodes, to find an occasional motor unit still active. Sometimes, as in longstanding neuromuscular atrophy, repeated voluntary effect may result in the firing of a motor unit, but this is presumably a reflex response elicited by inserting needle electrodes. Nonetheless, these reflex activations of motor units are an essential step in recovering muscle function. When these units fire reflexly, and are converted to audio-visual biofeedback signals, the rehabilitation therapist informs the patient that that particular muscle area is certainly functional, and with the right kind of effort the muscle activity can be brought under voluntary control. The process of bringing the reflex muscle firing under voluntary control is very similar to all other types of biofeedback learning and no different from learning any new kind of muscle skill.

The approach to the relearning is very similar to relearning any motor (muscle) skill, as for example, the older adult attempting to relearn roller skating or whirling a hula hoop. For one thing, the older adult has long been indoctrinated with the concept that intellectual analysis and determined effort are the essential ingredients for success. But when it comes to manipulations of the body's physical, physiological functions that have been put on automatic for so long, or, in the case of nerve-muscle problems, where patterns of muscle activity designed to compensate for deficits or protect against pain have replaced the normal muscle activity, there can be difficulties in recapturing the childhood ease of just letting muscle systems adjust themselves toward meeting the perceptual objective. It is a complex problem involving forgotten or substitute learned patterns of muscle activity that are linked to surprisingly dominant higher mental influences.

The significance of the dominant role of higher cerebral activities in relearning effective muscle activity is important to remember in rehabilitation therapy; moreover, the cerebral influence has been amply demonstrated in rehabilitation studies and has been reported. The important considerations are (1) that the patient can become easily fatigued as he continues to control specific motor unit activation (this is a mental, not physical fatigue, presumably from the cerebral effort involved in such exquisite discrimination of cellular activity along with suppressing nonproductive, habitual patterns), and (2) that the anxiety of effort actually prevents or interferes with motor unit activation. The problems of anxiety and fatigue that occur during the muscle rehabilitation process can be relieved by including relaxation training in the treatment program.

Thus, the rehabilitation learning process requires some skill on the part of the therapist in recognizing and working with the elusive, unconsciously mediated factors which regulate the participation and coordination of functionally related muscle subsystems. Muscle activity is complex under any circumstance, and recovery of muscle function entails not only recovery of ability to activate families of muscle cells, the motor units, it further involves recovery of effective *sequencing* of motor unit activation and constantly pulling newly recovered motor unit function into the effective patterns of muscle activity. It is not simply the process of converting the almost automatic reflex contraction of muscle fibers to voluntary control; but as recovery proceeds, new motor units become active and flutter in and out of the pattern, and these too must be brought under voluntary control. Oftentimes also, units seemingly under control will fatigue and falter, needing more practice to fit into the larger patterns that are useful.

Biofeedback muscle rehabilitation training requires a patient and temperate therapeutic approach because it consists of coaxing two rather disparate problems into a productive resolution. One problem is activating and recruiting motor units while the second problem is teasing their activity away from unproductive patterns caused by the disability, and together these objectives are directed toward useful, normal activity.

## Severe Muscle Problems (Paralysis)

Much more research attention has been paid to seriously incapacitating muscle problems, such as hemiplegia, dystonias, spastics, cerebral palsy, and nerve injury due to accidents or strokes. The most extensive studies, in terms of numbers of patients and varieties of neurologic disorders, have been reported by Brudny and colleagues. Using continuous feedback displays, with both visual and auditory signals, with the visual display as either a meter reading and integration of muscle activity or an oscilloscopic display of both the amplitude and rate of the muscle potentials or a digital numeric read-out of integrated muscle potential in microvolt-seconds. The auditory display was either an analogue signal in which the pitch of the tone indicated the integrated muscle value or the rate of a click. Patients were instructed about the relationship between the biofeedback displays and their own muscle contraction and relaxation. Because of the complexity of the underlying neurologic problems, training was directed both toward decreasing any spastic muscle activity and increasing strength and contraction of atrophied or paralyzed muscles. Treatment sessions were usually three times a week for about thirty minutes each. Most patients were able to control abnormal activity after one to three sessions; they were continued in training until they could maintain control over several sessions, which included demonstrating the functional improvement, then were gradually weaned away from dependence upon the feedback training sessions.

Considering the severity of the muscle disorders treated and the average duration of the problems, and failure of the patients to respond significantly to other treatment modes, Brudny and colleagues report quite dramatic beneficial results. Varying degrees of recovery of muscle function were achieved, the criterion of effectiveness of treatment being as much rehabilitation of function as possible under the circumstances of the injury or disease. Having seen films of some of the patients treated by the Brudny group, I can comment that these investigators are conservative in their estimate of successful treatment. Many patients who were literally helpless because of their paralysis were trained to the point where, by the addition of prosthetic devices, they could take considerable care of themselves. The films do not do sufficient justice to the dedication and treatment wisdom of the Brudny group, who are particularly inventive and sensitive during the training of the patients.

The Brudny group has also reported on a fairly prevalent but quite distinctive movement disorder, spasmodic torticollis. This abnormal movement disorder is the constant turning of the head to one side, resulting, after a period of time, in an extraordinary development of muscle on the one side and incipient, if not actual, atrophy of muscles on the other side of the neck. As described by Brudny et al., "spasmodic torticollis remains a clinical enigma," there being no consensus about its etiology and no prior significant available treatment. Using the combined audio-visual biofeedback technique, Brudny and colleagues treated nine patients with severe and moderately severe spasmodic torticollis for an average of ten weeks, at the rate of three to five times a week. In four of the nine patients, the disorder was recent, one to three years in duration, while for the remaining five patients the disorder was long standing, having persisted for ten to fifteen years. Seven of the nine patients learned to overcome their spasms of the neck voluntarily. A second study of ten patients yielded similar results. The investigators comment on the psychological gains that occurred concomitantly with mastery of the disorder.

Altogether, Dr. Brudny and his colleagues have reported on the use of sensory feedback techniques in more than seventy neurologic patients with a high success rate; it should be pointed out that their research analyses and criteria are quite stringent. For example, measurements are made of the number of motor units active during different maneuvers and during different stages of treatment. Also, measurements are made of the duration of the biofeedback effect following training sessions. In the treatment phase, patient instruction and motivating support are given, and home exercises are encouraged. As with the treatment programs for muscle tension reduction in stress-related problems, treatment supports and aims toward development of intentional, volitional control.

There are numerous other clinical studies which document the effect of biofeedback as a treatment modality in muscle rehabilitation, confirming and extending work as described above. Successful results have been obtained in stroke victims, spastics, and hemiplegics. The treatment procedures are all relatively similar, and combine oscilloscope pattern feedback displays with instruction and information for the patient which is cognitively useful about the objective of the therapy and the relationships between sensory information and muscle activity.

For stroke paralysis and for neuromuscular problems that result in spasticity of muscle groups, EMG biofeedback relaxation training has been found to be a helpful training aid. In the stroke paralysis patient, for example, there is a tendency for the opposite and non-affected muscles to undergo a contracture. It is not enough to attempt reactivation of the lost muscle fibers in the paralyzed muscles, the companion and opposite muscle groups must be re-educated as well toward normal function. Kleinman and associates have reported that EMG biofeedback training for the interfering spasticity provided significant decreases in muscle activity and resulted in increased range of movement of the affected muscle groups.

Simard and colleagues have published a number of studies in which the cognitive and environmental aspects of the treatment have been evaluated for influence on the rehabilitation learning process. They have demonstrated that absolute fidelity of information given about the rehabilitation process, about the equipment, about the objectives is necessary for the best results; also the meaningfulness of the task is important, not only in terms of personal achievement but also in terms of medical progress in general. They have also found that the environment of learning is critical. The atmosphere should be relaxed and relaxing, the instructions should be clear, successes should be confirmed, encouragement is important, and best results are achieved when the patient makes a commitment to the task.

## Relatively Uncomplicated Muscle Problems

There are, of course, a wide variety of muscle aches, pains, spasms, or nonextensive injuries which ultimately respond to therapeutic measures such as rest, massage, physical therapy, heat, etc., although the healing process often takes considerable time. Now research studies indicate that such types of muscle ailments can be much more rapidly treated by using biofeedback techniques. These treatments may use the muscle rehabilitation techniques described above or combine these with relaxation techniques.

One example is that reported by Jacobs and Felton in 1969. Patients with injury of the upper trapezius were tested for the degree of muscle relaxation they could achieve when aided by oscilloscope displays of their muscle activity. A single trial demonstration of the effect of a tense-relax sequence on the oscilloscope tracing of muscle activity was used to familiarize the patient with the significance of the biofeedback moni-

tor, then the patient proceeded with some ten trials of
the Jacobsonian tense-relax exercise, confined to the
trapezius, with the major amount of time allowed for
the relaxation aspect.

Results of this clinical study are intriguing. Immediately, during the first tense-relax trial, the injury patients showed a muscle tension level almost identical to
that of normal subjects who were not shown oscilloscope displays of their muscle activity. Further, within
three trials, the muscle activity was indistinguishable
from that of the noninjured subjects. On the other
hand, control, noninjured subjects actually increased
muscle tension slightly over the ten trials, and their
muscle tension was significantly higher than that of the
injured patients. In contrast, those patients with injured
trapezius muscles who were not given the oscilloscope
feedback display maintained levels of muscle tension
that were 5 to 30 times that of *either* the biofeedback
treated patients or the noninjured patients.

It does stretch the imagination to accept a positive
result occurring simultaneously with the beginning of a
treatment no matter how striking the raw data are.
There are, however, similarities in the rapidity of this
relaxation effect upon perceiving biofeedback information to results of certain EEG alpha, heart rate control,
gastrointestinal biofeedback learning experiments, and
the promptness with which motor units can be brought
under voluntary control. In the case of a limited muscle
injury, there is little disruption of nerve impulse transmission, and probably no interfering compensatory
muscle patterns. Unfortunately for the purpose of documenting the consistency of biofeedback effectiveness in
relatively uncomplicated muscle problems, these are
the kinds of problems that are put into immediate
therapeutic practice and not made the object of further
research. In lieu of "vertical" research documentation,
the validity of new techniques, such as biofeedback,
can be nearly as well validated by inferring from what
I call "horizontal" evidence, i.e., positive results from
many different but related studies.

One such related study is that by Swann and colleagues reported in 1974. These investigators studied

the effect of muscle potential biofeedback in patients suffering from long-standing aberrant muscle activity which interfered with normal activity. All of the patients suffered from "undesirable" contractions of the peroneus longus muscle while stretching the knee joint. This condition interfered with the normal knee extension of walking. One patient had endured the problem for 70 years, while the others had suffered the ailment for an average of approximately 12 years. The biofeedback used was auditory signals of the motor unit potentials occurring in the peroneus longus muscle, and the objective of the training was for the patient to learn to suppress the auditory signal while he was stretching the knee joint. The measurement used to evaluate the effectiveness of the treatment was the angle of the knee achieved when accompanied by a predetermined number of motor unit firings. As compared to conventional physical therapy treatment, the biofeedback patients showed a significantly greater improvement. The data presented suggest that the beneficial effects occurred by the third of six treatment sessions. Unfortunately, the experimental design used in the study alternated the biofeedback treatment with the conventional physical therapy treatment, and may have obscured or enhanced effects of both. The authors of the study felt confident that the biofeedback effect was real.

Uses of biofeedback for corrective purposes in muscles not involved in movement activity are discussed in Chapter 6.

# CARDIOVASCULAR BIOFEEDBACK

*Heart rate.* The psychophysiology of heart rate control . . . Learned heart rate control and anxiety and stress . . . Self-awareness and heart rate control . . . Role of information and cognition . . Clinical studies
*Blood pressure.* Psychophysiological background . . . Experimental studies . . . Blood pressure biofeedback in essential hypertension . . . Other biofeedback approaches to essential hypertension
*Vasoconstriction and vasodilation.* Migraine headache
*Skin temperature vasodilation.* Basic research studies . . . Role of instructions and strategy information . . . Temperature control in migraine headache . . . Temperature control in other vascular problems

## *Heart Rate*

### The Psychophysiology of Heart Rate Control

The many dimensions of the cardiovascular system —heart beats, blood pressure, blood flow, and skin temperature—for so long have been considered at the mercy of reflex regulating mechanisms and beyond voluntary control that demonstrating voluntary control over any aspect has been a great surprise to medical and psychological research theoreticians.

The history of medical and psychological research that revealed human beings to possess the capacity to control their own heart rates is a history of Western attitudes that have long rejected concepts of mind over body, and, in fact, have viewed them as little more than mechanically functioning units. The history is given in detail in two chapters in *New Mind, New Body;* this new book is concerned mainly with reviewing the psychophysiology of heart rate that has a particular relevance to heart rate biofeedback and its applications.

Heart rate responses have long been the staple of psychophysiological research. They are exquisitely sensitive indicators of emotions, stress, and anxiety, and presumably because the nervous regulation of heart beats is relatively simple, heart rate has been easy to bring under control by classical conditioning procedures. It was to be expected that when experimental psychology began to turn its attention to newer models of learning and to the role of cognition in the regulation of physiologic activities that heart rate would be among the first functions to be studied. Since that time, in the mid-1960s, nearly one hundred reports on heart rate learning have appeared in the scientific literature. All kinds of variations of conditioning or biofeedback procedures have been used, always with positive results, as for example, in the conditioning of heart rate increases, decreases, or stability.

Heart rate is undoubtedly one of the easiest physiologic functions to learn to control, and certainly the easiest of the reflexly regulated body functions. The ease of learning heart rate control is probably related to the fact that the heart beat is one of the few internal functions that can be felt and an awareness of it gained through a variety of experiences.

Control over heart rate can be learned using several different training procedures. Among the hundred or more research studies, training procedures range from simply providing continuous information about heart rate to procedures that use a dizzying number of feedback signals as reinforcements in the form of flashing colored lights and/or tones and augmented by rewards such as slides of nude females or a cash register toting up nickel and dime rewards for performing correctly. All of the techniques are effective, but there are marked differences in the degree of their effectiveness. In general, those techniques patterned after laboratory operant conditioning procedures established for animals yield the smallest and least consistent results. As is true in the biofeedback of other physiologic activities, procedures using continuous or almost continuous biofeedback signals consistently yield much better results.

The practitioner and researcher new to biofeedback may find the past history of heart rate biofeedback difficult to put into an operational perspective. At least half of recent laboratory heart rate biofeedback studies use conditioned learning experimental methods of the pre-biofeedback era, while the other half explore heart rate biofeedback from the standpoint of the role of information and cognition. The new practitioner should be reminded that both approaches are designed to explore the basic mechanisms of learned heart rate control, and little research has been oriented toward maximizing conditions of the techniques toward clinical success.

Laboratory techniques designed to demonstrate particular influences or suspected mechanisms (e.g., whether muscle activity actually causes the changes) are often not appropriate or optimal for clinical use. Laboratory procedures are developed and modified to probe and uncover elements critical to the phenomenon being studied, and relatively few research studies are directed toward evaluating elements critical to successful application. This has been especially true in biofeedback where it has been assumed, often with considerable error, that the essential aspects for optimal clinical effectiveness have been adequately defined. On the other hand, basic research studies have contributed a great deal toward describing relationships between emotion, personality, or cognitive styles and the role of information in the process of learning voluntary control over heart rate.

Currently, the use of heart rate biofeedback is predominantly in the treatment of cardiac arrhythmias. The straightforward relationship between heart rate and nerve stimulation, and hence for the possibility of higher cerebral control, could predict success of biofeedback in some disorders of heart beat conduction. It could also follow that the chief limiting factor might be the integrity of nerve connections, and indeed this has been borne out by clinical investigations. Bleecker and Engel have confirmed that patients with neural blockage at the junction between auricle and ventricle do not respond to biofeedback training to control ventricular heart rate.

The conceptual and practical distance between psychology and medicine is nowhere more starkly represented than in the case of learned or voluntary control of heart rate. In experimental psychology, the sole interest in heart rate is because it reflects changes in emotions, and because of its sensitivity to emotional stimuli, heart rate is studied chiefly to demonstrate its role in behavior, and particularly its role in stress. With operant and biofeedback techniques it has been abundantly shown in the laboratory that learned heart rate control can be used most effectively to prevent or relieve the usual heart rate responses to anxiety and stress. Despite this considerable experimental background, to date there are only two clinical studies on the use of learned heart rate control to reduce the effects of stress and tension.

On the other hand, in medicine the major concern with heart rate, aside from its diagnostic value, is with problems of disturbed conduction of the heart beat. Curiously, all but the two clinical trials of heart rate biofeedback have been conducted in patients with disturbances of heart beat conductions, despite the lack of experimental studies which might suggest its usefulness in these problems. This is not to say that there is not a good rationale for going directly to clinical use of biofeedback for heart rate disturbances since some cardiac conduction disturbances are affected by elements of emotional reactivity; however, the prevalence of physical causes would ordinarily suggest some caution about applying psychologic techniques in heart beat disorders. The fortunate consequence of this paradox of psychologic-medical conceptual attitudes may be that the use of a nonintervention technique such as biofeedback may not only positively affect certain pathologic conditions of heart beat conduction by way of the neural involvement, but undoubtedly can relieve any emotional overlay aggravating such conditions. This would allow for a more effective and less dangerous use of drugs.

As advances have been made in biomedical instrumentation, it has become increasingly easy to detect and display accurately and conveniently even brief, small changes in heart rate. The sensitivity of the cardiac nerves to emotional stimuli reflected in changing heart rate and the ease of its handling by instruments suggests that the future will see many more uses of heart rate in areas of psychology, even lie detection, as well as new biofeedback uses, particularly in anxiety and stress-related illnesses.

## Learned Heart Rate Control and Anxiety and Stress

Psychophysiologic theory, particularly that relating to stress, anxiety, and arousal, owes much to the ease with which heart rate activity can be recorded and the fact that heart rate is a sensitive indicator of emotion and autonomic reactivity. And although experimental psychology stresses relationships between heart rate activity and anxiety, it has scarcely bothered with exploring heart rate biofeedback in the treatment of anxiety or stress-related illnesses. One of the reasons for the hesitancy to explore biofeedback in such a well-established relationship as heart rate–anxiety undoubtedly has been the inability to produce dissociations between skeletal muscle tension and visceral tension under experimental conditions comparable to that occurring in clinical disorders. Laboratory procedures used to study anxiety, tension, and stress almost always evoke *both* muscle and visceral tension, but when the body systems are disordered, as in types of anxiety or stress-related illnesses, system specificity of response occurs frequently. The relevance of the muscle-visceral tension dissociation is strikingly demonstrated in the studies of Le Boeuf, who found that patients with anxiety having chiefly visceral tension did not respond to muscle relaxation treatment, whereas anxiety patients with chiefly muscle tension were improved. Future research may show that heart rate biofeedback can provide access to visceral tension states, and that learning to control heart rate activity may be a useful treatment in tension states in which visceral tension is dominant over muscle tension.

The experimental evidence indicates that heart rate control can be learned regardless of whether anxiety is constitutionally present or is induced by experimental conditions. It appears that individuals with high levels of anxiety can learn as well, if not occasionally better, than individuals with low levels of anxiety. Several studies have induced apprehension or anxiety, finding that experimental subjects learned heart rate control as well as they did in nonstressful situations. One study conditioned subjects to anxiety following biofeedback learning of heart rate control and found that the subjects were able to continue their control through the conditioned anxiety. Another researcher reported on subjecting a volunteer to the immersion of his face in water, and found that previously learned heart rate control successfully prevented the usually occurring bradycardia reflex. Another study with patients showing both anxiety and tachycardia found that not only could the patients learn large-magnitude changes in heart rate, but could sustain the control after the biofeedback learning.

The relationship between heart rate and subjective feeling states has been dramatically illustrated in biofeedback experiments in normal subjects capable of producing large-magnitude increases in heart rate. These individuals consistently report sensations of apprehension and anxiety as they voluntarily increase their own heart rates. The two clinical experiments that have explored the usefulness of learned heart rate control in anxiety states are discussed on pages 146–7 under Clinical Studies.

## Self-Awareness and Heart Rate Control

A number of research studies have explored the relationship between cardiac awareness and the ability to learn heart rate control as well as the relationship between awareness of self-dcterminacy and ability to learn heart rate control.

While one study failed to find a relationship between heart rate awareness as determined using the Autonomic Perception Questionnaire,[1] a second study found that individuals with a low degree of cardiac awareness learned heart rate control quite well whereas individuals who were aware of their heart rates did not. A subsequent report by Blankstein may have resolved this discrepancy. Blankstein used the set of subscores of the Autonomic Perception Questionnaire reflecting a *general* awareness of autonomic nervous system activity in states of anxiety and pleasure and compared heart rate control ability to the set of subscores reflecting *specific* awareness of heart functioning. He found that there was no relationship between general awareness of the autonomic system and heart rate control ability, but a positive correlation was found between specific awareness of heart functioning during pleasure states and ability to control heart rate. It thus seems obvious that evaluations of awareness of different aspects of physiologic functioning not only need to be defined specifically, but the occasions of the awareness need to be qualified more precisely with respect to the emotional state in which the awareness occurs.

The difficulty in relating autonomic awareness to ability for heart rate control is shown by another study reported by Blankstein. He found that the chronically unemotional individual, with psychopath-like characteristics, can effect greater control over increasing heart rate than can the nonpsychopath personality. If the lack of emotional display is interpreted as indicating internalization of emotional responses, this might have some relationship to cognitive styles described as external or internal.

Several researchers have reported that "internals" (those who tend to attribute responsibility for their behavior to themselves) were found to learn how to

1. Mandler, G.; Mandler, J.; Uviller, E.: *J Ab Soc Psychol*, 1958, 56:367–373.

increase heart rate better than did "externals" (those who feel that external factors shape their behavior), while the latter appeared to be better able to decrease heart rate than could "internals." Self-reports of subjective activity indicated that these two types of individuals also used quite different strategies to accomplish their learning, as might be expected, especially in view of the fact that their primary ability to control heart rate was in opposite directions. A subsequent study has revealed, however, that the differences in heart rate control ability between externals and internals disappeared when biofeedback training was extended to two days. The discrepancies among these reports on the role of locus of control to learning ability points out the hazards frequently encountered in short-term laboratory experiments. The terminology of biofeedback learning is often confused with terminology of operant conditioning in characterizing responses to specific experimental learning situations. Frequently the laboratory worker is content with some statistically significant change that correlates with the principal variable of the experiment, such as the frequency with which a physiologic change occurs when the reinforcement is given. When biofeedback techniques are used with the objective to establish learned or voluntary control, data become significant only when the physiologic change can be reliably evoked in the absence of the biofeedback signal, and this, of course, is the concern of the clinician.

The kinds of subjective states or strategies reported to be effective in short-term conditioning experiments which have the objective to achieve small changes of physiologic function, such as heart rate, may be quite different from strategies developed during longer training periods or repeated training, since in the latter there is more opportunity for trial and error and selection of successful strategies.

One interesting sidelight on the importance of strategy in heart rate biofeedback was reported by Davidson and Schwartz at the 1975 BRS meeting. Using an operant conditioning paradigm, subjects were asked to increase then to decrease heart rate in one-minute trials first with and then without an auditory biofeedback signal. Following this the subjects were asked to relive angry then relaxing scenes as a device to compare possible subjective influences. Inspection of simultaneously recorded EEGs revealed females to show right hemisphere activation during emotional conditions, left hemisphere activation before feedback, and right hemisphere activation during heart rate conditioning. The investigators interpret these results as indicating females may be adopting learning strategies that are more affective than cognitive. In view of the fact that evidence for this conclusion is weak, the conclusion may simply be a case of male chauvinism.

Aside from strategies, the ability to learn heart rate control and awareness of either self or of a selected autonomic function also relates to other personality factors and to factors involved in the physiologic function. In a study using continuous feedback, Stephens reported finding that individuals with the highest heart rate variability along with more frequent emotional skin electrical responses were best able to increase heart rate, whereas those who had the highest *levels* of heart rate along with high variability of rate were best able to decrease heart rate. Although marked individual differences in ability to control heart rate were found, high ego strength scores appeared to correlate with learning-to-control ability. Another investigator has found that high achievers are better learners, while still another has concluded that some individuals are simply poor visceral learners.

## Role of Information and Cognition

Laboratory studies have uncovered a surprising number of psychophysiological factors important to the learning-to-control process in heart rate biofeedback. The exciting direction of the new research is toward defining the importance of cognitively useful information, both consciously and subconsciously appreciated, to learning to control a vital body function that usually functions automatically and is reflexly regulated.

Heart rate and heart rate biofeedback are exquisitely sensitive to cognitive factors. The vast majority of heart rate biofeedback studies, taken together, indicate that the more kinds of information about the process that are available, the more rapid and more effective is the learning to control heart rate. Although the kinds of information provided in such studies are not separately identified, they closely resemble the categories of information outlined in Chapter 1, and identified in Chapter 2 as currently necessary to successful use of biofeedback. The sensitivity of heart rate activity to cognitive inputs also illustrates the concept of biological awareness, i.e., that kind of subconscious awareness of biological activities which cannot be expressed by ordinary means, but is expressed by specific, intentional alterations of biological functions, as in biofeedback learning or in responses to subliminal stimulation. It is to be expected that human beings have some sense or awareness of heart rate activity, since often they can feel their pulse pound, or can have other experiences with pulse and heart beat, and this experiential background may be the factor which makes learning to control heart rate a relatively easy task.

One of the most striking pieces of evidence demonstrating the close link between sophisticated cerebral activity and heart rate is the studies in which heart rate is shown to respond to false information about itself. Using various kinds of experimental designs, it has been found that not only the heart rate, but its accompanying subjective feeling state as well, can respond to cognitive information about itself which is false. For example, the heart rate is generally relatively faster in anxiety states, yet when the anxious individual listens to a slow heart beat and is told that it is his heart beat, his own heart rate can slow and his subjective anxiety decreases. This kind of psychophysiological evidence strongly supports my concept that many body activities are shaped by cognized acceptance of body states and activities induced by social impact and consensus, and further, that the influence of the cognized information about many physiological states is frequently dominant over internal, reflex regulating information even when the cognized information is false and its effects deleterious. In this light, heart rate biofeedback learning may contribute substantially as a preventive technique, allowing individuals to learn to suppress inappropriate heart rate reactivity and maintain an optimally functional state with minimal effects of stress.

The sensitivity of heart rate control factors to cognitive nuances makes it seem likely that the inability of some individuals to learn heart rate control may be related to the accuracy and detail of information they are given in their instructions and how this relates to their general background of understanding. Since most experimental laboratory studies consist of as short a training time as ten minutes and rarely as long as an hour of single sessions, it is possible that the added experience of extended training might equalize out the degree of control attained, with learning differences confined to rate of learning. No studies yet have carried out training to establish when maximal learning occurs nor even what is maximal. Some research studies claim their results indicate that presence of the biofeedback signal is the most important element contributing to the learning-to-control ability while other studies claim that practice is the most important element.

These differences are perhaps not important considerations in clinical practice since once commenced, biofeedback training is likely to be continued until learning occurs or does not appear to be forthcoming. The same applies to motivational factors. Frequently laboratory situations are minimally motivating, even with nickel rewards for various increments of performance. In practice, the patient who will benefit from learning heart rate control supplies much of the motivation necessary.

No factor in biofeedback has been confirmed more amply than has been the role of information in heart rate control. Some five groups of researchers have reported in seven separate publications that information, in the form of either instructions or the biofeedback signal or both, is the crucial element for learning. Brener, for example, has reported that heart rate control is a direct function of the percentage of time that feedback is available. This further emphasizes the importance of continuous feedback. It has been found, in fact, that instructions without biofeedback are adequate for most subjects to exert control over heart rate. Depending upon the type of experiment, biofeedback may or may not facilitate this learning to control heart rate. As has been pointed out, most human beings have had some experience with heart rate, consciously or unconsciously, and the associations made between subjective feeling states and heart rate level probably serve as a source of information for heart rate awareness. To learn control, only instructions may be necessary. After all, yogis have been controlling their heart rates for centuries.

The consensus is that cognitive factors are the essential elements in heart rate biofeedback, and that, in fact, typical reinforcements used to elicit heart rate learning are unnecessary. As Katkin and Murray concluded after reviewing early work in biofeedback heart rate, new statistics support "the notion that the subject's cognitive and somatic activities influenced heart rate change more than the reinforcement contingencies utilized."

## Clinical Studies

To date heart rate biofeedback has been used principally in cases of atrial arrhythmias, auriculo-ventricular arrhythmias, premature ventricular contractions, and (unsuccessfully) in a few cases of heart block.

Weiss and Engel have reported several times on patients with premature ventricular contractions (PVCs) treated with heart rate conditioning techniques. Using continuously available heart rate signals, patients were trained both to increase and decrease heart rate. All patients learned this task; however, in some cases the incidence of premature beats increased as heart rate decreased while in others the incidence of PVCs increased during learned increase of heart rate. Some patients were more consistent in slowing heart rate while others were more consistent in speeding heart rate, and about the same percentage of patients was capable of learning control in both directions. It appears that, overall, better results occurred with slowing of heart rate. Of those patients who successfully learned to decrease the incidence of PVCs, the effect was sustained after learning for at least three months.

In patients with ectopic auricular beats or with tachycardias, the same technique was used and patients learned to regulate heart rate. Part of the treatment procedure was giving the patients information by explaining the nature of arrhythmias. Those patients with anxiety accompanying their fast heart rates also showed decreased anxiety about their hearts and there was evidence that a belief in self-control was also developed.

Application of the same technique to patients suffering block of heart beat conduction at the auricular-ventricular junction showed that such patients could not learn control of ventricular rate. It appears obvious that an intact nerve supply and conduction pathways are required for learned heart rate control.

Heart rate biofeedback was explored as the physiologic manipulation during a desensitization procedure in patients with spider phobia. Heart rate biofeedback failed to be of value, although its failure might possibly be attributed to the use of only two one-hour training sessions.

Wickramasekera has reported an interesting case study of a patient with cardiac neurosis which he treated by first inducing relaxation by means of instructions to change the heart rate, then conducting a desensitization procedure using heart rate biofeedback as the monitor of the cardiac anxiety. Following 16 sessions the patient was free of anxiety episodes for several months, and the changed personality was maintained for the year's follow-up study. The length of the treatment is markedly different from the one noted above for spider phobia, and suggests that adequate practice is crucial to effective treatment.

# Blood Pressure

## Psychophysiological Background

As one of the more pernicious illnesses peculiar to human beings, essential hypertension may find its greatest treatment hope in biofeedback. As the term "essential" implies, the causes of this type of high blood pressure have eluded discovery. Long considered to reflect, in part, a normal aging process in which the muscles of the blood vessels lose their elasticity and tend to become rigid, suddenly, within only the last decade, medical opinion has begun to consider psychosocial factors as possible causes. A review of research studies favoring psychosocial influences as the etiologic agents of essential hypertension is given in *New Mind, New Body*. The effect of stress as a cause of essential hypertension is complex, appearing to relate more to the ability of an individual to cope with stress than to the amount or degree of stress he may be subjected to.

Briefly, the theoretical thinking about the relationship of stress to essential hypertension, based on numerous investigations, is that hypertensive patients develop some awareness of their tendency to overreact physiologically, a reaction which pushes blood pressure higher, and so they develop behavioral patterns by which they avoid stress situations or become overtly relatively unreactive. On the other hand, it has also been theorized that rather than developing an internal awareness of the potential harm to their blood vessels of reacting overtly, hypertensive patients may actually have a defect in their ability to perceive their environments completely, and that this serves to protect their cardiovascular systems.

There is some evidence to suggest that hypertensives are often personalities suggesting hostility, and the interpretation is made that such individuals internalize their anger, and that this in turn activates those nervous mechanisms which constrict blood vessels. It has frequently been suggested this is the reason for the high incidence of essential hypertension in blacks, and particularly in black women.

Taking all of the experimental evidence together, the person with essential hypertension would seem to be the kind of person who would like to fight back against his environmental stresses, but who cannot. The reasons he cannot may be that the stressful situation is beyond his ability to cope with it, or that he may lack the know-how, or that he may actually have some emotional or mental disability for such social complexities.

If this is a reasonably accurate description of the internal turmoil of hypertensives, and the evidence seems to dovetail well enough to support the assumption, then at least one major aspect of the cause of essential hypertension is the individual's reaction to stress. It would then logically follow that a majority of essential hypertensives would benefit to some degree by stress-reduction treatment techniques.

As reviewed under Essential Hypertension in Chapter 3, this seems to be well borne out by results of varieties of stress-reduction techniques when they are used in this disorder. Through the years there has been clinical success using either Jacobson's Progressive Relaxation or Schultz' Autogenic Training procedures, although the practical constraints of these techniques failed to engender widespread enthusiasm for them despite their successes. Within the past ten or fifteen years, it has been recognized that the tediously long relaxation programs such procedures required could be shortened and still be effective, and this change in perspective occurred hand-in-hand with a better understanding of stress; together these changes have sparked a renewal of interest in relaxation procedures as antistress treatment. Curiously, this happened only shortly before biofeedback procedures were developed. These new concepts then in turn stimulated the exploration of yogic body control techniques for use in the treatment of essential hypertension.

Basically, all of the relaxation or antistress procedures are related. Muscle biofeedback is simply a technologic advance in relaxation techniques, and as such, remarkably facilitates relaxation learning. In fact, as is emphasized in Chapter 3, it is almost always used in conjunction with other relaxation techniques.

The chief departure in biofeedback use in the treatment of hypertension is in the procedure which uses blood pressure levels as the biofeedback information. Even in this situation it is suspected that the blood pressure biofeedback signal is simply the target for a particular kind of relaxation. Certainly the target is relief of the tension either of the blood vessel muscles themselves or equally as likely, a general reduction in body tension.

At the present writing there are three major biofeedback approaches to the treatment of essential hypertension, and, when indicated, in other types of high blood pressure as well. The three approaches are: (1) the use of muscle (EMG) biofeedback to produce muscle tension relaxation, (2) the use of blood pressure level readings for the biofeedback signal, and (3) a multimodality approach using various biofeedback signals combined with yogic relaxation exercises.

The first is aimed chiefly toward general body reduction in muscle tension, assuming a relationship between skeletal muscle and visceral tension; the second is aimed toward affecting the degree of neural stimulation to the major blood vessels; while the third is aimed toward relaxation of both muscle and cerebral tension. Blood pressure biofeedback for the neural control of blood vessels directs itself chiefly to hypothesizing relative changes in activity of the two divisions of the autonomic nervous system, the sympathetic and parasympathetic; however, no suggestion has yet been put forward to explain how training with a blood pressure biofeedback signal can affect one or another set of nerves selectively enough to produce a fairly specific effect of changing blood pressure levels.

Continued research into the precise effects of both muscle and blood pressure biofeedback may well hold the key to understanding both stress and biofeedback. If it is found, for example, that muscle biofeedback procedures produce greater and longer-lasting reductions of blood pressure, then the mechanisms of both stress and biofeedback will be presumed to lie in complex cerebral processes. On the other hand, if biofeedback of blood pressure levels produces a greater and more lasting reduction of blood pressure, then the evidence will point to highly specific mechanisms, and possibly of a reflex cerebral nature for both the effects of stress and the effects of biofeedback.

Some extremely interesting clues have already been developed. Love, Montgomery, and co-workers have reported that there is a considerable lag time between muscle relaxation and blood pressure reduction effects following muscle biofeedback. It appears that long after muscle tension has been substantially reduced and biofeedback treatment suspended, blood pressure levels continue to fall. In contrast, in a study using diastolic blood pressure levels as a biofeedback reinforcement, diastolic levels fell significantly although systolic levels did not, and the effect occurred in a close temporal relationship to the biofeedback training. If these discrepancies can be confirmed, it will be strongly suggestive that the complex mechanisms sustaining high blood pressure as a result of failure to manage stress can be isolated into component elements. If, for example, it is confirmed that EMG biofeedback and practiced relaxation affect central blood pressure mechanisms indirectly, accounting for the lag time, the effects may result from relieving cerebral inhibitory effects on autonomic mechanisms. On the other hand, if the feedback of diastolic blood pressure information does indeed result in a more immediate, consistent, and sustained reduction of diastolic blood pressure, then this is strong suggestive evidence that some kind of biological awareness of system relationships exists and can be used to effect compensatory measures. The situation, as Alice said, gets curiouser and curiouser.

Particularly intriguing are the results of diastolic blood pressure biofeedback as they relate to the assumed generalized effects of stress and the rationale for the use of EMG biofeedback in the treatment of essential hypertension. In one study using diastolic blood pressure biofeedback that was directed toward measuring effect on anxiety and tension of the hypertensives, there were no indications of change in either anxiety or in physiologic indices relating to anxiety following biofeedback treatment while diastolic pressure did decrease, although the number of patients used was relatively small. Since it was *mean* (average) blood pressure that was the biofeedback signal given, the investigators suggest that diastolic levels were frequently reinforced by the feedback signal. This interpretation is based in part on the usual blood pressure relationships and reactions, that is, systolic pressures are much more labile, and respond to changes in stress levels far more readily than do diastolic levels.

This raises the most serious problem connected with using blood pressure readings as the biofeedback signal. Currently used methods require that the blood pressure cuff be inflated at frequent intervals, or sustained within a fairly narrow inflated range. This is stressful to the patient; cuff pressures must be sustained in order to read blood pressure levels because the reading is dependent upon listening for heart beats appearing or disappearing through the brachial artery. Since blood pressure levels often vary widely depending upon general body and emotional tension levels, blood pressure levels are difficult to assess under normal conditions. Moreover, the technique has a low degree of accuracy when compared to other techniques for measuring physiologic activities. Owing to the mechanics of the measuring device, the cuff and the stethoscope, the accuracy of any single blood pressure reading is at most 5 mm Hg.

## Experimental Studies

The diffuse and complicated network that keeps blood circulating effectively would seem to have so many presenting difficulties in its regulation that the idea of learned or voluntary control of blood pressure would be doubtful. The measurement of blood pressure is indirect, and at best is only modestly approximated. Blood pressure regulation is effected by widespread neural networks, by chemical, pressure, and hormonal reflex activities, and by biochemical processes occurring in the walls of the vascular system. And while blood pressure regulating mechanisms are largely under autonomic nervous system control, and thus blood pressure reacts to emotional and higher cerebral stimuli, its anatomical locations put blood pressure under direct muscle effects as well. Effects of stress, for example, on blood pressure are probably at least threefold: direct autonomic effects, hormonal, and muscle effects. With such a high degree of complexity to its regulation, it would seem unlikely that any one of the regulating elements could serve as a specific parameter for learning control of blood pressure levels. It would seem more likely that the information about blood pressure to be used in biofeedback learning should represent either a sum of cardiovascular events reflecting the dynamic interaction of many factors leading to particular levels, or the information should represent or provide an index of a major indirectly influencing factor. As it is, only two types of relevant information are available: blood pressure levels themselves and muscle (EMG) tension levels.

The problem of working with two dominant patterns of physiologic activity affecting blood pressure, skeletal muscle and autonomic mediation, was neatly approached by DiCara and Miller in experiments with rats. Using animals paralyzed by a curare-like drug, thus eliminating most of the muscle contribution, and using an operant conditioning experimental design, they discovered that rats could "learn" to change blood pressure levels appropriately in order to receive an appealing reward. This work was closely followed by a report by Shapiro and colleagues, also using an operant conditioning paradigm in human beings. Small but statistically significant changes were found for single training sessions. A number of other reports to scientific journals and meetings were made by the same group of investigators in which experimental manipulations using human subjects were described that led to the conclusion that blood pressure control was a fairly specific response to the procedures employed. The most significant publication dealt with the use of diastolic blood pressure levels as the conditioning signal. Results of these experiments also showed extremely small changes in blood pressure levels, but a comparison between learned increases and decreases of blood pressure (i.e., the difference between the conditioned increase and the conditioned decrease) showed the differences to be statistically significant, indicating that response discrimination between the two demands of the stimulus (the conditioning signal) had been made. It was also found that respiration was not a contributing cause to the learning effect.

The technique used for the biofeedback of "direct" blood pressure levels is in itself a stressful procedure. The technique used by the Shapiro group and in many of the studies of clinical application is an especially disturbing one. It consists of inflating the blood pressure cuff and adjusting the cuff pressure until just 50 percent of the heart beats can be detected below the cuff. This criterion is determined by comparing electronically the Korotkoff sounds with the R pulse wave detected from the brachial artery. At the 50 percent heart beat level, the cuff pressure reading is assumed to represent the median systolic blood pressure. A similar determination is made for diastolic level using the cuff pressure at which 50 percent of the beats pass the cuff on the downside of the pressure. Cuff pressure must be maintained for almost a minute to constitute a conditioning trial.

In 1970 Brener and Kleinman reported on the effect of augmented sensory feedback (biofeedback) using a finger cuff technique in which finger pulse was correlated with values obtained from the brachial artery cuff method. In their study the effect of the biofeedback information was determined by providing both continuous absolute and relative blood pressure changes as biofeedback signals and further augmented by providing *full instructions* about the procedure. Although the results of such training were not deemed statistically significant because of the usual blood pressure variations, the trend effects were positive and of the magnitude reported by others. In a subsequent study

Brener investigated the relative significance of instructions and of the biofeedback information, and found that learned control of blood pressure levels appeared to be specific to the availability of the biofeedback signal.

Specificity of cardiovascular control has been inspected in considerable detail by Shapiro, Schwartz, and Tursky using conditioning techniques. Subjects were rewarded for either decreasing or increasing heart rate and blood pressure simultaneously, then for differential responses, i.e., for simultaneously increasing heart rate while lowering blood pressure and the other three combinations. Significant heart rate–blood pressure integration and differentiation are claimed for single conditioning sessions although actual values of change are quite small.

## Blood Pressure Biofeedback in Essential Hypertension

Nearly a dozen reports or abstracts have appeared since 1971 describing the effects of blood pressure feedback in patients with essential hypertension. The original study by Benson and colleagues used the Shapiro technique of cuff inflation for detecting systolic blood pressure levels, as did several of the other studies. These early studies also used operant conditioning reinforcement techniques, i.e., increments of change in blood pressure level were reinforced by light and sound signals. The majority of reports indicated that substantial lowering of blood pressure resulted from biofeedback training although some reports were disappointing. For example, the Benson group found an average of a 16.5 mm Hg reduction in blood pressure of hypertensives while a report by Schwartz and Shapiro found a 5 mm Hg reduction within training sessions to be the greatest change. Similarly, McGrady et al., using twice-weekly conditioning sessions for a month and augmenting the treatment with home practice, found that all patients could lower blood pressure during training sessions, but for all sessions the average reductions were only 7.4 mm Hg systolic and 4.2 mm Hg diastolic. In a subsequent study, however, McGrady and colleagues employed the diastolic level as the biofeedback parameter and found significant reduction in both systolic and diastolic levels.

A similar experimental study by Elder and colleagues used extensive control procedures and a more stringent reinforcement criterion (a fall of 5 mm Hg systolic pressure before reinforcement). They instructed their eighteen hypertensive patients "to lower blood pressure any way [they] could" but gave no other explanations. The resulting changes in *systolic* blood pressure were not considered to be significant, presumably because of the variation factor, but as much as a 25 percent reduction of *diastolic* pressure did occur and persisted for the week's follow-up blood pressure check.

A similar curious change was found in the studies of Kleinman and colleagues using systolic blood pressure levels as the biofeedback reinforcing information. Their technique used weekly blood pressure biofeedback training sessions for nine weeks supplemented by home recording of blood pressure five times daily. They also found that while reductions in systolic pressure were not significantly changed, the diastolic levels were significantly reduced.

Akagi and colleagues have recently reported a study using direct blood pressure biofeedback in seven essential hypertensives. Each twenty-five-minute training period was followed by a ten-minute period of attempting voluntary control without the feedback signal. Despite considerable individual variation, five of the seven patients showed an average reduction of systolic pressure of 25 mm Hg. These investigators emphasize the importance of cognitive factors, especially as evoked by training instructions. Most experimental clinical studies have also found hypertensive medication could be significantly reduced in a significant number of patients.

Although the studies described above have obtained promising results for the use of blood pressure biofeedback in the treatment of essential hypertension, blood pressure reductions have been rather modest.

While the physiology of blood pressure would dictate the use of diastolic blood pressure levels as the most appropriate monitor of blood pressure activity, currently used techniques are not only difficult and somewhat traumatic for the patient, but accuracy is also a problem. Most indirect blood pressure measuring techniques have a poor sensitivity, 5 mm Hg at best, and in view of the variation of systolic blood pressure that so frequently characterizes the essential hypertensive patient, current techniques are not only difficult, but do not provide high-quality biofeedback information. For "direct" blood pressure biofeedback to be successful, there is an urgent need to improve the blood pressure detection techniques. The technique used by Brener may prove adequate, or a new technique described by Jernstedt and Newcomer may prove to be both accurate and convenient. These investigators have developed a non-cuff technique measuring the pulse transit time from EKG to digital pulse wave, and have found that it correlates well with actual blood pressure levels.

Walsh and associates have also developed a similar technique using pulse wave velocity as an index of blood pressure levels. In comparing pulse wave velocity biofeedback training with the effects of Progressive Relaxation they also, as did both the Elder and Kleinman groups, found diastolic levels to be reduced more significantly than systolic levels with both treatment procedures. A puzzling event occurred, however, when they combined the two treatment techniques. When combined pulse wave velocity biofeedback and Progressive Relaxation were used following training with either procedure separately, the patients seemed to lose their ability to lower blood pressure and some returned to pretreatment levels. The investigators felt that the procedure may have become aversive. In view of the beneficial results using relaxation procedures alone, the results suggest that perhaps some informational component of the pulse transit time contains information that may neutralize the relaxation effects.

One important element of biofeedback training that seems to have been generally overlooked in most of the experimental work in essential hypertensives is that of ensuring adequacy of the learned control. Using systolic biofeedback, Kristt and Engel approached this factor by training their hypertensive patients to both increase and decrease blood pressure levels until they were able to perform at will. In addition to significant changes, the control ability persisted for the three months of follow-up studies. Moreover, since no other functionally related physiologic changes occurred during the training, it was concluded that the learned control was specific for blood pressure.

## Other Biofeedback Approaches to Essential Hypertension[2]

The difficulties entailed in "direct" blood pressure biofeedback, along with the presumptive role of stress and tension in the cause of essential hypertension, have stimulated researchers toward other approaches. The rationale for using muscle relaxing techniques and a discussion of EMG biofeedback studies in essential hypertension have been indicated in the beginning of this section and are also presented in Chapter 3.

Two groups of investigators have been carrying out systematic studies on various combinations of biofeedback techniques and treatment regimes. These are Love, Montgomery, Weston, and associates in this country and Patel in England. The former group has been concerned chiefly with relaxation biofeedback procedures, but has included "direct" blood pressure biofeedback training during extended treatment regimes. A fairly complicated experimental design allowed for examining the effects of various relaxation procedures, including autogenic training, home relaxation practice, biofeedback, muscle assisted relaxation, and blood pressure biofeedback, and it was found that there was not much distinction among procedures or training techniques with respect to blood pressure reduction.

---

2. See also Chapter 3 and pages 163–170 re temperature biofeedback.

One of the most interesting outcomes of the Love group study was the "lag effect," noted earlier. After some sixteen weeks of relaxation treatment both with and without biofeedback at different stages, the reduction in blood pressure for the hypertensive patients averaged about 15 mm Hg systolic and approximately 13 mm Hg in diastolic pressure. Twelve months later at follow-up, the reductions amounted to 27.5 for systolic and 17.7 for diastolic pressure.

There seems to be little question that learned blood pressure control can persist for long periods. All experimental studies which have included follow-up examination at periods following biofeedback training for periods up to a year have found that reduced levels have been sustained.

Patel, working with a combination of yogic relaxation techniques and biofeedback, has found similar maintenance of lowered blood pressure levels. Patel has worked with large numbers of essential hypertensives, using first yogic breathing and muscle relaxation exercises, then a variety of biofeedback procedures (a multimodality approach), including skin electrical, muscle, and brain wave alpha. All hypertensives received three months of treatment, working three times a week for 30 minutes a session, and few patients failed to respond. There was, moreover, a 41 percent reduction in total drug requirement for all patients along with good subjective improvement. Patel also tested her patients for their reactions to stress and found that following training they responded less physiologically to stress stimuli than before treatment. Naturally Patel emphasizes the importance of the subjective state, but it should be pointed out that her studies, using large numbers of patients, were conducted with patients in private practice and hence are important indicators of the value of biofeedback and supplementary relaxation techniques in the clinical treatment of essential hypertension. Patel also found that the lowered blood pressure levels were maintained for at least twelve months.

A recent report by Sedlacek using multimodality biofeedback and yogic exercises confirms Patel's results.

## *Vasoconstriction and Vasodilation*

It was not until 1968 that learned control of blood vessel activity was reported. The magnitude of finger pulse volume was reinforced when it changed in the predetermined direction, and the resulting conditioned vasoconstriction was shown to be independent of body movement, muscle tension, heart rate, and respiratory irregularities. From Prague at about the same time Machac reported that individuals, using finger and forearm blood volume monitors, were capable of intentionally changing degree of vascular constriction at will by changing mental states. Volow and Hein have demonstrated that some individuals can be bidirectionally conditioned for control of finger pulse volume by using augmented feedback and prolonged training. Operant conditioning of finger blood volume has also been confirmed by Stern and Pavloski but with the unusual finding that effect occurred almost immediately within the first five-minute conditioning trial. The conditioning technique used a light signal as reinforcement of blood volume change in the desired direction. Analysis of subjective reports revealed that those subjects who received contingent reinforcement believed their thoughts of body activity caused the reinforcement light to come on, while the controls or those receiving only occasional reinforcement felt that the light signal occurred randomly.

## Migraine Headache

The application of biofeedback for control of vascular function is particularly appropriate for migraine headache. According to the classical carotid hypothesis of Wolff, the headache pain of migraine is primarily a result of vasodilation of branches of the external carotid artery. Using this model, Koppman and associates devised a technique to detect and feed back information about the diameter of the anterior temporal artery. Using a reflectance photoplethysmometer over the temporal artery, the continuously alternating blood volume pulse was used as the biofeedback signal. Training consisted of alternating eight-minute trials for learning to constrict and to dilate the blood vessels.

Migraine patients were given two to three one-hour training sessions per week for a maximum of twelve sessions, and were instructed to make no muscle movements but to attend and concentrate on dilating or constricting the blood vessel. It was suggested that imagery such as thinking big or small or of nothing or of pleasant things might help to find the conscious or mental state that would accomplish the task. Seven of nine patients developed significant voluntary control as shown by producing reliable differences between dilation and constriction. Since no correlations were found between temporal artery and finger pulse amplitudes, or between temporal artery blood volume pulse and any EMG change, it was concluded that the learning was specific to the temporal artery, and moreover that such specificity reflected a specific cerebral control. Although it was demonstrated that migraine patients could learn to control their vasodilation, no measurements were made of the effect of the training on headache pain or incidence.

A comprehensive study of the temporal artery technique biofeedback to reduce the dilation of the extracranial arteries and to relieve migraine headache has been made by Zamani (1975). Zamani used a technique similar to that of Koppman but further compared the effects of temporal artery control to effects of a relaxation training program on the treatment of fourteen migraine patients. The deep muscle relaxation procedure was employed on the basis of the reported personality characteristics of migraine patients: anxious, tense, shy, perfectionist, achievement oriented, resentful, easily fatigued individuals who react to stress, unvented hostility, and resentment with headaches. Half of the patients received the relaxation procedure while the other half received the vasomotor biofeedback procedure. The treatment program consisted of a pretreatment phase of six to eight weeks during which baseline information was accumulated, particularly with

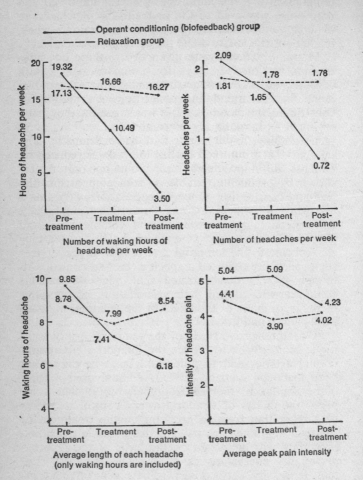

*Fig. 9.* Summary of results of Dr. Reza Zamani's study using temporal artery pulse pressure biofeedback for learning control of blood vessel constriction in migraine headache patient. See text for further description (from doctoral dissertation; personal communication).

respect to headache incidence, severity, duration, and medication used. This was followed by a four-week treatment phase consisting of two sessions per week, and finally a post-treatment phase of six to eight weeks consisting of a weaning period and follow-up measurements. The biofeedback patients were trained in both dilation and constriction of the temporal extracranial artery and received verbal encouragement as well as instructions about home practice which consisted of using the finger to detect the temporal pulse.

The results of this study were quite dramatic. The average total of hours of headache pain was reduced by 82 percent for the biofeedback group but only 5 percent for the relaxation group used for comparison; the number of headaches per week decreased by 66 percent for the biofeedback treatment group and by only 2 percent for the relaxation group; the average length of headaches was reduced by 37 percent for the biofeedback group as compared to only a 3 percent reduction for the relaxation group of patients; headache intensity was reduced by 16 percent with biofeedback and 9 percent for relaxation; and finally, the amount of medication used was reduced by 92 percent with biofeedback treatment and 9 percent for the relaxation treatment.

A new technique has been developed by Sovak and colleagues in which the pulse amplitude of digital arteries activates an audio signal, and it has been found that changes in digital pulse volume react more consistently and more directly than temporal artery pulse volume, and more quickly. Work is currently being conducted using this technique in the treatment of migraine and other peripheral vascular disease.

## Skin Temperature Biofeedback

### Basic Research Studies

Skin temperature provides by far the most convenient monitor of peripheral cardiovascular activity, and as such can reflect both disturbances in peripheral vascular function as well as changes in distribution of blood flow in a variety of other conditions. It has the distinct advantage that the average individual is familiar with the concept of temperature and has some idea of the relationships between his feeling states and his body and skin temperature.

It has been long known that hypnotic and self-hypnotic suggestion to change skin temperature is almost always successful in both normal individuals and in patients with disturbed peripheral vascular function. The degree of control possible by suggestion alone has been demonstrated by Maslach et al., who trained subjects under hypnosis to change the skin temperature of the two hands in opposite directions. They concluded that this feat implicated a powerful influence of cognitive processes on the autonomic nervous system.

The ability to learn control of skin temperature in selected areas has been repeatedly confirmed in temperature biofeedback studies although background control research that explores the influence of environmental and physiological contributing influences is sparse. For example, only three research studies have dealt with the relationship between environmental ambient temperature and effect on either the ability to control skin temperature or the relative degree of change possible, and results of these studies are conflicting. Newman compared hand-warming ability with temperature biofeedback in rooms at about 73, 58, and 50 degrees Fahrenheit and found no differences in learning abilities, and that both voluntary and involuntary responses were of about the same magnitude regardless of room temperature. Taub has not only demonstrated that learned hand temperature warming can be maintained in environments of 55 degrees Fahrenheit but the capability is retained even after vasoconstriction occurs after a twenty-five-minute exposure to the cool environment. These results directly conflict with those of Shapiro and Surwit, who found that subjects did not learn to warm hands in a cool environment.

It might be expected that the normal individual tone of the peripheral vascular system and its sensitivity to heat and cold stimuli would also influence learning of peripheral temperature control. One study compared learning to warm the hands in individuals with high and with low hand temperatures and found that little temperature change occurred in those subjects with high hand temperature. On the other hand, in an extensive study using numerous training sessions and training both to increase and decrease skin temperature, no differences were found between individuals who were sensitive to heat and those who were not.

While environmental and individual physiologic tendencies might be expected to influence differentially the ability to raise or lower skin temperature, here also results of experimental studies are in disagreement. Using a cross-over experiment in which some subjects first raised then learned to lower skin temperature, while a second subject group used the reverse procedure, no real differences were found although the data suggested that perhaps raising temperature was an easier task.

In a more extensive study, Engel and Schaefer in Germany alternated warming and cooling instructions over five training sessions and found no significant differences in learning to control either direction although they point out that temperature changes were small and there was considerable variation among subjects. In contrast the Surwit group found their subjects had more difficulty in learning to increase finger temperature; these results also were of low magnitude and no significant changes were found across days, only within the training sessions.

Two groups of investigators have used forehead temperature rather than finger temperature and have reported consistent changes indicating adequate learning. The studies differ, however, in their results with control procedures, one finding that subjects who received no instructions did not respond while the other group found that as long as changes of temperature in the desired direction were reinforced, instructions made no difference on the responses.

## Role of Instructions and Strategy Information

Clinical application of hand temperature biofeedback was initiated by Elmer and Alyce Green, who augmented the biofeedback signal with autogenic training procedures. Since then a number of research studies have investigated the role of autogenic training procedures in temperature biofeedback and the consensus appears to be that the autogenic training procedure plays a very minor role in learning to control finger or hand temperature. Only partial success was obtained using A. T. alone without biofeedback; two other studies found that neither autogenic training nor anti-autogenic training suggestions nor full instructions had any effect on temperature control learning ability, and one study which measured hypnotic susceptibility and "absorbed imaginative involvement" found that neither was important, concluding that only adequate training and motivation are required. On the other hand, in a related study using autogenic hand temperature training, the most important factor was found to be the instructional set communicated by the experimenter.

Despite the many studies, temperature biofeedback is still in its elementary stages. The laboratory studies differ widely in the number of training sessions given, many using only a single training session of fifteen minutes' duration. As the disagreement in results noted above illustrates, it is difficult to make comparisons under these conditions, although clinical studies with peripheral vascular disease will resolve these differences since under clinical conditions patients receive extended training.

It seems quite likely that normal individuals in laboratory experimental situations can readily adapt to the situation and become relaxed, with hand or finger temperature quickly reaching the individual maximum. This would be particularly true in warm, comfortable rooms. Under these circumstances, without adequate adaptation periods and controls for room temperature or controls for individual differences in hand temperature, hand temperature would rise naturally and quickly; thus when temperature biofeedback is used results could be dramatic. It is unfortunate that no study has controlled for all of these factors; in fact, none has conducted adequate controls for the adaptation phase.

If, however, the individual suffers a peripheral vascular disease with poor hand circulation, as in the Raynaud's phenomenon, then it is already known that adaptation does not occur and that the vasoconstriction is a chronic condition. Under these circumstances, any change elicited by temperature biofeedback training could be assumed to be a valid effect of the training.

Two other factors which may explain differences among experimental studies are the influence of differential awareness of dominant and nondominant hands and differences in vascular activity between the sexes. The Surwit and Shapiro study used the nondominant hand for conditioning, but in measuring skin temperature, found the dominant hand always to be warmer, and they have raised the issue of the importance of body image in voluntary control learning. These investigators also found a difference between the sexes which may relate to successful strategies. When trying to warm the hands, females tended to increase heart rate while males showed heart rate slowing.

The relative importance of cognitively useful information can also be deduced, in part, from studies using special types of experimental subjects. French and colleagues compared temperature control learning between normal students and mentally retarded patients, and found both groups learned equally well and, moreover, retained their learned ability over the follow-up period. Young children also can quickly learn and retain finger temperature control for considerable periods.

## Temperature Control in Migraine Headache

The Green technique of temperature biofeedback supplemented by autogenic training was used by Sargent, Green, and Walters in the first application of the technique to migraine headache. As originally employed, the biofeedback signal was information about the temperature differential between index finger and forehead sites, the objective being to increase this differential. This assumed that the effect would be warming the hand and cooling the forehead, thus redistributing vasomotor activity and presumably causing vasoconstriction of the extracranial arteries. The patients were taught and memorized autogenic training phrases, and considerable emphasis was placed upon vivid imagery and home practice. Patients were supplied with temperature trainers for home use, and were also required to keep records of home practice sessions, and of headache incidence and severity and amount of medication used. After the patients had mastered temperature control, they practiced only on alternate days, and after one month the trainer was withdrawn. Results presented showed 74 percent of the migraine patients were improved with respect to both headache frequency and severity, and medication was concomitantly reduced.

The technique was subsequently streamlined into a five-day intensive autogenic-biofeedback training program which additionally included instructions for changing lifestyle by "body stress scanning," and in a followup study of patients treated by this technique it was found that 82 percent were still relieved of the migraine or tension headaches a year later.

At least six additional clinical studies have confirmed the effectiveness of the Green-Sargent method, one investigator reporting that two migraine patients first trained with EMG biofeedback without success responded dramatically to the temperature training technique. Another researcher claimed excellent results with the temperature training alone without using autogenic training, while still another group of researchers found that the technique was quickly successful in treating two young girls with headache, and Diamond has reported the techniques successful in the treatment of childhood migraine.

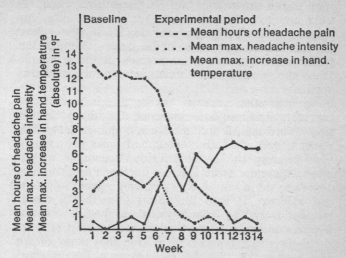

*Fig. 10.* Effect of temperature biofeedback training in a migraine patient. Number of hours of headache pain per week (dashed line) and estimates of intensity of the headache pain (dotted line) averaged for each week are graphed along with the average increase in hand temperature (from Wickramasekera, *J Behav Ther & Exp Psychiat,* 1973, *4,* 343–345).

## Temperature Control in Other Vascular Problems

Temperature control training has been tried sporadically in a variety of other vascular problems, all with considerable success. Because of its relative simplicity, its inexpensive implementation, and its high rate of success, there is an abundance of clinical anecdotal material on the success in disorders such as Raynaud's syndrome,[3] other types of headache, and as a relaxation procedure. Russell found temperature training helpful in relieving "psychic tension" during psychotherapy. French, Leeb, and co-workers have used the technique to raise scrotal temperature to the

---

3. A number of recent reports confirm the high success rate of temperature biofeedback in the treatment of Raynaud's syndrome. See also example in Chapter 1.

point where sperm could no longer survive, while another group used hand temperature training in an attempt to relieve menstrual distress. While temperature training was unimpressive in the latter condition, the investigators felt that improvements in the technique might evolve an effective treatment for menstrual distress.

An interesting concept has been put forward by Eversaul, who provides evidence for the idea that many functional disorders have a common denominator in a state he calls "habituated vasoconstriction." His data suggest that such individuals generally have a skin temperature some 8 to 10 degrees lower than individuals who do not have symptoms related to vascular problems. It is a bit unfortunate that Eversaul includes everything from arthritis and bursitis to hypoglycemia and even hemorrhoids in this category of functional disorders; however, it is true that many of the illnesses he cites can be characterized by disturbed vascular function. Eversaul's treatment program is equally as global as the list of functional disorders, consisting of operant conditioning and biofeedback techniques, self-suggestion, imagery, education, social reinforcement, and nutritional supplementation, and he describes documentation indicating considerable success with the technique.

The utility of temperature biofeedback training, particularly when viewed as an inexpensive and quickly learned technique for vasomotor activity control, may indeed be much broader than seemed at first glance. The eminent Indian cardiologist Datey has recently reported on the use of temperature biofeedback training in essential hypertension. Using the technique in ten patients, most on drug therapy, he found that 60 percent of the patients responded by significant reductions of blood pressure and in 20 percent the drugs could be discontinued.

# GASTROINTESTINAL BIOFEEDBACK

Functional diarrhea . . . Fecal incontinence . . .
. . . Esophageal spasms . . . Gastric acid secretion

With the full length of the gastrointestinal tract under control of the autonomic nervous system, it would be natural for biofeedback to expand into this vital system which too has its problems with stress and tension. It is equally obvious that the problem with the gastrointestinal tract is its relative inaccessibility; only the lower end can be studied conveniently. Nonetheless, the gastrointestinal tract can be beset with problems of tonus, of flaccidity and spastic muscle disturbances, of failure of sphincter tonic activity, and it can suffer disorders of its secretions, which also are under autonomic control. Most current gastrointestinal techniques are more inconvenient and uncomfortable than they are difficult, using as they do catheters and balloons, or needles in the anal sphincter.

## Functional Diarrhea

One delightfully ingenious study circumventing these unpleasant procedures has been conducted in patients with functional diarrheas. Furman devised a technique using an electronic stethoscope placed on the abdomen to detect sounds of peristaltic activity, and amplified the sounds, playing them back to the patient through a loudspeaker. After first perfecting the technique in normal subjects, he used it to treat five patients with varying degrees of bowel incapacity, most of whom suffered severe social restrictions because of their problem. Subjects were simply asked to increase or decrease their peristaltic activity, using the sounds as the biofeedback signal, and were given "social reinforcement" (verbal encouragement) for correct performance. Within five training sessions of about 30 minutes each, all patients achieved some degree of voluntary control over bowel (intestinal) motility. It is particularly interesting that symptomatic relief was usually obtained just before autonomic control became apparent, and in no case was it necessary to effect complete voluntary control to achieve relief from symptoms.

## Fecal Incontinence

In a not too dissimilar study Engel and Nikoomanesh treated six adult ambulatory patients suffering from fecal incontinence. Using balloons positioned at the external and internal anal sphincters, the pressure changes were recorded on a conventional polygraph, and the patients used the polygraph tracings as the biofeedback signals. The biofeedback was augmented by verbal encouragement. Training sessions lasted two hours, including rest periods, approximately three weeks apart, and all patients completed their training within four sessions. During follow-up periods ranging from six months to five years, four of the six patients have remained completely continent, the remaining two patients showing continuing improvement.

A similar procedure, except that the sphincter pressure was used to move a large column of water, was used in the case of a young (13 years) boy fecally incontinent. The first phase of treatment consisted of a single fifteen-minute session where the boy could watch the water column; since no significant changes occurred, the procedure was modified and the boy was monetarily rewarded for increasing sphincter pressure. Other modifications were instituted as needed, being particularly designed to favor increasing durations of height and pressure in the water column. The subject reached his maximal result at about the ninth or tenth training session and was markedly improved. Reports from the parents indicated that the improvement was sustained and that the boy could remain continent for periods up to eight hours.

## Esophageal Spasms

Schuster, in addition to using the balloon-visual feedback polygraph technique for fecal incontinence, also used a similar approach in the treatment of reflux esophagitis, a condition of lowered tone of the esophageal sphincter causing reflux of gastric contents and giving rise to symptoms of heartburn. Tandem balloons were swallowed so that one rested in the esophageal sphincter, and the pressure in the balloon was recorded on a polygraph. This constituted the visual feedback signal for the patients. Increased pressure, indicating increased smooth muscle tone of the sphincter often occurred simultaneously with turning on the feedback signal, or else was an almost immediate effect. Apparently most patients completed their training by the sixth session, with total relief of their symptoms.

## Gastric Acid Secretion

Several studies have demonstrated learned control of gastric acid secretion. Welgan used a biofeedback technique in which patients swallowed a pH electrode which was connected to a meter giving visual feedback of acid secretion. The subjects were duodenal ulcer patients used to a nasogastric tube in the stomach. For two fifteen-minute periods, interrupted by a fifteen-minute rest period, the subjects watched an expanded meter recording pH and were reinforced by tones for producing the desired changes. Subjects were exposed to the training procedures only once. In a second experiment conducted to determine magnitude of effect of the pH biofeedback signal, subjects not receiving the signal but having received the same instructions also showed positive changes. The effect of instructional set appeared similar to that found in most other biofeedback studies.

Whitehead and colleagues used an interesting technique to monitor gastric acid in four normal subjects. Gastric acid secretion was neutralized by injection of sodium bicarbonate through a nasogastric tube connected with a pH meter to show when neutralization had occurred. The amount of sodium bicarbonate was then used to express acid secretion. Because of individual variations, five to thirteen baseline sessions were required for adequate control data. This technique circumvents the problems of continuously aspirating stomach contents and effects of fluid volume on intra-gastric pH.

Feedback was via a counter for accumulated reinforcements of monetary rewards and lights signalling performance—of changing gastric acid secretion. Results showed that when money reinforcement was dependent upon a change in acid secretion the subjects could increase gastric acid secretion but could not reliably reduce it, whereas if the reinforcement was given on a temporal basis even if no change occurred, then the subjects could decrease the already increased acid levels to baseline values. No consistent correlations to other physiologic activities were found although individual subjects showed significant correlations between gastric acid secretion and one or more other physiologic activities. Moreover, none of the subjects reported using strategies involving cognitive mediation.

Only one other experimental gastric acid biofeedback study is available at this time and it completely supports the other two studies although only a single subject was used. This subject had been a four-year volunteer subject for gastrointestinal intubation research, and was experienced in the procedure. The study dealt largely with the psychic influence of appetizing food under various conditions of expectancy and camaraderie but also included a biofeedback session. Information about gastric acid levels was provided every two minutes, and irregularly over a four-hour period the subject was instructed to increase or decrease his gastric secretion. The subject was readily able to exert significant control over his gastric acid secretion, particularly to increase secretion, but reduced gastric secretions significantly under the biofeedback condition only when threatened with loss of an anticipated appetizing meal. The strategy used by the subject to change gastric acid secretion apparently was chiefly imagery: to increase secretion he visualized tantalizing food items and to decrease secretion he concentrated on thinking about nonfood items.

# BRAIN WAVE BIOFEEDBACK

The ultimate biofeedback may well be brain wave
biofeedback. Certainly, the brain electrical activity of
human beings is the greatest potential resource for understanding the dynamics of all human behavior. The
biofeedback learning process that can be invoked to
control skeletal muscle activity and to control the activity of organs and body systems innervated by the autonomic nervous system can also be applied to the
more complicated and sophisticated functions of the
central nervous system. Human beings can learn control over a wide variety of extraordinarily complex
brain functions. With brain as the substrate of the
mind, the potential of biofeedback techniques for regulation and modification of mind and consciousness
looms enormous.

Throughout the history of brain research, the difficulties of relating brain function to mental activity have been the difficulties innate to the continuously changing patterns of brain electrical activity and to the inexpressibility of ever-changing feelings, thoughts, and emotions. The remarkable contribution of biofeedback to brain-mind research is its ability to produce relatively "steady states." Once individuals learn voluntary control to sustain the presence of specific patterns or of specific elements of brain activity, such as alpha activity, the identification and precise definition of accompanying feeling states and mind activities becomes much easier.

The lack of reliable data about the mechanisms of complex mental functions has been as much a barrier to progress in developing new techniques for modifying and improving mind-brain function as was the lack of effective fuel propellants in the development of the space exploration program. By means of biofeedback techniques we are now learning, for example, that people with irregular brain function, such as epilepsy, or people with disordered mind function, such as neuroses or psychoses, can learn to generate brain states and brain electrical activities that can effectively reduce both physical and emotional distress. Nor are the benefits of brain wave biofeedback confined to disordered functions; uses are being developed to produce, sustain, and control brain states accompanying mind states conducive to tranquillity and creativity.

## The Electroencephalogram (EEG)— Patterns and Problems

Brain electrical activity patterns are usually referred to as the EEG, the abbreviation of the recorded brain wave pattern called the electroencephalogram. EEG generally implies the standard recording of brain electrical activity from eight or more electrodes or electrode pairs placed on the scalp according to a standard configuration. One of the troublesome obstacles to sound research relating brain waves to behavior that is difficult also for EEG biofeedback is that EEG patterns recorded from different scalp areas over the brain can vary remarkably, and this means that before EEG patterns can be related to behavior or states of consciousness a proper analysis of EEG activity is required to compare EEG activities among different brain areas. Unfortunately for biofeedback, such extensive recording and analysis are not generally possible either in research studies or in clinical use. This infeasibility means that considerable care must be taken in interpreting both the research and clinical results of EEG biofeedback.

What we know about EEGs is almost totally dependent upon the instruments used to record them. Throughout the history of EEG machines, attention has been focussed on relatively slow brain waves, and for the most part, on those slow, very large components that are signs of brain pathology. Most EEG machines dampen the amplitudes beginning at about 30 Hz (cycles per second) and eliminate all brain electrical activity occurring above frequencies of 50 or 60 Hz. The rationale for limiting EEG recording to slow brain wave frequencies has been mainly the inability of recording pens to reproduce high frequencies and the impossibility of electronic circuitry to discriminate very low voltage, fast EEG activity and the apparent relatively greater importance of the slow, high voltage waves for human activity. It is likely that neither of these latter assumptions is any longer valid; newer electronics can achieve more adequate signal-to-noise ratios, and research interest has turned to the more subtle and complex aspects of human behavior that are accompanied by the higher frequency EEG components.

Even with the present limitations of EEG recording, if a reasonably rapid recording speed and adequate amplification are used, the EEG pattern can be seen to be an almost never-ending variety of patterns. No two moments seem the same; indeed it is almost impossible to find exactly duplicate patterns of even a few seconds' duration no matter how long the recording is continued. What one sees visually is the occasional or frequent recurrence of rhythmic waves, and these alternate most irregularly with periods where no rhythmic activity can be seen.[1]

EEG patterns are, in fact, extremely difficult to define properly. Research into the significance of brain waves to subjective experience, mental events, and social behavior has been concerned mainly with certain arbitrarily defined, physically identifiable components of the EEG, such as alpha activity, and treating such specific components *as if* they were decisive elements in brain, and hence, mind activity. In truth, such EEG components are exactly that: components of *patterns,* and as such they *reflect* the changes and shifts of the activity of large but unknown numbers of brain neurons interacting among numerous brain structures. Brain wave components, such as alpha, are not causative elements in themselves, but when they are treated as such their importance can be made misleading. The mythology that has grown up around these kinds of research studies has generated a conflict between the alpha mentalists and the EEG neurophysiologists. While I would prefer to side with the EEG scientists, it must be admitted that they have contributed little meaningful research on the significance of either brain wave components or brain wave patterns of the relatively *normal* EEG. On the other hand, the new priests of alpha biofeedback have very nearly neutralized their contributions by failing to consider the neurophysiologic background of brain wave activity.

As every even incidentally reflective human being knows, it is difficult to capture and sustain thoughts and feelings and emotions. These products of the brain's activity play leapfrog into consciousness, moving so quickly that it takes a sharp concentration to sustain any particular thought or feeling long enough to identify its origins or consider its consequences. Thoughts, feelings, and sensations are almost constantly being replaced by new shadings. Concentration is the

---

1. Examples of different kinds of normal EEG patterns are given in Appendix 5.

mental maneuver of trying to pay strict *internal* attention to these phenomena long enough to identify and characterize them or put them to use.

Brain wave patterns reflect these dynamic racings of mind activities because they, the brain electrical activities, are the energies given off as the brain neurons process sensory and memory information. As the brain processes its enormous resources of information—perceptual, sensory, memory, experiential, judgmental—the sum of these activities, as determined by the numbers of active neurons, brain sites, densities of brain structures, levels of brain excitation, etc., all determine what brain electrical activity is available at the scalp to be recorded as the EEG pattern. The EEG pattern is thus a constantly changing pattern and at best a faint mirror of brain events occurring at some distance from the recording.

## The EEG Rhythms

It is mainly the rhythmic waves that have been labelled. The first to be identified is the alpha wave, variously defined as rhythmic EEG activity having a frequency of somewhere between 9 and 12 Hz, although some researchers include 8 and 13 Hz waves in their definition. The reason that alpha is defined in terms of a frequency range rather than as a specific frequency is precisely because alpha frequency does vary. It varies from person to person and it varies in the same individual depending upon a number of factors, such as level of attention, state of consciousness, mood, etc. Characterizing alpha as a 10-cycle-per-second (Hz) brain wave is merely for convenience, since it is rare that alpha occurs at exactly this frequency. The exact characteristics of alpha activity can also differ depending upon the location of the scalp recording electrodes. Frequently alpha in the frontal and pre-central areas can differ remarkably from that found in the mid-scalp or occipital regions.

The most precise expression of the behavioral state most closely identified with alpha activity is relaxed wakefulness. It implies that the brain state is a receptive one, and that it is not actively engaged in any specific mental or emotional activity. Alpha activity can be present, however, when a concentration of attention is not required for a mental task, or when a particular mental activity is habitual (it is reported that Einstein maintained an EEG pattern with considerable alpha while solving even moderately complex mathematical problems, but that when he was confronted with a new kind of problem, then his alpha disappeared), or when attention is focussed inwardly, or paradoxically in some cases where emotional adjustments block responsiveness and result in continued alpha in the EEG pattern.

Reports of biofeedback studies continue to support neurophysiologically derived notions that the subjective feeling state during the presence of alpha activity in the EEG is a generally tranquil, pleasant, almost floating feeling, although there may be occasional exceptions.

The second rhythmic EEG activity to be identified is theta activity. On the average, theta waves are about one-half the frequency of alpha waves, and are generally defined as having a frequency range of from about 3.5 to 6.5 Hz, although some researchers extend the range up to the lower end of the alpha frequency range, i.e., to about 8 Hz. Theta waves are sparse in the normal waking EEG pattern, and pose problems for biofeedback because theta usually appears as single or pairs of waves and trains of theta waves are usually poorly defined in recordings and occur only rarely. They rarely exceed more than 5 percent of the total pattern under any circumstances and are found most frequently during drowsiness and during dreaming. Even in these states, theta is not abundant. Theta activity also occurs during alert behavior, generally sporadically, but it frequently appears at moments of sudden insight or recognition of events in memory. Research evidence suggests that these quite different behavioral states and activities may relate quite directly to specific frequencies of theta, particularly within the same individual.

There is a good deal of evidence to indicate that the

rhythmic EEG wave with a frequency of 6 to 9 Hz (between the theta and alpha ranges) has mental and emotional correlates distinctive from either alpha or theta; however, research has not yet treated this frequency range as a separate EEG component.

There are few other easily identifiable rhythmic EEG components. Delta waves, having a frequency range of about 0.5 to 3 Hz, occur almost exclusively during the deeper stages of sleep, and usually appear as single waves and rarely as trains of four or more waves. Another rhythmic activity that occurs in short bursts has a frequency range of about 12 to 14 Hz, and occurs predominantly during the intermediate sleep stages, although it is occasionally found in awake states and is treated by some investigators as a higher frequency variant of alpha. The same frequency can be elicited by biofeedback techniques, although it does not normally occur during waking behavior, and is being used in the treatment of epilepsy.

Except for infrequently occurring large voltage waves (such as the K complex), nearly all other EEG activity is lumped together under the name "beta." The term is poorly defined but is generally used to indicate all EEG activity of (assumed) frequencies higher than that of alpha. As the term is used by different investigators, it can refer to rhythmic or nonrhythmic EEG activity and to different frequency ranges. Recently researchers have been characterizing beta according to specific frequency ranges such as 13 to 28 to 40 Hz, but often it is not specified whether the beta is rhythmic or not. In general, beta activity is quite low voltage, and because of this and its close relationship to the characteristics of electrical noise in frequency and voltage, it is difficult to quantify precisely. Beta activity is also loosely related to behavior. It is generally accepted that beta activity accompanies alert behavior and concentrated mental activity, such as in solving problems in mathematics. Beta activity is also the dominant pattern in anxiety and apprehension.

One of the higher beta frequencies that has been investigated adequately is the 40 Hz rhythm. Work with the 40 Hz rhythm depends upon sophisticated and high fidelity instrumentation because it is a very low voltage brain wave, close to the "noise" level of most instruments. It must be "extracted" from electrical noise, as well as from neighboring EEG frequencies and from extraneous scalp muscle electrical interference. This high frequency activity has been found to occur in states described as "circumscribed cortical excitability or focussed arousal," and the inference is that it is related to conditions favorable to short-term memory consolidation and problem solving. Most of the research has been done by Sheer, who reports that its use in biofeedback training is an effective tool for increasing problem-solving capacity in some individuals; he cautions, however, against generalizing on his preliminary results.

The current general level of EEG expertise is starkly inadequate to allow accurate conclusions by the casual investigator, and this applies particularly to researchers and therapists who plunge into such EEG biofeedback as alpha or theta. There are three major problems that are outstanding: instrumentation (discussed in the section on procedure), documentation of EEG changes, i.e., analysis of the EEG, and lack of an established background on the composition and variation and reactivity of EEG components in the normal EEG.

Serious evaluation of the dynamically behaving ongoing EEG pattern began only a short time before the emergence of biofeedback. The scientific literature built up for EEG components such as alpha or theta is based largely upon use of stimulation or other manipulations designed to elicit different kinds of EEG activity; in fact, at one time it was believed impossible to characterize the normal EEG pattern because of its constantly varying nature. Few laboratories in the world have concerned themselves with work with the normal EEG, and the current status of knowledge about normal EEG patterns is poor as a result. There are no truly reliable figures which quantify either the patterns or elements of the EEG pattern as it fluctuates normally. The literature is so recent and at so elementary a stage, that when I published a paper in 1966 on the alpha content of normal subjects with their eyes open as compared to when their eyes were closed (in visualizers and nonvisualizers), it was only a year following a paper by Mulholland on the single point that alpha activity could actually occur when the eyes were open.

There remains an enormous amount of basic research to be done simpy to characterize the normal EEG adequately. Each brain wave component can differ in its particular characteristics or aspects, i.e., each can vary irregularly in its aspects of (1) abundance, (2) specific frequency, (3) amplitude, (4) variability, (5) location (topographical distribution), (6) propagation or conduction time to the different recording sites, and (7) circumstances of appearance.

It is virtually impossible at the present time to obtain adequate values on more than one of these aspects of even *one* EEG component. Manual analysis of the EEG (measuring changes on the EEG record) is generally confined to measuring one, or possibly two, aspects, such as the amount of alpha present in the EEG (abundance) or its amplitude. EEGs recorded on paper are extremely difficult to analyze precisely, first because they are very small, requiring considerable accuracy in measurement, and second, because many features of the waves can be obscured by either ambient or normally interfering factors. Even electronic or computer analysis of EEG patterns fails to provide adequate data. The most commonly used computer analysis is the power spectrum analysis which deals only with EEG frequencies, and entails a computation which often gives a false impression about the relative importance of the different frequencies present. Electronic analyses generally or rarely deal with more than two of the aspects of EEG components noted above.

## Why Do EEG Biofeedback?

These analytic deficiencies have contributed to the misuse and misinterpretation of EEG biofeedback. Yet, despite the tendency toward scientific inaccuracies, EEG biofeedback has probably contributed more toward understanding the relationship between brain electrical activity and the products of brain activity labelled mental and emotional than any other prior scientific approach. The greatest contributing factor of biofeedback, as noted earlier, is that it can be used to produce a relatively steady state of brain electrical activity, sustaining particular EEG patterns long enough to be studied and analyzed and reliably reproduced so that confirmations of conclusions can be made.

The same advantage is what makes EEG biofeedback so potentially useful. Even in the relatively early stage of development of EEG biofeedback there is adequate rationale for exploring and using various kinds of EEG biofeedback.

The fact that, *in general,* the presence of alpha activity in the EEG and the absence of beta activity indicates a mental-emotional state of relaxed wakefulness is almost reason enough to suggest its use in individuals who complain of anxiety and whose EEG shows an abnormally low content of alpha. The appropriateness of EEG biofeedback for a particular patient is, of course, established first by conducting medical and psychologic examinations to ensure that the complaint does not have a specific or serious medical or psychiatric origin. Should the problem involve a more serious emotional disorder, certain types of EEG biofeedback may still be appropriate.

A second indication for the use of EEG biofeedback is where a brain wave index of normal activity is lacking, such as possibly the 40 Hz rhythm, or the 12 or 14 Hz activity used in the experimental treatment of epilepsy as described below. Conversely, it can be clinically meaningful to use EEG biofeedback techniques as a means of suppressing EEG components related to disturbed behavior.

A major use for EEG biofeedback is in the area of psychologic self-exploration, or with the therapist as an adjunct in psychotherapy. A consequence of learning how to sustain different brain states is the subjective effect. Even though EEGs are recorded at a distance from important brain structures and are a mish-mash of many different kinds of brain electrical influences, there are a number of defined and potentially definable relationships between brain electrical activity and subjective feeling and thought activity. When any of these EEG components (or more probably, a specific mixture) is sustained over any appreciable period of time, as with biofeedback, then it would seem likely that the presence of the feeling or thought states in consciousness, even liminal consciousness, could easily elicit or attract associated subjective material, be integrated with the ongoing subjective activity, and result in new "insights" or change in perspective.

## EEG Biofeedback Procedures

The major elements of the EEG biofeedback procedure are electrode placements, instrumentation, the training procedure, and the objective to be achieved.

*Electrode placements.* Because brain electrical activity has a small value by the time it reaches the electrodes on the scalp, both the securing of the electrodes and the locations of their placement on the scalp are crucial. First, both scalp oils and fine hair movement readily cause either poor contact with the skin and a movement interference directly into the electrode leads to the instrument. Second, if contact between electrodes and scalp is not firm and solid, the tiny gaps of poor contact increase the resistance of the electrodes, which attenuates the brain electrical signals, causes differences in resistance between electrodes, and an imbalance in the input to the differential amplifier resulting in increased electrical noise in the system.

Scalp muscle activity can often contribute "noise" problems in EEG recording and feedback. Certain scalp areas with more active muscle show a high frequency, occasionally high voltage firing, particularly in temporal electrode placements. Muscle artifacts of this kind are frequent in anxious individuals, as are large dc shifts due to minuscule accumulations of sweat under the electrodes and fine hair movements. Other frequently encountered EEG artifacts are eye movements, eye twitches, and occular tremors. Many people are "eye movers" with frequent eye movements, and this muscle activity is picked up by the electrode connections and can often obscure the EEG tracing in one or several areas for the half or full second of the movement. Other problems with eye movement are the reflexlike triggering of alpha or theta bursts and the occurrence of alpha following defocussing the eyes. Although seriously interfering eye movements occur in only 25 to 30 percent of the population, the reflexly elicited alpha can be quite misleading in alpha biofeedback training.

Satisfactory recording electrodes are hard to come by. The more reputable manufacturers of EEG biofeedback equipment have had to research the electrode problem because faithful sensing of the EEG signal is critical to instrument performance. For this reason, a good source of information about new kinds of EEG electrodes is the literature obtainable from a number of manufacturers by which comparisons can be made concerning noise characteristics and versatility (e.g., whether the connectors fit various instruments). Since improvements are constantly being made in electrode construction, it is advisable to seek out the new information.

Research and clinical electroencephalographers place EEG electrodes on the scalp generally according to the standard international 10–20 system; however, for general kinds of biofeedback EEG training, such electrode placements as used for clinical diagnosis are not so critical; moreover, in EEG biofeedback work, it is impractical to use more than one or two electrode pairs. For most EEG general biofeedback training, especially alpha or theta, the most convenient and productive placement is bipolar, with one electrode placed in the parietal region (sightly higher than midway on a line from the intra-aural plane to the top of the scalp), and the second near the inion (the most prominent bony protuberance of the rear skull), just above the insertion or origin of the neck muscles and roughly on a line with the parietal electrode. The ear lobe is an acceptable reference, commonly called the ground.

Some early manufacturers of EEG biofeedback instruments recommended electrode placement on the forehead, with the second electrode near the inion in the occipital region. This kind of placement can be almost disastrous for EEG recording. First, the electrode near the eye senses the many varieties of eye muscle artifacts, and because these produce large electrical signals, any EEG activity is frequently obscured. The forehead location is actually quite remote from EEG activity. Second, the detection of electrical activity between electrodes placed at such a great distance from each other is distorted by the averaging effect of the scalp and underlying fluids between the scalp and brain. The effect is similar to that of a filter, and tends to average the EEG activity toward an 8 to 10 Hz frequency, amounting to an artificial alpha or theta content.

*Instrumentation.* The biofeedback instrument is obviously critical to accurate feedback and for accurate information about a selected brain wave. In fact, the biofeedback instrument must act first as an EEG recording instrument. Because of the difficulties of recording the very small electrical signal and the high probability of electrical and movement interference, the instrument necessarily must be electronically sophisticated and accurate. Some of the electrical characteristics to look for are high input impedance, low noise level of no more than 1 or possibly 2 microvolts, either moderately narrow band pass filters or a variable filter arrangement, also with sharp edges, reasonable integration times, and a biofeedback display that can be demonstrated to follow the actual EEG signal or interest with high fidelity.

Most of the currently available EEG biofeedback instruments do not have provisions for proper monitoring of the EEG signal as it passes through the device. It constantly amazes me and other EEG researchers to find that individuals new to the field can and do trust the biofeedback display as a faithful indicator of the EEG event of interest. The best advice is *not* to count on the machine either to eliminate interfering artifacts or to isolate the selected brain wave properly. In addition to the problems of electrodes and their placement, instruments must and do amplify much of the electrical interference along with the EEG components; this may "block" the amplifier of the instrument which can make the device either reverberate or temporarily block its internal transmission. Moreover, if the filters are not sharp or if their amplitude thresholds are not properly set, both artifacts and normally occurring slow dc signals can "ring" the filters, causing artificial feedback signals.

It is recommended that the potential user of EEG biofeedback devices either request the following information from the manufacturer or conduct the test himself.[2] First, it is important to obtain a record of the EEG immediately after it has passed through the amplifier section of the device (often called the "raw" EEG). If the potential user is not experienced in reading EEGs, he should take adequate records (at least 10 minutes of recording) to an expert in reading both *normal* as well as abnormal EEGs. The inspection of the EEG record should note the approximate range of EEG frequencies passed through the amplifier, an estimate of signal to noise ratio (how much electrical noise is present), and whether the amplifier is responding to electromagnetic or movement interference (e.g., wiggle the wires). The second piece of information should be recordings from the filter(s) of the instrument. The manufacturer should supply either a graph indicating the exact amplitudes of EEG signal which pass and do not pass through the filter for *all* of the EEG frequencies concerned. A good filtering system will show a very sharp attenuation of signal at the edges of the range of interest. Further, a record of the filter(s) should be made *at the same time* that the EEG tracing from the amplifier is made, so that the effect of large dc currents or fast transients can be inspected. Finally, *simultaneously* with the recording of the "raw" EEG and the filtered EEG, a record should be made of the dc voltage used to activate the biofeedback display in order to ensure that the feedback monitor is faithfully following the original EEG, and is doing so linearly.

---

2. An example is shown in Figure 23, Appendix 5.

*Training.* The objective of EEG biofeedback training is generally quite different from the objectives of EMG biofeedback training. One way of stating this difference is that a primary objective of EMG training is deep relaxation, while that of EEG biofeedback is to develop an awareness (and control) of either some subjective feeling state or subconscious mental process that results in a shift in EEG activity and a consequent emotional improvement. There are, however, similar, if not the same, elements involved in accomplishing the objectives of the two kinds of biofeedback, particularly evolving a "passive" mode for effecting the EEG changes, as contrasted to active attention and conscious participation and effort. In practice, this means that certain of the supporting procedures of EMG biofeedback may or may not be appropriate to certain types of EEG biofeedback. It may be important to use portions of relaxation exercises in the early phases of training in order to assist the patient in understanding the passive mode, but once this has been accomplished further exercises in relaxation may interfere with attaining the objective of the EEG training.

Length and structure of the actual training and of the individual sessions should be at the discretion of the therapist. The most successful results have been obtained using one or more periods of 20 to 30 minutes with the patient alone with the biofeedback device. This can take the form of several 10-minute training sessions interspersed with rest periods in the earlier stages of training, or a 30- or 40-minute session broken by discussion with the therapist. Discussions of changes in subjective feeling states, mood, sensations, thoughts are an important part of the training sessions, and sufficient time should be allowed to integrate these into the training program.

Analysis of successful EEG biofeedback indicates that successful training is achieved when the biofeedback procedure itself is supplemented by (1) cognitively useful information, (2) strategy information, and (3) psychological counselling (as described in Chapter 9 for EMG biofeedback). The cognitively useful information seems to be especially important in EEG biofeedback, providing the patient with information about what brain waves are, what they look like when recorded, how they are recorded, how they originate and change, what it is thought they relate to emotionally and behaviorally, how the instrument works, and other relevant physiological and instrumental information. The strategy information can initially be similar to that of EMG training, e.g., relaxation exercises, but in EEG biofeedback the emphasis is on gaining awareness of the significance and mode of producing the particular brain wave relevant to the clinical problem. Strategy in this case often must be especially tailored for the individual case, such as using specially designed imagery or autosuggestive phrases, thoughts, or concepts. The counselling or psychotherapy is an important adjunct since it provides for review of the subjective events during training and allows an opportunity to improve strategies and use any new thoughts, insights, or feelings productively.

*Objectives of the training.* In addition to defining the desired EEG change projected to assist in improving the patient's condition, establishing the objective in terms of precise objective and subjective terms is important to successful treatment. Since the desired changes depend upon the state of the patient, these are derived by establishing baseline values for both subjective and EEG activities. Generally speaking, the patient will have either an excess or a deficit of the relevant EEG activity, and the amount of change to be achieved is best stated in terms of percentage change from baseline since individuals vary considerably in maximum and minimum attainable values of different EEG components and these values also vary with the severity of the problem. Usually, the more serious the problem, the greater the deficit or excess, and the more difficult it is to evoke the desired EEG changes.

In anxiety, for example, there may be a minimum, or occasionally no, alpha present in the EEG. Obviously, without other techniques, such as relaxation exercises, it will be difficult for the patient to produce additional alpha because he has very little information about alpha and subjective relationships to go on.

When he learns how to produce alpha, the patient may proceed rapidly to his maximum, but the maximum he can achieve may be on the low side of the range of alpha abundance for normals or on the high side. Or, the effect of subjective changes may influence the rate of increased alpha production. For these reasons, the general approach is to set a series of objectives in which increased alpha production is to be achieved in reasonable increments. Individuals vary in maximum alpha content for many reasons, including inherent EEG pattern, inherent arousal level, personality, and intelligence. Similar variations and problems occur with all EEG components.

Prior to any EEG biofeedback training, accurate records of EEG activity should be made, usually 15 or more minutes, and records analyzed for content and characteristics of the more obvious EEG components. If the biofeedback instrument has been determined to record faithfully, values from the instrument can be used to document the selected EEG component.

It is equally important to document initial subjective states. Because of individual variation, relationships between specific aspects of EEG activity and subjective states or activities are general at best, particularly during the initial phases of training. The objectives for the subjective changes should be established independently on the basis of appropriate tests. There are the various psychological and psychiatric tests noted in the section on EMG procedures in Chapter 9 which can be given before and after EEG biofeedback training. The most important objective of subjective change is that the training is useful in real-life situations, and this should be considered as the most important documentation.

The changing awarenesses which develop during EEG biofeedback training often can change the patient's concept of his illness, the treatment, and his dependencies, all of which may require special psychologic attention. Moreover, these subjective changes can change the patient's attitude about his concurrent medication, if any. Strict records of medication should be kept, particularly since the effectiveness of the biofeedback training may substitute for drug effect, rendering the ongoing medication excessive with resulting side effects from the drug.

## Perspective on Clinical EEG Biofeedback

While EEG biofeedback is still in its early stages of development, and adequate research documentation of its potential benefits is small, there are many valid reasons for including relevant EEG biofeedback in a wide variety of treatment programs. There is no question but that both general and specific EEG activities relate to both general and specific aspects of an individual's mental and emotional life. Any objections or adverse results using EEG biofeedback can generally be attributed to confusion created by either inappropriate methodology, unsupported conclusions, or inadequate instrumentation.[3]

Researchers in the psychophysiology of alpha have, for example, frequently applied neurophysiologically inappropriate methods or artificially constructed constraints, and this has led to the use of inadequate methodology for clinical situations. For example, the early alpha conditioning work of Kamiya was exactly that: conditioning, in which a psychologically appropriate experimental design was used, but which was not neurophysiologically and hence clinically appropriate. The technique alternated brief (60 to 90 seconds) trials of reinforcing increases with decreases in alpha abundance. The purpose of the experimental design was to meet the theoretical criterion that the phenomenon could be called a conditioning phenomenon only if enhancement and suppression occurred using the *same* reinforcement (i.e., to the same tone or sound), demonstrating that the two directions of EEG change could be discriminated even though the same reinforcement was used. Neurophysiologically, this design equated the mechanisms underlying alpha production and alpha suppression, an assumption which, in fact,

---

3. Other confusing elements stemming from research methods and concepts are discussed in Appendix 4.

does not hold. The neurophysiologic mechanisms which produce alpha and those which cause the disappearance of alpha are quite different. In essence, this kind of experiment asks the individual to learn two EEG tricks at the same time, a procedure which slows the learning of each task since as soon as one learning task is initiated, the other is required. While the Kamiya experiment was excellent for experimental psychologic theory, its methodology poses serious problems in clinical application, although it is a superior technique for demonstrating control *after* learning. Clinically, the objective is to learn control of one EEG component or pattern at a time; hence clinically, procedures should be designed to facilitate learning.

Another factor which has caused confusion in the clinical application of EEG biofeedback is the type of research studies that have been published. Contrary to the usual course of events when experimental techniques are evolved for clinical use, a large share of EEG biofeedback research has been directed toward confirming or denying theoretical points. Some studies have been directed toward determining the relationship between EEG alpha and visual mechanism; some toward experimental anxiety in which little relationship between experimental and clinical anxiety has been established; some concerned only with arousal theory; or some toward proving that alpha is a principal brain wave correlate of meditation. Unfortunately there has been no systematic clinical work evolving practical procedures, or synthesizing the various conceptual bases, or evaluating changes in clinical EEG and subjective activities.

Another point of confusion has arisen from popularization of EEG, particularly alpha and theta, biofeedback. Many of the popular reports about these EEG biofeedbacks have been presented by nonexperts, or are based on work with remarkably inadequate instruments, or lacking any serious scientific documentation.

And finally, many "scientific" reports on EEG biofeedback are seriously limited by the inadequate backgrounds in neurophysiology and electronics of the scientific investigators themselves. The problem of scientific publication in this field is compounded by a serious lack of experts in the fields, hence it is relatively simple to find a scientific journal without experienced editors that will accept reports of poor experimental work. Unfortunately even some of the more prestigious journals have failed to apply expertise in accepting such papers. There is, moreover, a further problem in the publication of scientific articles. Science is now inundated with thousands of "specialty" journals, and there are no standard descriptive terms for indexing articles, especially in areas such as psychophysiology, and as a result it is extremely difficult to search the literature properly.

## Alpha Biofeedback in Neuroses, Psychoses, and Behavior Problems

A review of reports on experimental clinical uses of alpha biofeedback reveals two consistent and significant themes running throughout all studies. The first is a process that follows upon the training or instructions that turns the attention inwardly. This reduces the amount of attention paid to external factors and leads to a decrease in mental tension or rumination about social pressures, and this effect in turn alters the significance that the individual attaches to external environmental situations and stimuli. The second significant theme in the various clinical reports is the importance of the *idea* of self-control which develops during the training and that is apparently used by the patient as a motivating factor, facilitating his learning process.

One of the earliest clinical reports on alpha biofeedback was that of Korein, Miller, and others describing the effect of alpha biofeedback in twenty-three patients with psychogenic and systematic disorders. The report indicates that the patients learned control of their symptomatology within two weeks, and reported the experience as tranquil. Unfortunately a follow-up report has not appeared.

Recently (1974), Mills and Solyom reported on the use of alpha biofeedback in the treatment of ruminating obsessives. Their concept was that mental relaxation might be reciprocally inhibitory to the ruminating activity that is characteristic of the obsessive neurotic. Using five ruminating obsessives and a treatment course of seven to twenty alpha feedback training sessions, they found encouraging results. It was discovered, rather surprisingly in view of the habitual behavior, that some obsessives could indeed learn alpha control, and the patients reported their subjective states during alpha training as relaxed, daydreaming, and not thinking. Although the ruminative activity could be successfully inhibited during the alpha training sessions, the effect did not appear to persist after the treatment periods. The investigators also compared the effectiveness of special, augmented instructions for the learning process to that of standard minimal instructions and found no differences.

Other variables that may facilitate increasing persistence of the biofeedback success are the various strategy procedures and augmented psychological support. The results of this study demonstrate a remarkable effect of alpha biofeedback in altering circumscribed preoccupation with mentally and emotionally disturbing problems, indicating some distinctive relationship between rumination and brain wave activity as well as inhibition of the preoccupation by the accompanying new subjective state. In this light, further study of EEG biofeedback in obsessive behavior may well uncover more specific and enduring procedures or techniques.

Another dramatic pilot study is that of Childers using alpha biofeedback in the treatment of severe social problems. The patients were classified as psychopathic, four showing long-standing symptomatology. Two were schizophrenic. The treatment was ten 45-minute sessions of alpha biofeedback. The investigator reports that by the sixth session: "assaultive, abusive behavior had completely ceased with a dramatic change in their behavior and appearance on the ward." All five patients were discharged from the hospital within two to three weeks and two of the four adults in the study became gainfully employed. Measurements of the changes in alpha activity were not made, and so no conclusions can be made concerning the relationship between degree of alpha control achieved and the behavioral changes. Dr. Childers cautions that the study was a pilot one, and that despite the dramatic effects that occurred, placebo effect still could not be ruled out.[4]

Weber and Fehmi have recently reported the successful use of alpha biofeedback in patients who were either severely neurotic or had psychosomatic or character problems. The EEG alpha activity from five different brain sites were used either simultaneously or sequentially, and the patients received two full-hour sessions per week for approximately twenty training sessions. When the patients demonstrated good control of alpha activity, they were changed to EEG theta biofeedback training. Results were considered good in six of the ten patients, with partial improvement in one and questionable results in three patients. The treatment program was amply augmented by instructions and verbal discussions of the patient's problems and experience.

A related study used biofeedback of the "alpha-theta" EEG frequency range. This is a range between 6 and 9 Hz, midway between the frequency ranges designated as alpha and theta. Green, Sargent and others of the Menninger Foundation have explored this frequency range for its subjective correlates, and Twemlow and his colleagues refer to their investigations as justification for using this kind of biofeedback in the treatment of chronic alcoholics. The justification was that the "alpha-theta" range fostered a "psychophysiological growth process, enabling psychological maturation to occur in a nonverbal milieu." This conclusion is apparently based on reports by Green that this EEG frequency is dominant or occurs during reverie and hypnogogic imagery.

---

4. This kind of comment occurs frequently in all medical treatment studies, but it is particularly relevant to the biofeedback phenomenon. If such striking therapeutic effects frequently occur when experimental treatments are instituted, or more attention is paid to the patient, the implication is that a mental-emotional shift accounts for the improvement. This may be the fundamental mechanism of biofeedback, i.e., a shift in the emphasis or attention of mental processes.

The study used sixty patients in a V.A. Hospital, who received five hours of biofeedback training per week for a period of five weeks. Biofeedback training was supplemented by intensive supporting programs described by the investigators as designed to encourage meditation and reflective reverie as problem-solving devices. The investigators used a variety of personality and behavioral tests, and post-training testing revealed a number of significant trends of changes in feeling states and emotional reactivities. Personality and emotional profiles showed a reduction in depressive effect, a reduction in the fear of previously emotional situations, an improvement in impulse control, an increased sensitivity to the patient's own needs and feelings, and a better ability to handle aggressive feelings.

A number of large-scale research projects on the effectiveness of alpha biofeedback in addictive behavior, including heroin, are currently underway throughout the country. Descriptions of the projects and progress reports can be obtained by writing to Smithsonian Science Information Exchange, Inc.[5] One study, for example, is that of Graham, who reports that alpha biofeedback at times used alone but most often used in combination (simultaneously) with EMG biofeedback was successful in assisting the detoxification of addicts and improved mood and relief from symptoms.

In addition to the published reports described above, a number of private reports from various hospitals and clinics deal with the experimental use of alpha biofeedback for a variety of psychosomatic problems, neuroses, pain, etc.

For example, Werbach et al. have summarized a dramatic case report of the use of alpha biofeedback in an obsessive compulsive neurosis. The patient, unresponsive to conventional treatments, including hospitalization, was being maintained on doses of 800 mg of chlorpromazine and 45 mg of trifluoperazine daily. Following ten alpha biofeedback sessions, the patient evidenced side effects from the medication, and it was ultimately reduced to approximately one-tenth of the

5. Room 300, 1730 M Street N.W., Washington, D.C. 20036.

original dosage. The patient showed remarkable changes in effect, tension, and social behavior, and obtained a full-time job. A follow-up 18 months later revealed the improvement to be maintained.

Both Werbach and Barnes[6] have independently reported on the use of alpha biofeedback in a variety of psychiatric and psychosomatic disorders as encountered in private clinical practice or clinic. Results are uniformly encouraging; however, it should be noted that both clinicians are psychiatrists and employ supportive psychologic and psychiatric treatment in addition to the biofeedback. Barnes and colleagues have used alpha feedback successfully in such diverse psychosomatic problems as colitis and headaches. Reporting on its use in tension headache in the journal *Headache* (1974), these investigators not only describe the change in headache activity as being reduced by approximately 80 percent by the fifth week of treatment, but report that the relief provided was both greater and longer lasting than that with relaxation training. Furthermore, in a subsequent study of migraine headache, these clinicians have found alpha biofeedback to be as effective as they found it to be in tension headache.

Benjamins compared alpha biofeedback with EMG biofeedback in a systematic desensitization procedure treating snake phobia. The subjects were first given three 40-minute training sessions with Progressive Relaxation, followed by the alpha EEG or EMG training. After seven sessions both treatment groups had reduced their avoidance behavior, but the alpha biofeedback group showed a more substantial reduction in state anxiety. It was also found that amount of alpha was a reliable measure correlating with the subjective rating of fearfulness.

## Alpha Biofeedback and Pain

For centuries chronic pain has been treated medically, with drugs as the primary and continuing choice

---

6. UCLA Symposium, Asilomar, June 1975.

of treatment. "Painkillers," from Demerol down to aspirin, comprise the largest single class of drugs used. Thoughtless medical overuse of drugs has subverted society's health with drug-dependent illnesses and flagrant drug abuse. The prodigious reliance on drugs is an extraordinary statement on the immaturity and indifference of medicine in the light of both experiential and scientific understanding of the perception of pain. There is virtually no human being who has not had the experience of pain being shut out when attention suddenly and intensely becomes focussed on an event or thought unrelated to the circumstances of the pain. The youngster howling after a nasty bump can almost always be diverted from the pain response by a more powerful focus of attention. Yet chemicals work with great ease, and the awe the average person has for the authority of physical and chemical forces has long eclipsed the individual's own psychological resources. Our attitudes about the relief from pain have rested comfortably on molecules, along with ignoring the little gray cells in the brain and their pain-relieving potential. Now with the changing social consciousness have come concepts of awarenesses and interior resources and the recognition that mental activities, if used precisely, can influence the performance of other cerebral activities, including those that attend perceptions, such as the perception of pain.

The potential of alpha biofeedback to alter the perception of pain has attracted the attention of a number of clinical investigators. Two studies, of quite different types, have been detailed examinations of the role of alpha in the perception of pain. For one case study the investigators proceeded on the basis of the reported high tolerance to pain developed by yogis who simultaneously exhibited a high content of alpha activity in the EEG. Using a single patient with intense headache pain persisting over a period of years, the patient was given 67 "alpha conditioning" sessions during which he increased alpha activity from 20 to 92 percent with the eyes closed and to 50 percent (presumably from zero percent) with the eyes open. Although the patient was not able to influence the head pain once started by al-

pha feedback, in some instances he was able to prevent
pain by enhancing his alpha before the headache began.

The second single case study, reported by Pelletier,
used a subject who was already capable of exerting almost complete control over his autonomic functions.
The individual was given 100 two-minute sessions of
alpha, and an equal number of theta biofeedback sessions, and following training, voluntary control of
bleeding and pain was demonstrated by piercing the
bicep with a stout needle. Physiological data showed a
significant increase in alpha and theta, and this was
interpreted as indicating mediation of the autonomic
control by alpha activity.

Other investigators cited the rationale for using alpha biofeedback in the treatment of chronic pain as the
reported shift in attention from external to internal
events during alpha activity, the idea being that attention paid to the perceptual aspects related to chronic
pain could be altered. Moreover, it is well known that
there is a circular interaction between anxiety and pain,
that each tends to increase the other until one or the
other is relieved.

In a pilot study conducted by Coger and Werbach,
chronic pain patients received alpha biofeedback three
times a week for a total of ten sessions. Approximately
one-half of the patients showed significant changes in
the abundance and amplitude of alpha with some slowing in alpha frequency, and these patients also reported
an increased tolerance of pain and reduced reactivity
to emotional situations.

A more comprehensive example of the new direction
to therapy and therapeutics stimulated by the biofeedback idea of self-control is in the study by Melzack and Perry entitled "Self-regulation of pain: the
use of alpha-feedback and hypnotic training for the
control of chronic pain." Melzack, a psychologist, has
published extensively on the nature of pain, and has
concluded that in addition to the distress of the actual
physical damage, there is extensive evidence that pain
"is also determined by expectation, suggestion, level of
anxiety, the meaning of the situation in which injury

occurs, competing sensory stimuli and other psychological variables."

The Melzack and Perry study is a progressive attempt to bridge the therapeutic gap between psychology and medicine, even though it carries considerable bias in favor of psychologic, hypnotic techniques. These researchers felt that alpha biofeedback training would be relevant to the problem of pain relief in several ways: by shifting attention to different inner feelings and presumably away from the pain milieu, by responses to the suggestion of relief from pain that would accompany the alpha training, by relaxation occurring with enhanced alpha activity which should decrease the effects of sensory influences and thereby decrease anxiety, and also by a sense of developing control over pain which would shift the significance level of the perceived pain.

The study itself compared "hypnotic training" with "alpha training" and also with a combination of the two. The patients all had medically documented, severe chronic pain of long duration. The quotes around hypnotic and alpha training indicate that a specialized version of training was used, and included several auxiliary techniques. In actual fact, the "hypnotic training" began with extensive Jacobson's relaxation exercises, was followed by ego-strengthening techniques directed specifically toward suggestions of feeling healthier, stronger, etc., and finally suggestions about calmness, ideas of control, self-confidence, independence, and other relevant, positive suggestions. Each of these procedures, of course, has independent therapeutic effects.

Although eight alpha training sessions were used for the chronic pain patients, they too pose some difficulties, both in misleading terminology and for accepting them as legitimate alpha training sessions. Instructions consisted of strong, explicit indications that alpha training would actually assist the patient in achieving control over his pain. The feedback signal was a special music (a Bach flute piece "rearranged with a slight jazz beat"!); the sessions lasted only 20 minutes, but more distressing from the standpoint of what alpha means, each session was ended by a practice period with *no* feedback signal followed by a five-minute practice of *suppression* of alpha, that was followed immediately by the patient answering the critical post-session Pain Questionnaire used to evaluate the effects of alpha training. All training was conducted with the eyes closed.

The results of the study are surprising. From their results the investigators concluded that while alpha training contributed very little in the way of relief from pain, and their hypnotic training procedures contributed substantially but not significantly statistically, the combination of hypnotic *with* alpha training was a quite effective treatment for relieving chronic pain. In actual numbers, there was an average of a 33 percent significant reduction in pain in 58 percent of the patients so treated.

*Critique of Study as Example of Current Inadequacies in the Art of Biofeedback.* From the standpoint of scientific merit, this clinical study leaves much to be desired. Not only are the terms of the treatment procedure misused, but the data presented is misleading. For example, only six patients were used for the "hypnotic training" and six for the "alpha training," but twelve patients were used for the combination of the two treatments. Generally speaking, because of the normal physiological variation among people, the greater the number of patients, the more valid and reliable are the results. When data are averaged, variation among patients tends to be exaggerated when small groups are used and less so when larger groups are used. Thus, the average for the group receiving the combined hypnotic-alpha training *appears* to be more significantly different when compared to pretreatment subjective pain reports than does either of the treatment procedures used separately. If, however, the amount of variation is observed, it can be seen that the amount of variation about reporting pain was considerably less in the alpha training group of patients, even though the averaged effectiveness against pain was remarkably less than for the hypnotic training group. In contrast, the amount of variation in reporting pain encountered for the group receiving the combined treatment was very large. One interesting observation about the variation of pain relief is that relief amounting to 80 or 100 percent appears to have been frequently encountered. If so, then all the statisticizing indicates is that although some patients reported a marked *increase* in the quality and sensation of the pain, *on the average,* i.e., in some 50 percent of patients with chronic pain, the combination of hypnotic and alpha training can yield an average of some 30 percent *reduction* in pain sensation.

It is unfortunate for the potential practitioner that the "alpha training" technique used in the pain study misrepresents and misuses alpha biofeedback in at least six areas important to its successful application. These kinds of errors arise from many reasons, as outlined in Appendix 4, but they are generally due to the remarkable lack of comprehensive organized background information both about alpha activity and about effective biofeedback procedures.

The misuse of the alpha-subjective relationship and biofeedback procedure can be best illustrated by critiquing each of the steps of the "alpha training" procedure described above.

The instructions given to the patients that learning alpha control would definitely help them to control pain actually qualifies as misleading information. There has been no prior evidence to indicate that alpha activity plays any role at all in the perception of pain, and to suggest, categorically, authoritatively, that it does is the equivalent of false information. The effect of false information appears to be one in which a conflict develops between the development of intuited relationships, action of the physiological monitor (the feedback signal) and subjective awareness on the one hand, and expectations based on authority on the other hand. False information has been demonstrated to be inhibitory to almost all biofeedback learning. The situation is not unlike the effect of false slow heart rate given as an auditory signal to anxious people who, believing the slow heart rate to signify calmness, became less anxious.

The *kind* of biofeedback signal is also extremely important to the biofeedback learning process. If the objective of the training is to learn control over a physiologic function, and particularly if the objective includes achieving relaxation and/or a change in focus of attention (and both are stated objectives in the pain study), then the feedback signal should be one that can contribute to gaining these objectives or at least not distract from them. The use of music, lilting and jazzy, contains elements which distinctively evoke various kinds of mental activities, such as memories, imagery, or daydreaming, as well as drowsiness and relaxation. Unless individual reactions to the particular kind of signal are determined, it remains unknown whether patients respond to the music by mental alerting or mental relaxation. Because music is constantly changing in melodic line and instrumental accompaniments, it has a high probability for evoking different kinds of mental images, and as each is evoked, it is accompanied by some alerting effect. Repeated listening to music does not guarantee adaptation or habituation, else musical pieces would not be played over and over. And for each shift in mental activity, there is an accompanying shift in EEG activity, including changes in alpha activity.

In view of the numerous other elements of the study, the alpha training sessions were unusually short and few in number. The investigators used an operant conditioning technique, similar to that of Kamiya and of Hart and others, except for quality of the feedback signal, and these researchers found that upward of 20 individual sessions were required to produce a significant change in alpha production. Even in my own alpha studies, in which the biofeedback signal was continuously available, most preliminary learning required at least 45 minutes.

The real difficulty of the study's methodology involves the time at which the post-training Pain Questionnaire was given. The effects questionnaire was *not* given following the "alpha training" for production, but was delayed until after giving two 5-minute sessions using quite different conditions, the first being attempts to produce alpha without the benefit of the feedback signal (which could introduce uncertainty), and then a period of attempting to suppress alpha activity, a procedure which directly opposes the direction of the primary learning. It would be as valid to say that the questionnaire would reflect sensations accompanying the effort of trying to suppress alpha, and all of the different mental activities involved in that exercise. The reported results of the experiment would seem to bear this out, since the smallest changes in alpha actually occurred with the "alpha training."

Next, all of the "training" was carried out with the patient's eyes closed. I and other researchers have demonstrated repeatedly that there is not much "learning room" when the eyes are closed, and the considerable difference in alpha activity between the two conditions of the eyes closed and the eyes open (such as significance of seeing and using visual cues for either intentional or spontaneous recall) are such that the learning is not generalized. As Travis and colleagues have shown, there is no carry-over from learning to produce alpha with the eyes closed to producing it with the eyes open. In other words, these are essentially two different learning tasks.

And finally, despite the fact that the explicit objective was to determine whether control of alpha activity contributed to changing perceptions of pain, no effort was made to document whether or not the patients had developed control or not. Simply asking the patient to try to continue to produce alpha in the absence of the feedback signal cannot qualify as a control measure because it lacks any reference to the intent to control. The conditions of the experiment, a long, fatiguing session, eyes closed, the darkness, and adaptation to the environment, are all conditions in which alpha production is normally maximal, and the individual bursts of alpha are frequent. Demonstration of actual *control* of alpha production would require some index indicating that the *intent* to produce alpha could be discriminated from its spontaneous appearance, which, under the experimental conditions, would be near maximal anyway.

Melzack's study points out the extraordinary confusion about the mechanics and mechanisms of alpha activity. The objective of biofeedback therapy, the idea of control, is for the patient to develop sufficient control over selected physiologic activity that it can be useful to him in those real-life situations where he experiences his problems.

Despite its many methodological flaws, the Melzack and Perry pain study does contribute importantly to new directions for the treatment of chronic pain. The contribution is contained in the results of the combined hypnotic-alpha procedure. It should first be recalled that neither training procedure is exactly what it implies, since the hypnotic training was supplemented by relaxation, ego strengthening, and other suggestion techniques, and the alpha training was marginal alpha training at best. Nonetheless, the combination procedure produced a significant relief in pain perception, and this suggests, as Melzack and Perry note, that multiple approaches to the treatment of pain are more effective than single approaches because of many interacting determinants of pain.

## Insomnia

At the Biofeedback Research Society meetings of 1974, Stoyva and colleagues reported a preliminary study on the effectiveness of EEG theta training in a population of twelve patients. Marked improvement was found in six of the patients, three others reporting faster falling to sleep after nocturnal awakening, and only three reported no improvement.

It would seem fairly obvious that it is not the absolute amount of theta activity present in the EEG that produces sleep, rather, that enhancing a normal EEG component (theta) accompanying behavioral drowsiness intensifies the neuronal activity predisposing to sleep. But in order for sleep to occur, continuing neurophysiologic changes in the direction of sleep must occur, and these are reflected in the EEG pattern continuing to change toward a sleep pattern. This sequence of events suggests that increasing the EEG content of a specific component, such as theta, initiates a shift of total pattern. In the case of shifting brain electrical activity toward sleep activity, the biofeedback training may be primarily effecting or giving a direction for change in EEG activity.

A similar sequence of events may account for the success Feinstein found in a pilot study using biofeedback training of 12 to 14 Hz rhythm. She reported that training with this rhythm, which is similar to the 12 to 16 Hz sleep spindles, produced a significant improvement in both subjective sleep quality and in EEG sleep patterns. This type of biofeedback study is of exceptional interest because of the quite different circumstances between the training sessions and the effect of the training. Training was done in the waking state when the 12 to 16 Hz rhythm has such a low voltage that it can be extracted only by electronic filters. The relationship to the high voltage 12 to 16 Hz sleep spindles is unclear; nonetheless, the effect of the biofeedback training indicates some fairly specific relationship between this rhythm and the sleep state. Since the subjects apparently did not sleep during training, the effect of the training appears to be that of isolating a specific EEG component, being able to recapture it more or less at will, and when the component is evoked under the proper conditions, it serves as a catalyst to shift the EEG pattern toward sleep.


## Epilepsy

Clinical research studies on the use of biofeedback techniques in the treatment of epilepsy have followed three quite different approaches. Each approach appears to have a reasonable utility although they differ considerably in technique and degree of treatment difficulty. The similarity of effectiveness of such different approaches suggests that in the future each technique will be found more or less specific for particular types of epilepsy.

The three approaches are: (1) learning to control alpha activity, (2) learning to suppress specific seizure wave EEG activity, and (3) learning to produce and control 12 to 16 Hz EEG rhythm.

The apparent efficacy of all three approaches opens up promising directions for understanding both the etiology and treatment of epilepsy and other types of seizure activity. The common denominator of the three approaches is that each results in a shift in direction and pattern of brain electrical activity, i.e., a change in brain state.

The several preliminary reports on the use of alpha training in the treatment of epilepsy all indicate a fairly dramatic effect in suppressing seizures. Although other pilot studies with alpha also suggest positive effects, it should be stressed that much of the alpha-epilepsy research is of a preliminary nature. One investigator has interpreted the positive results from alpha training as a learning by the epileptic to function at a lower level of arousal.

A much more pragmatic investigation of biofeedback techniques in epilepsy has been carried out by Poirier, an electroencephalographer and neurologist specializing in epilepsy and seizure disorders. Poirier uses an eclectic approach in which the seizure patient is encouraged to learn to control either the suppression of seizure specific brain waves or the production of various brain wave components, such as alpha or theta activity. From rather extensive clinical experience, Poirier reports a high rate of success in patients' learning to control EEG activity and the consequent seizures. Although Poirier's treatment programs are individualized for the patient, and hence do not constitute a systematic investigation of specific forms of biofeedback for the treatment of epilepsy, it is important to recognize that quite different types of control of quite different aspects of brain wave activity can produce significant improvements in seizure control in different types of patients.

Poirier's eclectic approach is criticized by laboratory researchers who are oriented toward a more systematic approach. The objective of the laboratory researcher is to develop highly specific forms of treatment which can be demonstrated to produce positive results reliably. From the patient's standpoint, both approaches have merit; the Poirier approach in which the EEG component to be controlled is selected on an individual patient basis assures some immediate effects; the basic neurological approach presently requires special instrumentation not readily available, nor has the technique received adequate clinical trial.

A highly practical and rational therapeutic program devised by Johnson and Meyer was used in a young epileptic with severe *grand mal* seizures. Beginning with a relaxation training program for two weeks, the patient was then given four half-hour EMG biofeedback sessions using the forearm extensors, then three sessions with the frontalis muscle. EEG training was then begun, first giving twice-weekly training for 12 weeks, then weekly for 17 weeks, then on alternate weeks. The patient started with alpha training, followed by alpha-theta, then theta biofeedback. During the treatment program the patient's seizures decreased from an average incidence of 2.79 per month to 1.5 per month; moreover, the patient reported subjective feelings of being in control of seizure onset.

The specific EEG component approach has been developed primarily by Sterman. Sterman and his colleagues first observed the 12 to 16 Hz EEG rhythm in cats taken from electrode recording sites over the sensorimotor cortex, and thus called it SMR (sensorimotor rhythm) found to be associated with relaxation and the absence of movement. Subsequently it was found that cats trained to produce abundant quantities of this rhythm became resistant to seizures induced by convulsant drugs. A number of follow-up neurophysiological studies led to the conclusion that learned production of the sensorimotor rhythm could lead to a significant central neuronal reorganization, and these observations stimulated a search for an analogous rhythm in human beings.

It was found that a quite low voltage 12 to 16 Hz rhythm could be detected over the rolandic cortex in man, but it generally requires special electronic filters for its isolation and identification. Research has not yet clarified whether SMR is the same or different from the infrequently occurring variant of alpha activity formerly called the mu rhythm. Sterman has reported that the optimal electrode placement for recording the SMR is by means of bipolar electrodes placed over the left and right central cortical areas from a point 10 percent off the vertex to a point 30 percent off the vertex, using the intra-aural distance as the reference line.

Training of the SMR for use in seizure patients has used particularly interesting biofeedback displays. Some experimental work has been carried out using rows of lights which monitor increments of production of SMR and in other studies, progress in producing the rhythm has been indicated by using a projector showing scenes of increasing progress in completing a picture puzzle. Although special electronic filters are required to extract the very low voltage 12 to 16 Hz rhythm from the EEG, even for raw observation, biofeedback training does result in the emergence of clear trains of the SMR. When activity of both hemispheres is recorded, it can be seen that the increased production of SMR occurs in the hemisphere being rewarded by the biofeedback display. The subjective reports of the patients indicate feelings of relaxation, although drowsiness apparently does occur frequently enough to interfere with their performance.

The majority of epileptic patients receiving this experimental treatment by Sterman and his colleagues had been virtually refractory to conventional treatment, and had suffered severe seizures for long periods of time, yet SMR training produced generally excellent results, ranging from a significant reduction in seizure activity to a complete freedom from seizures, and an accompanying normalization of the EEG pattern.

Effectiveness of the Sterman technique has been confirmed by two other investigators, one of whom additionally used learned blocking of theta activity at the same time. Follow-up studies indicate that the treatment, particularly with continued practice, maintains its effect of preventing seizures or reducing their frequency. Two investigators have reported failures in treating epileptics by training the SMR rhythm in preliminary studies. Differences in treatment results may be due to differences in patient selection or in persistence in the training procedure or in instrumentation which requires considerable electronic sophistication. On the other hand, one interesting discrepancy does appear. Sterman originally reported that non-epileptic patients learned to control the 12–16 Hz rhythm much better than did epileptic patients. Another study, by a different researcher, devoted specifically to this result turned up with completely negative results. A third recent study, however, was directed specifically toward identifying and localizing the 12–14 Hz rhythm and using biofeedback techniques to train normal subjects to produce rhythms of this frequency in their EEG patterns. Kuhlman reports that the only 12–14 Hz activity found in six subjects exhibited the classical reactivity of the mu rhythm (alpha variant), and none of the subjects trained with 12–14 Hz rhythm learned to increase this activity whereas subjects trained with 9–11 Hz mu rhythm all increased this activity. Owing to the complexities of the instrumentation, negative results may be much easier to account for on the basis of procedure and technology than positive results.

It seems worth repeating, in light of the effectiveness of such different forms of EEG training to control such different EEG components, that perhaps EEG biofeedback is primarily a process of learning to shift brain states in a directed manner.

In a later study Kuhlman used a somewhat different technique and obtained results which promise to keep the controversy and uncertainty about which precise brain wave frequency range is best suitable in the treatment of epilepsy. As a control or baseline procedure, he first subjected the patients to a month of random EEG feedback, at the rate of two or three sessions per week. The patients then received 9 to 14 Hz biofeedback. Three of five patients responded, and these showed a reduction in seizure incidence averaging 60 percent. Upon returning these patients to the random EEG biofeedback, he found that the seizure reduction was maintained and further that there were significant increases in amounts and frequency of alpha which he interpreted as suggesting that the biofeedback facilitated normal resting EEG pattern development.

At the same time Sterman has reported that patients trained with 6 to 9 Hz EEG frequency range responded by an exacerbation of the symptoms.

In view of the apparent beneficial effects of alpha biofeedback in epilepsy, i.e., using the 9 to 12 Hz EEG frequency range, the beneficial results with the 12 to 16 Hz range and the generally positive results of Kuhlman using the 9 to 14 Hz range, but the adverse effects to the 6 to 9 Hz range, use of the higher (e.g., 10 to 16 Hz) frequency ranges holds considerable promise in the treatment of epilepsy.

## Evolving Uses for EEG Biofeedback

1. *Shifting dominant EEG activity between the hemispheres.* Ever since the discovery that the speech center in man's brain was localized in only one of the hemispheres, usually the left, there has been growing evidence and awareness that many of the more sophisticated mental elements, contributing to cognitive styles and skills as well as aspects of conscious-subconscious relationships, may be attributed to differences in relative dominance of the hemispheric activities. If the two cerebral hemispheres are distinctively dominant for different cognitive activities, then this difference should be reflected in differences in the EEG patterns. Once the EEG differences are established, biofeedback technology can be used to manipulate the hemispheric relationships, either suppressing undesirable differences or enhancing desirable differences or similarities.

Although no biofeedback studies have yet been published, the groundwork and the rationale for biofeedback manipulations of EEG synchrony between the two hemispheres has been developed.

Based on the neuro-psychophysiological studies of Gazzaniga and Sperry, Dimond and Beaumont. Geschwind and Levitsky, and Giannitrapani and Galin, Ornstein, and colleagues have recently confirmed that the two cerebral hemispheres process different kinds of cognitive information. Comparing the EEG activity of the hemispheres, it has been found that tasks classified as analytic, such as language or arithmetic tasks, result in a greater suppression of EEG activity in the left hemisphere, while the brain information processing during tasks classified as intuitive, such as spatial or music tasks, result in greater suppression of EEG activity in the right hemisphere. An analysis of the EEG components involved has revealed the primary EEG difference between the two hemispheres to be in activity in the alpha range.

Only one experiment has been reported using hemispheric alpha synchrony biofeedback, and it is unfortunately not clear from the report either when the feedback was used or what its effect was. The data did, however, show that relative changes in EEG activity of the hemispheres during different kinds of mental activity are relevant to the potential of alpha hemispheric synchrony biofeedback. In the experiment, when subjects were asked to focus their attention on *performing* either mental arithmetic or a physical task, such as clenching the fist, the alpha between the hemispheres became de-synchronized. When, however, the subjects focussed their attention upon a mental object or mental concept or some perceptual memory the alpha of the hemispheres became synchronized. These results were taken to indicate the differences in brain states when attention is on actual performance, physical or mental, and the role of alpha activity when the focus of attention is on a relatively stabilized field of internal awareness.

The problem of defining differences in functions of the two hemispheres has been a particularly difficult one since the great majority of brain functions are either shared or duplicated between the hemispheres. The specialization of the hemispheres is essentially an emergent one, reflected chiefly in the more complex abilities of man. Over and above possible differences in the speed of information processing, and in ability to sustain specific kinds of activities, specialization of hemispheric functions can be demonstrated for quite different situational demands. For some time it has been known that speech and language processes, as well as complex motor organization, are associated with left hemisphere function, while the capacity for spatial integration is associated with the right hemisphere. Dimond and Beaumont have more recently shown that "high level vigilance and a capacity for paired associated learning appear to be associated with the left hemisphere, while calculation (contrary to other evidence) and the ability for creative-associative thinking are associated with the right hemisphere."

The two different kinds of studies, the one demonstrating differences in the processing of cognitive information, and the other showing differences in hemispheric relationships with different focus or different kinds of attention (active or passive), provide ample rationale for the use of EEG biofeedback in a wide variety of problems involving learning, cognition, and communication. It seems probable that certain learning conditions or learning techniques can favor a cognitively dominant hemisphere, such as a reliance on the intuitive skills or a reliance upon the analytic skills, with a concomitant deficit in the other. Training to alter the EEG contributions of these mental activities should alter the intuitive-analytic relationships toward a more balanced or more useful state. Imbalances between the two types of cognitive styles may be the cause of certain learning disabilities.

The experimental evidence further suggests that learned shifting of the hemispheric relationships will shift the focus of awareness, a procedure which can prove useful in psychotherapy. Moreover, since the dominant hemisphere is concerned chiefly with verbalizable material, i.e., conscious awareness, then altering the relationships between dominant and nondominant hemisphere may provide a therapeutic technique for gaining access to unconscious nonverbalizable material.

2. *Promoting empathy*. For more than twenty years the literature of psychobiology and psychosomatic medicine has contained scientific reports confirming the fact that stages of deep rapport and empathy be-

tween two individuals are accompanied by physiologic states in which both individuals respond physiologically to emotional stimuli in the same direction and to a similar degree. It would seem obvious that if two individuals are empathetic and understanding of each other's emotional concerns that both would respond similarly to emotional provocations.

It seemed reasonable to assume that the reverse situation might hold true, that is, if two people were in similar physiologic states and responding physiologically to the same emotional stimuli, then the *sensations* or appreciation of feeling and emotion might be similar. Given such similarities, communication could be facilitated. These speculations suggested that empathy or rapport might be facilitated by training *pairs* of individuals toward similar physiologic states.

I chose to train pairs of people, first randomly selected pairs, then psychiatrist-patient pairs, to synchronize their production of alpha activity. The training technique was a biofeedback signal consisting of a blue light that turned on only when the two subjects were producing alpha activity simultaneously with each other. The experiments were carried out in ordinary light with the subjects' eyes open in order to minimize the spontaneous simultaneous occurrence of alpha. One of the difficulties in obtaining reliable data in experiments of this type is that when 50 percent or more alpha is present in the EEG, such as when the eyes are closed or after training, the random occurrence of synchrony is very high, and it is difficult, analytically, to discriminate spontaneous alpha from feedback-signal-related alpha.

As a partial check on the accuracy of the simultaneity of alpha appearance in the EEG as a result of the biofeedback synchrony training, I tested each subject separately by asking him to indicate, by closing a switch, when he felt his partner had alpha activity in the EEG pattern. At this time no feedback signal was given. Most subjects achieved a 75 percent accuracy level of predicting their partner's alpha after training. I have interpreted this success rate as evidence that the training had entrained a biological rhythm. This is the best guess explanation, and it is not, as many people would like to believe, a suggestion that it is some developing psychic ability. The preferable explanation is that if each individual has an awareness of alpha in his own EEG pattern, as has been amply demonstrated to occur, then he is reasonably sure that his partner has alpha activity at the same time.[7]

Subjective reports only have been available to estimate convergence of feeling states and changes in communications, and these strongly suggest that feelings of "being in touch" with each other do develop from the synchrony training, along with a sense of improved communication. Using the technique to facilitate communication between therapist and patient disclosed an important effect of the psychiatrist's role. Working with patients with whom it had been difficult to establish a clinical rapport, it was the psychiatrist who had difficulties learning to control the synchrony of alpha, presumably because it is he who is also responsible for analysis of the relationship between himself and the patient.

3. *As a meditation aid.* Early in the history of alpha biofeedback, an excitement little short of ardent was generated by reports that yogic and Zen meditators showed large quantities of slow alpha in their EEG patterns. It is the feature of alpha biofeedback that has been exploited by a great many people newly interested in the practice of meditation.

The EEG picture of meditation is by no means clear. Part of the confusion and misinterpretation about brain waves and meditation stems from a distressing lack of understanding of meditation and an equally dismaying lack of understanding of brain waves.

Many people are unaware that there are many types of meditation practice, and many different levels of each type. These range from the relatively uncomplicated quiet state advocated in Transcendental Meditation to

---

7. The phenomenon may, however, suggest brain electrical events that might occur during kinds of telepathic communication. Two people might be in the same, or complementary, brain states at such times. Biofeedback research may clarify this possibility.

the highly developed concentration of advanced yoga or tantric Buddhism. Some introductory forms of Zen and an occasional yoga sect advocate "emptying the mind" and the "no-mind" state in which there is no primary focus of attention. In sharp contrast, certain advanced Zen meditations and nearly all yogic meditations involve intense concentration. These two quite different activities of mind are accompanied by quite different patterns of brain wave activity.

Meditation requiring concentration is most clearly defined by Gopi Krishna. According to the yoga sutras of Patanjali, "the mind has to pass through two stages of concentration, i.e., a primary state of concentration and a more stabilized and prolonged form of it . . . only then can it attain to samadhi or mystical trance." Gopi Krishna continues,

> the aim of the practices is to keep only one object or one line of thought before the mind to the exclusion of every other object or chain of ideas. In order to achieve one-pointedness of mind, a great deal of voluntary effort is necessary, and the practitioner has to keep himself always in a state of alertness to prevent his mind from slipping into passive or drowsy states or into other streams of thought and fantasy. It is clear, therefore, that there is a world of difference between a passive, inwardly-focussed mental condition . . . where the ideas are allowed to meander and drift, as in preceding sleep . . . and the alert, attentive, centrally-focussed state of mind necessary for concentration in all its forms. . . . There are others who prescribe negative forms of concentration, forbidden by the ancient masters, which allow the mind to think loosely or wander ceaselessly during meditation, leading to passive, somnolent or quiescent states indicated by the alpha signal in biofeedback.

The popular notion is that meditation is accompanied by a predominance of slow, rhythmic EEG activity, particularly slow frequency alpha and even considerable theta activity. This concept is based on a number of scientific papers, particularly from Japan, reporting a remarkable enhancement of alpha activity during Zen meditation. A distinctive feature of these EEG states is reported to be the failure of the meditators to adapt to auditory alerting stimuli, indicating that perceptual acuity is heightened but any sign of responding is blocked, apparently by the tranquil mental state.

Proponents of Transcendental Meditation also claim that the EEG pattern shifts to predominantly alpha and theta waves during meditation; however, it is generally considered that the experimental studies have not been controlled. Recent studies have failed to confirm the occurrence of increased alpha as a result of the meditation; instead, as noted in the EMG section in Chapter 2, at least two research groups have documented the occurrence of the various sleep stages during Transcendental Meditation by practiced meditators.

Wenger and colleagues some time ago studied the physiologic activities of practitioners of Hatha yoga and found abundant quantities of well-developed, well-modulated alpha activity along with slowed respiration and heart rate. More recently, Green has reported extensive studies with one yogi, Swami Rama, and consistently finds remarkably increased amounts of slow, rhythmic EEG activity, i.e., slow alpha and theta.

Contrary to the published reports about the predominance of slow, rhythmic EEG activity during Zen meditation, or during T.M., or as the early Wenger studies with practitioners of Hatha yoga found, EEG studies of advanced practitioners of yoga show significantly "alerted" EEG patterns.

An extensive study by Das and the famous electroencephalographer and neurophysiologist Gastaut, followed the EEG, muscle tone, and heart rate during the several distinctive phases of yogic meditation, from the fixing of attention to the meditation proper, on to the final ecstasy or complete concentration. Muscle activity was undetectable during meditation, while the heart rate accelerated during deep meditation, especially in the ecstasy state, and only then it slowed. The EEG pattern showed an extremely interesting and unusual

*Fig. 11.* Partial record of an Indian yogi during meditation. Throughout his meditation the yogi showed remarkable quantities of high frequency and relatively high amplitude EEG activity.

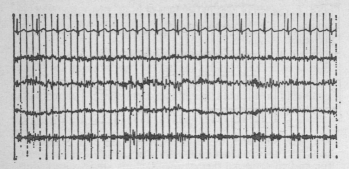

*Fig. 11A.* Top to bottom the tracings are (1) heart rate (EKG); (2) EEG lead 1 from temporal-parietal electrode pair; (3) EEG lead 2 from parietal-occipital region; (4) EEG lead 3 from occipital electrodes; (5) filtered beta of 13 to 28 Hz frequency taken from EEG lead 2. Tracing taken some 40 minutes after beginning meditation and is marked by rhythmic beta activity of approximately 20 to 25 Hz.

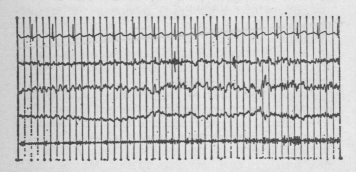

*Fig. 11B.* Some 15 minutes later background EEG activity has become small and poorly defined slow wave activity in the theta range emerges followed by slower beta activity than previously.

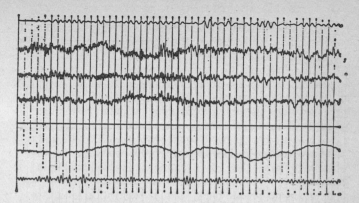

*Fig. 11C.* Still later, the EEG recording has been changed to include records of filtered EEG activity and of eye movements. Top tracing is filtered theta, the next three are the EEG leads 1, 2, and 3 as before, then a nonrelevant signal marker channel, followed by recording of horizontal eye movements, and filtered alpha. The record shows constantly drifting eye movements and the EEG has increased in amplitude and shows a wide variety of EEG components, including poorly defined theta activity, occasional alpha waves, and rhythmic beta activity in the 13 to 28 Hz range.

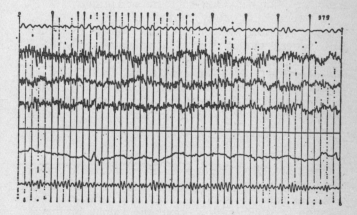

*Fig. 11D.* Still later during meditation, EEG amplitude has increased, components are quite mixed, and there is considerable eye movement. Throughout his meditation the yogi showed a virtual absence of alpha activity.

sequence of changes. First the alpha rhythm increased in frequency, followed by the appearance of 15, 20, and 30 Hz and 18–20 rolandic beta and diffuse, irregular 25 to 30 Hz EEG activity, proceeding to increased amplitudes of the 25–30 Hz activity to 30 to 50 µV(!) in the ecstatic periods. Following ecstasy alpha reappeared at slower frequencies widely distributed throughout the EEG. Also during the ecstatic period, the EEG failed to respond to alerting stimuli.

I have recorded EEGs from only two yogis in my laboratory, and the EEG changes exactly paralleled these reported by Gastaut and Das.

If one now refers back to the description of autogenic training (A.T.) it can be seen that A.T. proceeds quite orderly from the empty mind, relaxed state to the single pointed inward focus of attention to total loss of self-consciousness. In essence autogenic training is a Western version of traditional yogic training leading to enlightenment. Thus we now have two techniques for controlling activity of the mind for comparison of EEG patterns, one, A.T., largely devoid of the religious overtones, and the yogic technique in which achieving union with God is integral and primary.

A recent EEG study during advanced autogenic training practice revealed fast, low voltage frequency EEG patterns chracteristic of alerting states. The EEG changes were very similar to those described above for advanced stages of yogic meditation. These kinds of results, i.e., the yoga studies and the A.T. study, relate to the kinds of EEG activity one would expect if meditation as described by Gopi Krishna were practiced. The alert type of EEG pattern suggests an intense effort required to maintain concentration on a single object or thought.

Obviously, EEG patterns differ considerably during meditation, depending upon the type of meditation practiced and the level of meditation achieved. The question of whether slow, rhythmic (alpha or theta) and fast, alerted EEG activity reflect different types of interior concentration on mental events or the degree of concentration is not yet resolved. The information to date, as summarized above, suggests that slow alpha may indicate one type of internal focus of attention, possibly that of the passive observer, whereas fast EEG activity, as found during yogic meditation and ecstasy, may indicate active mental involvement in the perception of mental processes.

# 8

## A BRIEF SUMMARY: WHICH BIOFEEDBACK FOR WHICH PERSON

There remains the question of which kind of biofeedback is suitable for what kind of person with which kind of emotional or psychosomatic or physical problem, or perhaps with no problem at all. Is there, for example, a perferred form of biofeedback for a particular illness, or can any type of biofeedback be used for any illness? Who is a candidate for what kind of biofeedback? Is there a place in this new domain of biofeedback for well people who simply are interested in using the techniques to become better acquainted with internal states and gain a new consciousness of their whole being?

These questions are best answered by summarizing the relative effectiveness and effects of the different kinds of biofeedback in the broad spectrum of its applications. The basis for selecting a biofeedback technique appropriate to a specific situation is determined by the purpose in mind for the biofeedback training, and by a consideration of the specificity and extent of the illness process and the nature of the underlying cause of the problem.

It is common in medicine and psychotherapy to refer to different treatment approaches as treatment modalities. In biofeedback the term modality is used to indicate the body system or function or activity that is used to provide the biofeedback information. Muscle (EMG) biofeedback, EEG biofeedback, temperature biofeedback are examples of different biofeedback treatment modalities.

For the purpose of selecting the proper biofeedback modality, the uses of biofeedback techniques can be separated into three categories: stress-related problems, including emotional and psychosomatic problems; disorders which are primarily of physical origin; and interests in self-awareness. Except for the latter, which is discussed toward the end of this section, the most generally useful biofeedback modalities are those directed toward stress reduction. These are useful not only in emotional and psychosomatic problems, but in problems of physical origin as well since most physical disabilities are aggravated by the stress of the physical problem and trying to function with the disorder. Thus for the great majority of illnesses responsive to biofeedback treatment, the antistress relaxation procedures are the initial treatment of choice.

There are two principal biofeedback procedures whose primary focus is stress reduction. These are muscle (EMG) biofeedback to assist in learning muscle relaxation and temperature biofeedback, which produces a more internal relaxation effect. Some investigators feel that alpha biofeedback is appropriate as a stress-reduction measure, particularly for emotional stress. Each procedure needs to be augmented by other relevant procedures, as discussed in the text of the book, and each also has its problems in practical use.

When used in stress-related problems, EMG biofeedback is preferably supplemented by abbreviated forms of Jacobson's Progressive Relaxation and occasionally by autogenic training. The chief problem in EMG biofeedback has been the relative failure of the learned relaxation of the frontalis muscle, most commonly used, to generalize the relaxation effect to other muscles of the body. This is remedied in practical use by employing the full complement of ancillary procedures, including Progressive Relaxation, record keeping, home practice, and by using other muscle groups for the biofeedback information. Currently biofeedback research is exploring variations of EMG biofeedback to ensure greater degrees and more widespread relaxation, such as using biofeedback signals of the sum or average of the muscle tension of several muscles simultaneously.

Another technique is to use a preliminary scanning of tension to determine the muscle areas where the greatest tension occurs, then concentrate the training on those muscles.

It should be made quite clear that in the present stage of the art of biofeedback the advantage of using the frontalis muscle tension levels as the chief indicator of body muscle tension has been that it has provided a base for learning awareness and control of muscle tension despite the apparent specificity of the relaxation effect to the frontalis muscles. Moreover, in some way the patients have experienced subjective changes, including relief from anxiety and pain, although the subjective changes have not generally correlated with changes in frontalis muscle tension.

It appears to be the impact of the *total* relaxation training procedure that is responsible for the clinical improvement. It has been reported repeatedly that a combination of Progressive Relaxation with home practice, record keeping, and what amounts to TLC during the training is equally as effective as either EMG biofeedback alone or EMG biofeedback in combination with the other relaxation techniques. The evidence is strongly suggestive, however, that EMG biofeedback plays an important role both in accelerating and facilitating relaxation learning and in consolidating the relaxation learning experience.

EMG biofeedback is appropriate for all disorders listed on pages 65–66.

Temperature training for relaxation effects is generally performed using hand or finger temperature. There has been no solid physiological evidence that temperature biofeedback results in a general relaxation effect, but a particular type of internal relaxation effect is inferred to occur from the subjective reports following training and from the relief of pain in tension and migraine headaches. The relaxation appears to be a diminution of sympathetic tone in the cardiovascular system. The recent report of successful use of temperature biofeedback in the treatment of essential hypertension suggests that temperature training does produce an antistress effect, an effect in which vasodilation of the hand, underlying the hand temperature change, generalizes adequately to other vascular beds of the body. Temperature training thus may be useful in the treatment of stress reactions in which the reaction is one primarily of increased visceral tension.

The effects of stress manifest themselves quite differently in different people. Some people express their response to stress by bruxism (grinding of the teeth), others by developing tension headaches, and still others by low back pain. Nor are the differences confined to the muscle system; some individuals react to stress with high blood pressure, some by cardiac arrhythmias or uncontrollable sweaty hands, or cold feet, ulcers, or functional diarrhea or colitis. While all of these disorders can be treated by the general biofeedback relaxation techniques, the more effective treatment approach appears to be the use of the specific biofeedback modality appropriate for the organ or body system involved, and combining this with the relaxation procedures. The person reacting to stress by developing problems in peripheral blood flow can be easily treated using hand temperature training or finger vasomotor training. Certain cardiac arrhythmias can be readily treated using heart rate biofeedback, and migraine headaches may be best treated using finger or temporal artery pulse volume biofeedback.

The consensus of those clinical researchers who have had the opportunity for a broad, practical background in biofeedback is that the kind of biofeedback to use in a treatment program is that which provides biofeedback information about the exact physiologic function involved in the illness. There are, however, a few exceptions.

From this standpoint, diagnosis provides two indicators: the physiologic system problem and the underlying cause of the problem. For example, the patient may be found to have a gastric ulcer, and the reason for the ulcer may be diagnosed as an undue or idiosyncratic response to stress. Research evidence indicates that direct biofeedback of gastric acid secretion levels can be used to learn to control the acid secretion leading to healing of the ulcer. On the other hand, there is also evidence that biofeedback-assisted relaxation procedures using EMG biofeedback can lead to a general control of the stress response also with consequent healing of the ulcer. The choice of the biofeedback modality is made by the physician upon consideration of the disease process, his conclusions about the suitability of the type of biofeedback for the particular patient, and the availability of the different biofeedback modalities.

The most difficult and generally unsatisfactory biofeedback modality is blood pressure biofeedback. The almost constant inflation and deflation of the blood pressure cuff is a stressor in itself and may defeat the purpose of the biofeedback training. Fortunately, relaxation procedures appear to be useful in reducing moderate levels of blood pressure in essential hypertensives to normal ranges. Progressive Relaxation, and yogic exercises and meditation both alone or used with EMG biofeedback are also effective techniques. Here again, EMG biofeedback appears to exert a facilitatory effect on the other relaxation techniques.

Many people develop vague, nonspecific, nagging, and often floating symptoms of body distress, and it seems likely that in many instances such symptomatology is an expression of stress reactions. Biofeedback can play a dual role in the treatment of these kinds of disorders of obscure origins.

The first is using a biofeedback-assisted relaxation procedure, and the second is using biofeedback instruments as stress scanning devices. In the latter mode individual muscle involvement can be localized by measuring muscle tension of the various muscle masses, and those showing the highest levels of tension are used for the EMG biofeedback training. Areas of visceral tension can best be determined by scanning the visceral systems by conventional diagnostic procedures or by determining system reactivity via biofeedback instruments. For example, blood pressure or heart rate reactivity can be elicited by a variety of test procedures, such as those eliciting a mild arousal response.

Although the preponderance of biofeedback uses currently appears to be focussed in the area of stress-related problems, it should be pointed out that some biofeedback techniques or modalities appear to be specific for specific disease processes. The use of the SMR (12 to 16 Hz EEG rhythm) to reduce the incidence of epileptic seizures seems specific, as does the learning to control peripheral vasomotor activity via vasomotor activity biofeedback or the learning to control cardiac arrhythmias by means of heart rate biofeedback or learning to control gastric acid secretion through the biofeedback of gastric acid levels.

Individuals with disorders of the neuromuscular system, such as the paralysis following a stroke, cerebral palsy, or spasticity usually require a combination of biofeedback procedures. Whether the primary problem is paralysis or spasticity, the opposing muscle groups tend to be affected in the opposite manner. The resulting imbalance of the muscle system can be relieved to some extent by applying muscle relaxation techniques to the contracted muscle groups while at the same time using muscle contraction training or motor unit training for the paralyzed or stretch-adapted side.

Various types of specific EEG biofeedback are appropriate to several different kinds of brain and subjective state disorders. The treatment of epilepsy appears to be an example of a fairly specific disease entity that can be relieved by a specific type of EEG biofeedback. On the other hand, it is of interest that emotional problems such as anxiety, neuroses, and phobias, in which relaxation techniques are frequently effective, have been found by several investigators to respond extremely well to alpha biofeedback.

Patients with chronic pain are candidates for biofeedback treatment. Increasingly, clinicians are reporting varying degrees of success in treating chronic pain using EMG and EEG biofeedback. A number of pain clinics, usually in association with hospitals, have been established with biofeedback as the principal treatment modality. The reason why EEG alpha biofeedback should neutralize pain is not completely clear, but then we still do not know why aspirin relieves pain either.

Throughout the history of biofeedback the majority

of both experimental and clinical studies have shown that the biofeedback experience results in changes in subjective state and activity useful to the patient or subject. As a psychotherapeutic or self-analysis, biofeedback can be used in two quite different ways. First, when one or another of the specific EEG frequency ranges or components is used as the physiologic parameter for training or learning to control, the subjective activities most frequently associated with the EEG components (such as relaxation, imagery, etc.) used can be elicited or strengthened, and thus subjective sets or states can be redirected toward more useful mental or emotional functioning. This may be the process involved in the successful use of alpha biofeedback in neuroses and psychosomatic problems.

The second mode of biofeedback in psychotherapy is one that has not yet been fully developed or reported in the scientific literature although many clinical psychologists are exploring the technique. This is the use of the biofeedback device as a means of communication. The most familiar example is the use of the skin electrical response to emotional stimuli as used in the lie detector. Essentially the same principle can be used in psychotherapy or psychological counselling. During the psychologic interview and discussion, the instrument registers the consciously repressed emotional responses of the patient; the therapist and patient can then work together toward determining the course of therapy most successful in reducing the physiologic responses, and hence the emotional reactions.

# 9

# PROCEDURE PROTOTYPE FOR CLINICAL PRACTICE[1]

*Therapist's tasks for the biofeedback treatment sessions.*
The introductory session . . . First, or first several, biofeedback training sessons . . . Subsquent biofeedback training sessions . . . Final series of biofeedback training sessons
*Implementing the training sessions*
The introductory session . . . Treatment sessions . . . Importance of set and setting . . . Patient's record keeping . . . Relaxation techniques . . . Home exercises . . . Physiologic and psychologic testing . . . The biofeedback psychologic interview . . . Record keeping for the clinic

The procedures used in successful biofeedback treatment programs are a complex combination of physiologic, medical, psychologic, and instrumentation expertise. And because the psychophysiologic changes leading to recovery from emotional problems, psychosomatic or physical illness can be effected only by the patient, the procedures represent a new approach in therapy and therapeutics.

Details of an EMG biofeedback treatment regime,

---

1. The prototype is based on EMG biofeedback for relaxation and relief of muscle tension because of the widespread utility of the technique in the treatment of stress-related illnesses. The general scheme is also applicable to the various types of cardiovascular, gastrointestinal, or respiratory biofeedback and to some aspects of biofeedback in neuromuscular rehabilitation, but it requires modification for use in the various types of EEG biofeedback.

as a prototype biofeedback treatment procedure, are presented in this chapter as a general, comprehensive guide; certainly not all elements of the program may be necessary in everyday practice, however, the various ancillary elements described and sequenced have been found to contribute to a high rate of successful therapy.

The guide for clinical practice is concerned with the total technique of biofeedback treatment, i.e., all of the tests, procedures, and support that are needed to ensure optimal results as well as the documentation necessary to evaluate progress of the patients. The guide includes details of the information to be given to the patient, the therapist's or technician's role, and examples of tests, aids, and record keeping over a course of biofeedback treatment.

The first task is, of course, to determine the appropriateness of biofeedback for the presenting complaint of the patient. Following medical and psychiatric histories and workups, the determination can be made as to whether the physiologic manifestations of the patient's problem are those which have been demonstrated to be susceptible to biofeedback treatment or whether the patient's emotional character is amenable to this course of treatment.

Since biofeedback is a continuing treatment and is largely an educational process, its successful application requires considerable preparation. The professional therapist and his technical associates must be prepared by having a thorough understanding of the role of all of the elements of the treatment procedure, and preparing a "game plan" appropriate to the particular patient being treated.

Assuming proper patient selection, the following guide details the pretreatment routine consisting of establishing the treatment schedule and giving explanations, notes the events in each biofeedback session, and provides guidelines to be used for patient and clinic record keeping.

# Therapist's Tasks for the Biofeedback Treatment Sessions

Although biofeedback is a learning process, it is primarily a treatment program to relieve the complex effects of stress that also involve a rehabilitation process; as such, the treatment services and therapist's tasks are so extensive that the treatment program needs to be preplanned in considerable detail.

The following general scheme has been found to be effective in clinical practice. The scheme is first outlined, then follows descriptions which amplify elements of the program that are either new or specific to biofeedback training.

## The Introductory Session

1. Agree with the patient upon a concise statement of the problem to be treated along with precisely defining the objective of the biofeedback training.

2. Provide explanations and discussion covering (a) the relationship between the biofeedback therapist and the patient's physician if these are different, (b) what biofeedback is, (c) the role of the biofeedback instrument, and (d) the patient's role and involvement.

3. Agree upon a specific schedule, including length of sessions, how many sessions per week, and approximate duration of the treatment.

4. Give and record relevant tests for psychophysiological assessment of the patient, including tests for psychologic and physiologic reactivity.

5. Instruct the patient about record keeping and provide log or chart outlines and assign the homework.

6. Ensure that the patient has an understanding of the biofeedback process in order to avoid misconceptions early.

## First, or First Several, Biofeedback Training Sessions

1. Briefly re-explain biofeedback training and instrumentation, clarifying any confusion.

2. Attach individual to instrument while explaining how the feedback signals change with variations in physiologic activity and that these may be associated with slight differences in subjective feeling states. The individual tests the instrument, e.g., with the EMG instrument, he can mildly contract then relax the involved muscles to show how tension and relaxation are indicated by the instrument.

3. The first training period is begun by adjusting the instrument to read large changes for small differences in muscle tension (i.e., the amplification of the signal is increased until the biofeedback display changes with small changes in physiologic activity). The patient is instructed about relaxation and various strategies used to achieve it, and the therapist may elect to work with the patient through demonstrations of Progressive Relaxation, autogenic training, imagery exercises, or other appropriate and relevant techniques. The patient is then allowed to work alone with the instrument for several periods of 10, 15, or 20 minutes with short rest periods interspersed.

4. Between training periods the therapist can discuss the patient's response to the biofeedback experience and encourage his participation and interaction in the experience. The therapist may also elect to work more closely with the patient during the first training sessions, giving him verbal reinforcement and support.

5. At the end of the session any post-testing desired can be carried out, and the patient's subjective report is taken and discussed.

6. The patient is instructed in relaxation procedures for home use and may be provided with tape recordings for this purpose. He is also instructed to begin a record of his subjective responses to the relaxation exercises. Finally, the patient is instructed to make attempts to identify his stress situations during the day and begin

to identify his tension image patterns that are his reactions to the stress (see Jacobson's procedure, pages 53–55).

## Subsequent Biofeedback Training Sessions

1. Prior to beginning the training sessions, the therapist reviews with the patient the patient's overall assessment of his progress, including the difficulties encountered and the strategies he employs to relax when away from the training sessions. Both the objective and subjective changes should be summarized and reviewed, and the patient's record keeping is checked and reviewed. This may entail exploring possible alternative biofeedback training, adjusting strategies, new homework, etc.

2. During the actual biofeedback training periods, feedback signal levels are adjusted to the patient's needs, usually it is to make the task more difficult, or it may be appropriate to train the patient for both directions of activity, e.g., increase *and* decrease muscle tension imperceptibly as a way of achieving greater control and awareness.

3. At the end of each training session, the effect of the session is reviewed with the patient and compared to sessions of past performances.

4. Occasional records of physiologic changes can be made when convenient.

## Final Series of Biofeedback Training Sessions

1. The final sessions are devoted to making sure that the patient has learned adequate control. This can be accomplished in several ways; for example, it may be desirable for the patient to practice his relaxation or biofeedback when he does not have the biofeedback signal available, with the therapist monitoring the instrument. Or, the therapist may wish to institute a desensitization procedure in which he confronts the patient with, or the patient visualizes, those events he considers stressful while he continues to maintain control over the biofeedback signal. Another type of

weaning procedure is to have the patient rely on his learned ability to rate his tensions and to keep a log indicating the stress conditions and his evaluation of his reaction to them during everyday conditions.

2. One of the final sessions is devoted to final documentation of the physiologic and psychologic changes. Preferably, recordings are made of the physiologic activity and a final subjective evaluation is also made.

3. The patient should be encouraged to return for refresher training if he feels the need.

## Implementing the Training Sessions

### The Introductory Session

The key to successful and lasting biofeedback treatment is the understanding the patient develops about the meaning of biofeedback and his role in the treatment. The unique nature of biofeedback as a therapeutic tool and the relative scarcity of factual information about what happens in biofeedback training means that a good bit of time must be spent in acquainting the patient with the ideas behind biofeedback, the procedure, and what is expected. It is virtually impossible to provide the proper explanations, take the relevant history, accomplish the necessary testing, and still have enough time to proceed to the actual training during the first session. Moreover, record keeping by the patient is begun some time before beginning training since it is not only an important part of the treatment procedure, but is the basis for making evaluations about the therapeutic progress of the patient. Thus, the introductory session may precede the actual treatment sessions by days or weeks, depending upon the need for documentation of the patient's symptoms and related subjective reports.

*Explaining biofeedback and the equipment.* Since patient improvement is mainly a result of the patient's understanding, his motivations, and developing his own control, explanations and instructions are directed toward explaining the therapeutic situation as one in which information is provided for the patient's individual use. Moreover, nearly all clinical biofeedback literature indicates that the more information the patient has about the biofeedback treatment, the more effective and efficient is his progress. However, because many patients have anxieties about medical procedures, it is best to give the information casually, treating the patient as a partner in the process.

A useful device is telling the truth about biofeedback, i.e., that it is waking up internal control systems that consensual consciousness apparently has largely blocked from general, intentional use; that it is basically a process of "letting it happen" or of "letting go" of conscious and subconscious control and inhibition (passive concentration and passive volition), and that the ability to learn control over body functions is inherent in human beings although little used because of inhibitions generated by educational and medical traditions.

Biofeedback can be explained in several ways. First, the term biofeedback was devised as a shorthand expression for the process of "feeding back" the biological information about a selected internal function to the individual whose biological information it is. A good tentative definition of biofeedback is that it is a learning process in which one uses biological information to learn how to exert voluntary control over one's own automatically, reflexly regulated physiological activities. It can be explained that the physiologic information is obtained from monitors of physiologic activities, generally by means of devices or instruments, such as thermometers, stethoscopes, or EKG machines, and that the patient's job is to learn how to discriminate different levels of physiologic activity. He does this by "training," i.e., becoming acquainted with how the monitor changes and what that means to him. It is much the same as learning how much muscle pressure is needed to drive a golf ball. It can be pointed out that practicing to use our muscles in special ways leads to precise control over exactly those muscles involved, but we are never aware of exactly how this learning and control occurs.

The explanation can then continue by explaining the role of the instrument. It is pointed out that the electrodes actually sense unfelt muscle tension, and that the device amplifies this tension and uses it to activate the display or monitor, i.e., the lights or tones, which follow the levels of muscle tension as they normally fluctuate over time. The patient is told that this is information he has never had access to before, but it is much the same as the unfelt muscle tension levels his brain uses, along with visual information, to *move* muscles (as driving a car or playing tennis), and that learning how to use this unfelt muscle tension, now in the form of visual or auditory information, also occurs by means of subconscious mental processes.

The explanation of the instrument can be augmented by describing all aspects of the actual instrument used.

Because the concept of biofeedback is so new to the patient and is almost the antithesis of medical tradition, it is important to ensure that the patient really grasps the concept. It is very useful to cite analogies of the biofeedback process that are familiar to the patient in everyday life. A good example of how we all use biofeedback to exert voluntary control over automatic, reflex functions is winking. Blinking is a reflex, an automatic act performed to ensure even distribution of moisture over the eyeball. But we *learn* to wink by using biofeedback information, either from a mirror, or by asking someone to tell us what our eyelid is doing, and we also have a bit of internal muscle information about how the eyelid feels in blinking and when we try to wink. Or, we can use examples of learning how to drive a car or play the piano. We use internal muscle information and other sensory information, something in the brain activity integrates this information, and we end up *knowing how* to drive a car or play the piano, but we can't describe how we do it or even *how* we learned to do it.

*Explaining the objective of the treatment.* While the real objective of the treatment is to relieve the patient's problem, this probably should be explained in terms of learning to become aware of muscle tension, and that the process of learning this awareness is what affords relief, i.e., the awareness allows the patient to control the level of tension much as he learns to control the amount of pressure or tension on the accelerator when driving. It is also advisable to re-emphasize that this kind of voluntary control rarely comes totally into conscious awareness, although the *strategies* one uses do come into conscious awareness.

The objective is then put into terms of what one desires to accomplish with respect to the biofeedback instrument, i.e., that it is one's own physiologic, muscle tension that controls the instrument, and one must learn to discriminate by subjective, inexpressible feelings, different levels of the instrument's signals, and that when this happens, the control will happen automatically. Another objective of the treatment is to teach the patient first, that he is in control of his own muscle tensions, and second, that the burden of using his biofeedback learning in his everyday life is up to him. And to that end, he should make a commitment to both the training and to consistent, persistent home practice.

*Explaining the supporting therapy,* its purpose; the need for the patient to personalize the supporting measures (various relaxation techniques); providing strategy information. It is important for both the biofeedback therapist and the patient to know and to keep in mind that biofeedback is a new experience. Traditionally, in both medicine and psychology, the patient is the *object* of treatment; in biofeedback, the patient *is* the treatment. That is, whatever beneficial effect occurs, occurs because of intentional, albeit largely passive or subconscious, participation of the patient and generation of appropriate, desirable changes by the patient. This is such a fundamental but such a new and different approach in therapy and therapeutics that it may take some time before the patient realizes that he and his mind are the resources for his improvement. The therapist should always bear in mind that putting the major burden for recovery on the patient means that the patient has to re-educate his feelings and dependencies at the same time that he is trying to learn how to change his own physiologic activities "by mental means."

The newness of both the concept and the experience of biofeedback means several things of considerable importance to the patient. He has little if any idea of how to manipulate his mind and body to accomplish the objective of his treatment, and further, as he begins to become aware of internal events and begins to experience himself, aware of his ideas of his body image, aware of his mental capabilities, his ideas and perspectives of his relationships to other people begin to change. This, too, may be viewed as a learning problem with which the patient will be trying to cope. The changes in awareness are usually difficult for the patient to verbalize, thus the therapist, much as in counselling or psychotherapy, should not only be constantly aware that these events are going on in the patient's mind (usually only verging on conscious awareness) but should be ready both to help the patient express his changing emotions and awarenesses, and to provide clues whereby the patient can strengthen his new ideas and insights.

At this point in the developing understanding of biofeedback therapy, the other informational factors discussed earlier appear to be critical to successful biofeedback treatment in addition to the biofeedback signals. These are cognitive information, psychologic support, and strategy information that are needed to put the biological information to use. Each of these elements appears to play a very definite role in the biofeedback process.

Cognitive support is given in the form of explanations of what biofeedback really is, how the selected physiologic activity operates, and how the instrument *really* works. Cognitive information means the kind of information supplied to the patient which gives him an understanding of what is going on and what his role should be. In essence, the therapist should share his information and ensure that the patient understands what the treatment is, how the equipment works, how his body systems that are involved function, and has a clear-cut statement of his role.

Psychological support is provided in the form of encouragement, usually by gently indicating to the patient that he can indeed change his own biologic functioning and shape it very much the way he wishes for his greatest state of well-being. It can also be casually indicated that some people *choose* to keep their medical-biologic problems for a wide variety of reasons, but that new, beneficial insights and solutions spontaneously occur when people are released from the continuing internal pressure of tensions and anxieties, even when these are not consciously felt.

Psychological support is necessary because not only is biofeedback a new experience, but the entire concept is beyond the pale of tradition, particularly the traditional roles of physician and patient. This can be viewed as cultural shock, the idea that the average person actually can control his own body process, and hence his health and illnesses. The therapist can offer a good bit of support quite casually, such as "a clinic such as this wouldn't have started if people couldn't do it." More critical support is in the form of encouragement, especially noting that every individual has a slightly different way of achieving results, that the process is internal and often inexpressible, but that the learning how to control body functions is no different from learning how to walk or talk.

Psychologic support is less effective when it is assertive; it appears to have more impact when it is quite casual, since the patient has a good bit of new information to digest, and he has to fit the information into his own frameworks. In other words, the control must come from within; there should be no pressure to perform up to someone else's expectations.

Strategy information offers clues about how to relax, how to change one's own physiology and mental awareness of being. Again, *how* an individual learns to control body functions through biofeedback is an individual matter, and the science is too young to have developed high probability strategies. There are, however, a number of strategies that have been found to be generally helpful, such as the brief forms of Progressive Relaxation and autogenic training techniques, individualized imagery such as developed in desensitization procedures, yogic exercises, or a mixture of these as appears to be appropriate for any particular patient.

Each of the strategy techniques is best used in simplified form, with very clear instructions. The use of the biofeedback monitor markedly accelerates the effects obtained, thus it is chiefly the concepts involved and a moderate number of specific exercises that are needed. It is the consistency with which the exercises are employed that is the most important factor.

Each of the above factors is important to the patient's progress, although one or another factor may be more or less important to different patients. We have to remember that biofeedback therapists are new to the game also—and because so much of the patient's recovery is in the hidden areas of *his* mind, at this stage in biofeedback the best therapeutic results stem from continued exploration of what are most effective supporting measures for which kinds of personalities, subjective states, and disorders.

Obviously, since biofeedback is primarily an internally generated technique, the more the patient can be encouraged to do for himself, the greater the probabilities are for his improvement. But because "being his own doctor" is a new experience, many patients will be hesitant about actively making suggestions or actively participating in their own treatment programs.

Nonetheless, once patients begin active involvement in their own treatment, they begin to gain confidence in their own abilities and to explore new techniques for getting in touch with internal states. By this time they begin to lose feelings of inferiority about creating new ways of dealing with vague feelings and get into the spirit of making their own special relaxation or desensitization tapes or inventing personalized autosuggestion formulas.

## Treatment Sessions

The number and scheduling of treatment sessions should be agreed upon prior to beginning treatment. The reason is that successful results go hand-in-hand with learning of voluntary control and the learning requires an adequate training period. The average number of treatment sessions will range between 7 and 12, although often extended training may be warranted. The length of each session in actual biofeedback practice should be approximately 30 minutes, and it is best if the patient can be seen at least twice a week.

The number of treatment sessions of course depends upon the progress of the patient. The program index may be somewhat misleading, since some patients will report excellent relief from their symptoms after a few sessions; however, the objective of the treatment is to develop control over muscle tension so that the effects can be lasting. This means that the patients should be given increasingly more difficult control tasks, i.e., trained to achieve more and more relaxation for longer periods of time until they can maintain that same deep relaxation *when the feedback signal is removed*.

Wherever possible, the final training session should be devoted in part to demonstrating to the patient that he can maintain a relaxed state without the instrument, and during imagery of tension-producing situations. Since the treatment objective is to demonstrate the patient's learned ability to control muscle tension it may be advisable to have him train part of each session without the feedback signal, while the therapist follows the muscle tension levels to determine his progress. The desensitization process may not take long once control of muscle tension has been achieved, but the desensitization procedure is a large factor in ensuring the transfer of the control from the clinic situation to everyday-life situations.

## Importance of Set and Setting

The need for optimizing the psychologic aspects of biofeedback training has been amply covered in earlier sections. At the present stage in the development of biofeedback therapy, we do not know whether psychologic support is integral or ancillary to the process; therefore, it is important to use psychologic techniques fully or as needed in order to maximize successful treatment. A large part of the psychologic support lies in the attitude and concern of the biofeedback technicians or therapists, and even in the attitudes and feelings expressed by the furnishings and decorations of the clinic. At one recent meeting of the Biofeedback Research Society, an investigator reported a study illustrating this point. Two assistants trained in biofeedback procedures, with differing personalities, were each given a number of patients to train in finger temperature control. The outgoing, warm assistant successfully trained 20 of 22 subjects while the retiring, uninterested assistant was successful with only 2 of 20 individuals.

The direction of the psychologic support is to convey to the patient not only interest in and concern for his problems, but also to suggest that he, the patient, is a student-partner in the treatment process. One has to handle the latter strategy carefully, since most patients may not initially be able to accept a major role in their own recovery process. Bringing the patient into partner status must proceed slowly and wait for the patient to accumulate and digest the new information and the new attitudes he faces in biofeedback.

## Patient's Record Keeping[2]

The patient should be informed that all record keeping, logs, diaries, etc., are both to document his progress in training and to assist in modifying the procedure for the best effects. In actual fact, the record keeping contributes much more: by keeping the patient's attention on the exact nature of his problem, and in some way this attention contributes to the developing control. The record keeping aspect of the patient's biofeedback treatment is in fact co-equal with the instrumental biofeedback training in importance. In a large sense it is also biofeedback, and perhaps this should be pointed out to the patient if he does not begin to see the relationship for himself. Record keeping

---

2. Some examples of logs are given in pages 254–256.

helps to keep the patient focussed on the realities of his physical, emotional, and mental activities, and apparently even the concept of trying to appraise the reality of these activities accurately has a therapeutic effect. The reason for the therapeutic effect may stem from two factors: apprehension about the unknown and expectancy. Reducing the incidence and intensity of episodes of unwellness to actual numbers tends to bring unwellness into the sphere of the known, with some loss of anxiety. When this is known, the effects of expectancy are considerably diminished. The effect of expectancy is essentially a process of comparison of what actually is to what was expected. Somehow, human beings tend to rate anticipated events as more dramatic than the events actually are. Expectancy also carries a good deal of tension, and accurate record keeping can diminish the tension effects of both apprehension and expectancy. The therapeutic effect of record keeping may also relate to an unconscious drive to be in control (if the patient is not totally dependent upon his illness as a way of coping with his social problems); in any event record keeping seems to be therapeutic in and of itself.

Most people find diary keeping tedious or do not have enough time for it. Also, they generally do not know what is important to note. Therefore, they appreciate prepared charts for their record keeping. The charts are not only invaluable in helping the patient to become aware of his own problems, but they assist the therapist in tailoring further treatment. The charts are also important as a source of information to the referring physician as well as in problems of ethics of treatment.

It should be stressed to the patient that insights and thoughts he may have about his physical and emotional problems will arise spontaneously as a result of the attention (due to record keeping), awareness, and training. He should be advised that becoming aware of the reasons for his tensions may no longer be disturbing because much time has passed since the original stress causing the tension, and because of both the experience he has gained over time and the biofeedback training, his perspective on the reasons for the tensions may be changed considerably.

The record keeping of the therapist, at least that part of it which deals with muscle tension levels and expressed symptoms and problems, should probably be shared with the patient. The purpose of this is twofold, to show the interest of the therapist, along with or as a way of maintaining the patient's motivation, and to provide the patient with additional information which he can use in becoming aware of his tensions.

## Relaxation Techniques

It is probably a good idea to begin biofeedback treatment by being honest with the patient and explaining that all people are different and have had different experiences, so they should do a bit of experimenting (but not too much) to see which of the techniques may work best for them (Progressive Relaxation, autogenic training, transcendental meditation, tapes, or working with a therapist).

A review of clinical reports indicates that a judicious mix of techniques obtains best results. A more extensive review of the reasons for this is given in the preceding sections. Details of selected relaxation techniques can be found in Appendix 1 and can be found in books and tapes obtainable from various psychological services.

## Home Exercises

At the outset, it is important to convey to the patient the importance of home practice. It is an accepted fact in most medicine that patients fail to follow the physician's directions, and for this reason it is important to use every device one can think of to foster home practice. Some clinicians have used the small parking meter timer which can be set to buzz at hourly intervals to remind the patient to practice—anywhere from 30 seconds to 3 minutes—relaxation. Patel uses an interesting reminder system, instructing patients to use everyday sounds such as telephones ringing, church bells, trolley bells, etc., as reminders. These kinds of associations appear easy to develop. The least the patient can do when reminded is to either practice alternating tensing-relaxing or say the autosuggestion relaxation phrases slowly to himself. Obviously it is best if the patient will allot two or three 20- to 30-minute periods per day for serious relaxation practice. The therapist should try to elicit the best times when the patient can do such practice, then encourage him to do it. If a biofeedback instrument is also used in home practice by the patient, then a good device would be to have the patient write down some numbers indicating what muscle tension levels were during the practice periods.

Although most biofeedback clinical investigators use cassette tapes made from either Jacobson's or Schultz and Luthe's relaxation techniques which have been modified to reduce training times, it would seem like a good idea to use tapes for *both* techniques. The "tense-relax" sequences of Jacobson's Progressive Relaxation increase the probabilities of learning muscle tension awareness, whereas the autogenic training phrases of Schultz and Luthe are helpful in stimulating imagery and focus of attention. There is another reason for using standard relaxation tapes, and that is because of the cultural shaping of the patient which has accustomed him to reliance upon some kind of prescription for recovery from illness. As treatment proceeds, however, and both the patient and therapist work to personalize the biofeedback learning, the patient may become interested in developing his own techniques. In these cases, the therapist can offer suggestions to the patient about making his own tape, or the patient and therapist may want to make one together.

The use of portable instruments for home use is questionable. I personally believe that the use of biofeedback instruments in the home should be the exception rather than the rule, and should be reserved only for exceptional cases. Patients may abuse instrument use through inadequate understanding, or they may neglect use altogether. Since the major objective of the biofeedback treatment is to teach the patient voluntary control, weaning away from instrument use should be begun as early as feasible. The patient who must rely on the instrument will gain only temporary periods of relief from his problem.

## Physiologic and Psychologic Testing

There are many varied reasons for testing and documenting all phases of the patient's physical and psychological status. Not only are test results necessary for the general requirement of medical records, but also to demonstrate the effectiveness of the treatment programs to other therapists or to government agencies. From the standpoint of treatment, both the physiologic and psychologic tests are invaluable both to review with the patient as part of the biofeedback treatment process and also for use as a guide for developing a more simplified or effective program or criteria for future use. Biofeedback techniques are new, and the most predictive, significant ways to select patients or evaluate a patient's progress are not completely known.

It is first assumed that the patient has had a recent physical examination and these records are available for review to ensure that the patient's problem does not require other, specific treatment, and the records can be reviewed for reasons for medication he may be taking and to confirm the patient is actually a candidate for biofeedback training.

## The Biofeedback Psychologic Interview

Because of the nature of biofeedback, this should *not* be the typical psychologic interview attempting to elicit definition of emotional problem areas. Rather, because biofeedback is largely a process where the inherent, internal physiologic control mechanisms are to be activated, the interview emphasis for biofeedback treatment should be directed chiefly toward reminding the patient that because of our intense social situation, we all have unfelt tensions that interfere with optimal physiologic and psychologic functioning, and that biofeedback techniques are designed to help us become aware of the effects of these various social and environmental tensions, and with the awareness comes understanding of and actual release from the effect of the tensions. It can be pointed out that for the first time, biofeedback offers information about internal processes, particularly about tension, and that everyone has the ability to control or find release from the tension effects if they allow the muscle tension information and accompanying feelings to sink into the subconscious and allow the subconscious mechanisms to process the information. It must be stressed that it is directed attention, but not *conscious* intention or effort that brings good results and relief.

On the other hand, the biofeedback therapist should be sensitive to the patient's discussion so that he can document the patient's emotional situation, and use the presenting opinions and attitudes of the patient as reference in future discussions when the patient will describe his changing feelings.

At this point it should be noted to the patient that because biofeedback is a process where *he* is going to assume control, he should begin keeping records or a diary about his feelings of tension, and reasons why *he* thinks the tensions exist and how they are affecting him, so that *he,* and he alone, can watch his progress and gain new insights and strategies for dealing with his tensions.

*Psychologic testing.* Evaluation of the patient's progress depends upon changing psychologic reactions and self-appraisals, and aside from other modes for evaluating the patient's emotional status, it is convenient to employ standardized tests as ready reference for progressive evaluation of effects of treatment. One or more of the tests from sources listed in Appendix 3 may be appropriate for patient selection and prediction of ability to stay with the treatment regime, as well as for measuring the effects of the treatment.

*Physiologic testing.* This is highly desirable to provide an accurate indication of both tension levels and reactivity of both muscles and the autonomic nervous system. If at all possible, physiologic (polygraph) recordings should be made, or at least some semiquantifiable index, of levels of muscle tension, heart rate, blood pressure, and skin electrical tone (GSR). At the same time, muscle and autonomic system reactivity can be measured by simple tests such as knee jerk, cold pressor test, standard exercise tests, reactions to mental arithmetic problems, or reactions to mild electric shock or noise following a warning light and the patient's being advised about the test.

*Techniques for electrode application and for aiding patient to discriminate differences in muscle tension level signals.* Electrode application must always be done carefully for best results. The objective is to ensure a low resistance contact with the skin to prevent interference by ambient electrical "noise" in the instrument's operation.

If the frontalis muscle is used, electrodes should be placed bilaterally, with the reference ground electrode in the center of the forehead, about 1 inch above the eyebrow line. For placement of the frontalis electrodes, ask the patient to frown, then palpate the position of maximal muscle tension.

For other, larger muscles, electrode placement is unilateral, and electrodes are simply placed anywhere from 2 to 5 inches apart, with reference electrode placed on nearest bony structure. The skin is first cleansed with alcohol to remove oils, then the skin is mildly abraded, using sandpaper or a commercial plastic scrubbing pad. The electrodes are then applied using good quality electrode paste.

Special attention is paid to starting the patient's training. Since the objective of the treatment is for the patient to become aware of different levels of tension and relaxation, yet he has no previous knowledge of tension levels at rest, it is important first to demonstrate how the instrument records and monitors different tension levels, then to check from time to time that the patient is actually learning control. Initially, at the first session, rather gross muscle activity can be used. Ask the patient to frown or gently grit his teeth. This will cause the biofeedback instrument to change its monitoring signal dramatically. After some training, have the patient pretend or imagine that he is frowning or gritting his teeth or smiling, but not to move or noticably tense his muscles. This should produce a discriminable change in the feedback signal, and furnishes the patient with additional information, namely, that he really does use muscle energy when he is imagining, and also that he can detect and control quite small changes in muscle tension.

One very important consideration lies in the selection of muscle groups or muscle to be used for the feedback signal. Most of the early clinical uses of EMG biofeedback were based upon the work of Budzynski and colleagues, who used the frontalis muscles of the forehead in the biofeedback treatment of tension headache. These researchers had claimed that once relaxation of the frontalis muscle was achieved, relaxation generalized over the muscles of the upper body. It has subsequently been shown that this may not be true, and particularly in some disorders where tension is localized in other muscle groups. Moreover, a number of clinical studies report that muscle tension reduction in the frontalis muscles does not necessarily correlate with the beneficial treatment effects obtained.

Wherever possible it would seem expeditious to work with muscle tension in the muscles primarily involved in the disorder. The case of bruxism is a good example. The first experiments used the frontalis muscles, and with poor results.

Differences in judgments about muscle groups to use may account for certain relative failures that have been reported. For example, in menstrual distress, muscle tension of the forearm was used, and with poor to moderate results. Perhaps muscles of the lower abdomen might prove to be more suitable for EMG biofeedback training.

## Record Keeping for the Clinic[3]

Release forms can be an important way of documenting the precise role of the biofeedback treatment programs and ensuring an understanding by the patient of the training procedures. Every aspect of the training should be noted in the release form, along with some documentation that the referring physician or therapist has authorized the treatment, that he fully understands it, and that in his opinion the biofeedback training will not interfere with any other treatment being used for the patient.

For records of psychologic and physiologic tests the clinic office or the therapist should prepare simple but complete forms in which the results of all test procedures can be entered. At least pretreatment and final test values are vital to enter.

In each training session, muscle tension levels can be read and noted in the record as, for example, a few minutes after beginning the session, one-third of the way through the session, and two-thirds through the session. The reason for no final value is that some patients tend to let up toward the end and others experience a mental fatigue.

Records of other physiologic functions, particularly heart rate and blood pressure, should be noted during the first and final sessions, and if possible, midway through the treatment program. For final documentation, copies of the patient's record keeping should be included.

The following is a partial list of information the biofeedback therapist should note for each session of the patient. Obviously, some items will become redundant or less significant, or other items may have to be added: date and hour of session; biofeedback modality used; length of session; comments of patient about interim period; comments of patient about present sessions;

---

3. Some examples are provided on pages 254–256.

therapist's impressions of patient's progress and needs; note any changes in awareness; note any changes in medication; recommendations for subsequent sessions; physiologic test data; psychologic test data.

The therapist should also provide himself with a checklist of observations about each patient. This should include entries about the mood of the patient, notes about what he reports about his progress, about his understanding of what is going on, any problems he has, how consistent his home practice is, and finally any suggestions by patient or therapist about improvements in his treatment program.

*Summary reporting.* This is essential to have and to keep up to date both as information for the referring physician but also in the event of government inspections.

The summary report can be started after the first visit by the patient, when concise statements can be made about (1) the patient's problem and (2) the recommended biofeedback training and treatment procedure.

Thereafter, the most significant data concerning the patient's progress, both physiologically and subjectively, can be entered. These data can be tabulated or graphed.

*Special observations.* It has been reported that on occasion patients have dropped out of treatment programs because they felt they had gained enough awareness to carry on by themselves. In some cases this may be true; however, because the therapist's responsibility is to ensure optimal therapeutic benefits, it is probably best to caution the patient beforehand that really productive insights and awarenesses occur when they can actually demonstrate control over the physiologic monitor.

The problem of concurrent medication can be sticky. Some, such as migraine patients, may have become dependent upon their medication, whereas other patients may want to stop their medication altogether. In either case one must proceed with caution. A recommended procedure is, if this is agreeable to both the patient and his physician, to reduce drug doses by increments to 10 to 20 percent if and when his symptoms and medical indices have begun to normalize some 7 to 10 days earlier. Drug doses should never be reduced until biofeedback effect can be demonstrated, and then it must be initiated by the physician or by the patient in consultation with the physician.

The patient should also be advised that biofeedback is therapeutic just as drugs are therapeutic, and should he be taking medication, he should become sensitive to the possibility that his own control as a result of training may narrow his margin of tolerance for a drug. He should note any changes in feelings or sensations about the drug effects to his physician so that the physician can determine whether the drug dosage should be changed or even whether the drug should be discontinued. The referring physician may wish to be in direct touch with the biofeedback therapist, and in this event the biofeedback therapist must keep proper records so that the physician can make the right judgment about medication, concurrent.

## Examples of Charts for Record Keeping by Patients and for Biofeedback Therapists

### HEADACHE LOG

| Date | Time AM/PM | | Intensity* | Medication | | Type of headache | Location of headache |
|------|-------|----------|------|------|------|------|------|
| | Began | Subsided | | Name | Dose | | |

*Rate on scale of 1 to 10 with 10 as most severe.

### PAIN LOG

| Date | Time AM/PM | | Intensity* | Medication | | Type of pain | Specific location of pain |
|------|-------|----------|------|------|------|------|------|
| | Began | Subsided | | Name | Dose | | |

*Rate on scale of 1 to 10 with 10 as most intense.

### FEEL GOOD (PEAK EXPERIENCE) LOG

| Date | Time | Duration in hours | Cause or Reason | Medication if any | Intensity* | Comments |
|------|------|------|------|------|------|------|

*Rate on a scale of 1 to 10 with 10 as best feeling state.

## Post-Treatment Questionnaire
1. Do you feel you are better able to relax quickly?
2. Do you feel you can relax more deeply?
3. Do you feel you have a better understanding of relaxation?
4. Do you feel the biofeedback helped you to relax?
5. Did you like the biofeedback training?

## Subjective Units of Tension (SUT scores)
One biofeedback investigator has used this index with success. The patient estimates his subjective feelings of tension on a scale of 0 to 10 both before and after relaxation exercises.

## Insomnia—Sleep Record
1. Time to fall asleep
2. Number of hours slept
3. Number of nightly awakenings
4. How felt in morning (scale 1 to 5)

## THERAPY RECORD
(Therapist's Notes)

Patient's Name:

Session Number:

Date:

Therapist:

Type of biofeedback:

Notes re:

    subjective assessment of progress

    supplemental therapy (autogenics, breathing, etc.)

    observations on patient's response and interaction with equipment

    relevant dialogue with patient

    subjective assessment of patient's state of mind

    any other pertinent data and observations

## THERAPY RECORD
### (Equipment Notes)

Patient's Name:

Session Number:

Date:

Therapist:

Type of biofeedback:

Equipment used: EEG and EMG

| Instrument settings | Initial values | Final values |
| --- | --- | --- |
| Amplitude: | | |
| Display threshold: | | |
| Inhibit/limiter: | | |
| Time: | | |
|   Beginning | | |
|   End | | |
| Type of feedback: | | |
|   1. Visual | | |
|     a. lights | | |
|     b. meter | | |
|   2. Audio | | |
|   3. Verbal | | |

| | Temperature | |
| --- | --- | --- |
| | Initial | Final |
| Setting: | | |
| Temperature: | | |
| Thermistor | | |
| Placement: | | |
| Time: | | |
|   Beginning | | |
|   End | | |

# RELAXATION EXERCISES

## 1. Outline of Verbal Procedure Used in Developing Voluntary Control of Internal States in Autogenic Feedback Training*

We are all familiar with the fact that the human organism is equipped with regulating systems, mechanisms, and principles that work automatically . . . the heart . . . the breathing mechanism, etc. We are going to ask you to use certain formulas—that is, certain simple *phrases*—to support or reinforce this tendency of the organism. We are interested in securing cooperation between the "individual" and his automatic regulating systems.

In this experiment we are attempting to direct physiological changes through the focus of attention. It is important to realize that we do this *not* by force of will, but through the use of visualization and imagination during relaxation. It is important to have a casual, detached attitude—what in art might be called a "creatively passive" or expectant attitude—toward the change we are attempting. We simply use the formula, visualize and feel that it is happening, and then "let it happen," so that we will not interfere with the body's tendency to cooperate.

It has been found helpful to try to visualize clearly the part of the body which is to be influenced before using the formula relating to it. In this way a "contact" appears to be set up with that particular part. This seems to be important in starting the chain of psychological events which eventuate in physiological changes. These changes essentially result from the operation of the *psychophysiological principle* which affirms that "Every change in the physiological state is accompanied by an appropriate

*By permission of Elmer E. Green, Alyce M. Green, E. Dale Walters, Research Department, The Menninger Foundation, Topeka, Kansas 66601.

change in the mental-emotional state, conscious or unconscious, and conversely, every change in the mental-emotional state, conscious or unconscious, is accompanied by an appropriate change in the physiological state." This principle, when coupled with volition, makes possible psychosomatic self-regulation.

Concentrate on each phrase in whatever way seems most effective for you, repeating it verbally, or visualizing it as if it were written, or as if you are hearing it spoken —maintaining a steady flow of the phrases for the duration of the exercise. The aim is to train certain mental processes to operate in such a way that finally a very brief passive concentration on a formula will accomplish the intended physiological change almost instantly.

## Autogenic Training Phrases

The eyes should be gently closed and quiet. Relax the body in the following manner, visualizing and feeling the relaxation of each part as you proceed. Repeat each formula two or three times.

*Relaxation Phrases.* "I feel quite quiet . . . I am beginning to feel quite relaxed . . . My feet feel heavy and relaxed . . . My ankles, my knees, and my hips, feel heavy, relaxed, and comfortable . . . My solar plexus, and the whole central portion of my body, feel relaxed and quiet . . . My hands, my arms, and my shoulders, feel heavy, relaxed, and comfortable . . . My neck, my jaws, and my forehead feel relaxed. They feel comfortable and smooth . . . My whole body feels quiet, heavy, comfortable, and relaxed." Continue visualizing and repeating the phrases silently for a minute or two.

*Warmth Phrases.* While you remain relaxed and quiet, with your eyes closed, visualize your hands and repeat each of the following formulas. Concentrate in a passive way, visualize the event, and then just let it happen. "I am quiet and relaxed . . . My arms and hands are heavy and warm . . . I feel quite quiet . . . My whole body is relaxed and my hands are warm, relaxed, and warm . . . My hands are warm . . . Warmth is flowing into my hands, they are warm . . . warm." Continue visualizing and repeating the warmth phrases silently for a minute or two.

*Reverie Phrases.* While you remain relaxed and quiet, with your eyes closed, repeat the following formulas.

Again, concentrate in a passive way, visualize the event, and then just let it happen. "My whole body feels quiet, comfortable, and relaxed . . . My mind is quiet . . . I withdraw my thoughts from the surroundings and I feel serene and still . . . My thoughts are turned inward and I am at ease . . . Deep within my mind I can visualize and experience myself as relaxed, comfortable, and still . . . I am alert, but in an easy, quiet, inward-turned way . . . My mind is calm and quiet . . . I feel an inward quietness." Continue using the phrases for a few minutes, allowing your attention, your thoughts, to remain turned inward.

*Activation Phrases.* The session is now concluded and the whole body is reactivated with a stretch and deep breath and the phrases: "I feel life and energy flowing through my legs, hips, solar plexus, chest, arms and hands, neck, head, and face . . . The energy makes me feel light and alive."

## 2. Relaxation Exercises. Examples*

RELAXATION TECHNIQUE: Deep Breathing
(Five minutes)

1. Select a comfortable sitting position.
2. Close your eyes, and direct your attention to your own breathing process.
3. Think about nothing but your breath, as it flows in and out of your body.
4. Say to yourself something like this: "I am relaxing, breathing smoothly and rhythmically. Fresh oxygen flows in and out of my body. I feel calm, renewed and refreshed."
5. Continue to focus on your breath as it flows in and out, in and out, thinking of nothing but the smooth, rhythmical process of your own breathing.
6. After five minutes, stand up, stretch, smile, and continue with your daily activities.

RELAXATION TECHNIQUE: Mental Relaxation Place
(Five to ten minutes)

1. Select a comfortable sitting or reclining position.
2. Close your eyes, and think about a place that you

*Developed by Dr. Cary Howard McCarthy.

have been before that represents your ideal place for physical and mental relaxation. (It should be a quiet environment, perhaps the seashore, the mountains, or even your own back yard. If you can't think of an ideal relaxation place, then create one in your mind.)

3. Now imagine that you are actually in your ideal relaxation place. Imagine that you are seeing all the colors, hearing the sounds, smelling the aromas. Just lie back, and enjoy your soothing, rejuvenating environment.

4. Feel the peacefulness, the calmness, and imagine your whole body and mind being renewed and refreshed.

5. After five to ten minutes, slowly open your eyes and stretch. You have the realization that you may instantly return to your relaxation place whenever you desire, and experience a peacefulness and calmness in body and mind.

RELAXATION TECHNIQUE: Tensing the Muscles
(Five to ten minutes)

1. Select a comfortable sitting or reclining position.

2. Loosen any tight clothing.

3. Now tense your toes and feet (curl the toes, turn feet in and out). Hold the tension, study the tension, then relax your toes and feet.

4. Now tense your lower legs, knees, and thighs. Hold the tension, study the tension, then relax your legs.

5. Now tense your buttocks. Hold and study the tension. Relax your buttocks.

6. Tense the fingers and hands. Hold the tension, study the tension, and then relax.

7. Tense your lower arms, elbows, and upper arms. Hold it, study it, and then relax.

8. Tense your abdomen. Hold the tension, feel the tension, and relax.

9. Tense your stomach. Hold the tension, feel the tension, and relax.

10. Now tense your chest. Hold and study the tension. Relax. Take a deep breath, and exhale slowly.

11. Tense the lower back. Hold and study the tension, and relax.

12. Tense the upper back. Hold the tension, feel the tension, and then relax.

13. Now tense the shoulders. Tense, hold, and study the tension. Then relax.

14. Now tense the neck, back and front of your neck. Hold the tension, study the tension, and then relax.

15. Now tense your entire head. Feel the tension in the back of your head, top of your head. Make a grimace on your face so you feel the tension in your facial muscles. Study the tension, and then relax.

16. Now try to tense every muscle in your body. Hold it, study it, and then relax.

17. Continue sitting or reclining for a few minutes, feeling the relaxation flowing throughout your body. Know the difference between muscles which are tense, and muscles which are relaxed.

18. Now stretch, feeling renewed and refreshed, and continue with your activities.

RELAXATION TECHNIQUE: Thinking About Body Parts
(Twenty minutes)

1. Select a comfortable place to lie down. Remove shoes, loosen belt or light clothing. Stretch out on your back, arms resting by your sides, feet slightly apart, eyes gently closed.

2. Think to yourself, "I am now going to relax completely. When I awaken I will feel fully refreshed."

3. Think about your feet, wiggle your toes, flex your ankles. Then "let go"—let go of all the tension, and let your feet rest limp and heavy.

4. Think of the lower part of your legs, your knees and thighs, up to your hips. Imagine them just sinking into the floor, heavy and relaxed.

5. Now think of your hands. Wiggle your fingers and flex your wrists, then let go, relax.

6. Think of your lower arm, elbow, and upper arm, all the way up to your shoulders. Picture all the tension just melting away.

7. Think about your abdomen. Let the tension go, and allow your breathing to flow more smoothly and deeply.

8. Think about your stomach and chest, up to your throat and neck. As you continue breathing more deeply, just imagine all the tension flowing out and you are relaxing more and more.

9. Now think about your throat, neck, and head, feeling

limp and relaxed. Relax your facial muscles. Drop the jaw, parting the lips and teeth. Picture yourself completely relaxed.

10. If you are aware of any remaining tension anywhere in the body, go to the area mentally and relax the tension.

11. Continue to remain in this completely relaxed state for five to ten minutes. You may picture pleasant thoughts, or simply blank your mind and enter a stage of light sleep.

12. When you are ready to awaken, say to yourself, "I have been deeply relaxed. I am now ready to wake up, feeling completely refreshed and relaxed."

13. Begin to wake up by flexing the ankles, wiggling the toes. Then wiggle the fingers, and gently shake your wrists.

14. Bend the right knee, and then the left knee. Bend the right arm, then the left arm.

15. Open your eyes. Stretch each arm over your head. Then slowly sit up, stand up, and stretch again. You are ready to continue with your activities.

RELAXATION TECHNIQUE: Number Count Down
(Three to ten minutes)

1. Select a comfortable position.

2. Close your eyes, and breathe deeply and rhythmically several times.

3. Take another deep breath, and while exhaling mentally visualize the number three (3). "3" is your symbol for complete body relaxation. (Relax any tension in your body, remembering the state of deep relaxation felt after the tensing muscle exercise.) Mentally repeat to yourself, "3, complete body relaxation."

4. Take another deep breath, and while exhaling mentally visualize the number two (2). "2" is your symbol for complete brain and nervous system relaxation. (Any thoughts, fears, concerns, worries—let them all go. Relax all thought processes, feeling a sense of mental stillness and harmony.) Mentally repeat to yourself, "2, complete brain and nervous system relaxation."

5. Take another deep breath, and while exhaling mentally visualize the number one (1). "1" is your symbol for complete Oneness within yourself, complete mind-

body attunement and harmony. Mentally repeat to yourself, "1, Oneness, mind-body harmony."

6. In this deep state of mind-body relaxation, you are filled with calmness, peacefulness. You are one with the creative forces of your own being, and you may direct these creative forces to bring about positive changes and benefits in your daily life and health.

(At this time give yourself positive health suggestions you wish to hear. If there is a particular part of your body that needs healing, imagine that your own healing energies are flowing to that part. Create a tingling sensation, and imagine the body area bathed in pure light energy, restoring and renewing every cell and tissue.)

7. When you are ready to continue with your daily activities, say to yourself, "I have been in a deep, renewing state of mind-body relaxation. I will maintain the perfect attunement I have experienced, and will be in perfect health, feeling better than ever before. I will count from one to five, and at the count of five I will feel wide awake and in perfect health."

8. Then begin counting, "1 . . . 2 . . . 3 . . . 4 . . . 5." Open your eyes, and say out loud (or repeat mentally with your eyes open), "I am wide awake, in perfect health, feeling better than ever before."

SAMPLE POSITIVE SUGGESTIONS WHICH MAY BE GIVEN IN DEEP STAGES OF RELAXATION
*Health and Wholeness*

1. I have healing power.
2. My mind is in every cell of my body, and I build up my desired state of health by my positive, healthful thinking.
3. My body is fluid and pliable, and my thoughts move easily through it to build perfect health.
4. I can create right and harmonious thoughts and feelings within my own being, and change the whole pattern of my life and my health.
5. My body and my mind maintain complete harmony and health at all times.
6. Every day joy, love, and peace increase in my consciousness.
7. I see my problems as opportunities for growth, and

know that the best answers will present themselves to me in deep states of relaxation.

8. Every night I enjoy a soothing, relaxing, and rejuvenating rest. Every morning I awaken feeling happy and confident.

9. My imagination is the door to achieving my life goals. I imagine and visualize myself as happy, successful, healthy, and joyous.

10. I am filled to overflowing with a dynamic sense of love. I love myself as a unique and creative person, and I feel love toward others. Love relaxes and harmonizes my emotions. Love attunes me to the healing power of my own body and mind. I am filled with love. I am healthy and whole.

11. I am in control of my own life and health. I choose health and happiness.

12. Every day in every way my health, happiness, and prosperity increase.

# INSTRUMENTATION

Choosing a biofeedback instrument is a perplexing task for any professional researcher or therapist. In the few short years biofeedback has been around, the medical instrumentation market has exploded with devices for use in biofeedback. Many of the early devices were (and some still are) purely exploitive. Users have found many serious deficiencies, and more sadly, many have found some instruments not only useless but actually to give misleading biofeedback information.

If the following guidelines are followed, you can be sure of choosing a reliable and serviceable instrument. The time spent in researching your specific instrumentation needs and which instruments meet those needs can amount to a considerable dollar saving.

The first task is to become acquainted with the *exact* parameters of the physiologic system you have selected to use for biofeedback and for the result you want to produce. For example, if you are interested in hand temperature biofeedback, you should be aware that emotional and psychosomatic problems are often accompanied by a very low skin temperature, and the instrument should be able to accommodate low temperatures. On the other hand, temperature biofeedback training can often result in extremely large changes in hand temperature; therefore the range of *accurate* temperature readings should allow for fairly large extremes in hand temperature. The same precautions should be taken with respect to EMG and EEG devices.

The latter pose more difficult problems in defining the physiologic characteristics chosen for the biofeedback. With muscles, for example, the electrical activity associated with tension can vary remarkably from muscle to muscle; thus the potential practitioner should be armed with data indicating the frequency of muscle firing activity for the muscles of interest, and an idea of the voltage generated both in different muscles, and also during different states of tension and relaxation. The relative failure to find correlations between muscle tension levels of the frontalis muscle and subjective effects, or the findings that Progressive Relaxation exercises can result in a general deep relaxation of all muscles whereas reduced tension in the frontalis does not generalize to other tense muscles should be a reminder that muscles exhibit quite different activity (tension) under different circumstances, and the activity characteristics of the muscles chosen for biofeedback should be matched with the specifications of the instrument.

A second task is to become acquainted with the meanings of the electrical terminology used to describe the characteristics of the instrument. It is necessary to become proficient in translating these terms into descriptions circumscribing the physiologic activities of interest. This includes such expressions as noise level, amplification, filtering, and integration.

The criteria which I personally use in evaluating instruments are the records obtained from the several major stages of the biofeedback instrument. I personally insist upon seeing records of the EMG or EEG activity immediately after the amplification stage of the instrument and before filtering or integrating, and these records must show a fidelity to records obtained by the best physiologic recording techniques. It can be immediately recognized whether the noise level is excessive, whether the amplifier passes or causes artifacts, and whether there is too much or too little filtering in the amplifier. I then insist upon a simultaneous recording through the filters in the case of EEG instruments. By comparing the amplified EEG recording with the recording of the filtered activity the accuracy and precision of the filters can be determined. In addition, this is an excellent opportunity to check the effect of signal amplification on the operation of the filter; in many cases too much gain can drive the filter artificially. Further, it can be determined whether artifacts passing the amplifier "ring" the filters, i.e., activate the filters artificially. And finally, a record should be obtained following the integration phase and immediately before the signal is used to activate the biofeedback display, and this record should also be made simultaneously with the other two records as a check that the activity operating the display is faithfully following the original signal input.

Few biofeedback instrument manufacturers provide for recording these several stages of the original and treated physiologic signal; nonetheless, my personal standard would require output jacks from which the EMG or EEG signal can be recorded, i.e., the original "raw" activity, the filtered activity, and the voltage which activates the display. These recordings are not only necessary to ensure that the biofeedback signal is accurately reflecting the physiologic activity of interest, but they are also invaluable to sample the physiologic progress of the patient's improvement. If the biofeedback displays of the instrument have been previously confirmed to be accurate and reliable, then of course the various displays themselves can be used for the physiological documentation.

Other factors relevant to biofeedback instrumentation and particularly to EEG biofeedback instruments are discussed in Chapter 7.

## Biofeedback Instrumentation Companies

Those indicated with an * are those companies whose instruments I have found to be of generally high quality. This does not mean that other manufacturers may not also manufacture good quality, but simply means that I have not seen them personally. If you have any difficulty locating one of these companies, write to the Biofeedback Society of America (formerly known as the Biofeedback Research Society), Department of Psychiatry C268, University of Colorado Medical Center, 4200 East Ninth Avenue, Denver, CO 80220, for further information.

Alpha Metrics
  6311 Yucca St.
  Los Angeles, Calif. 90028

Aquarius Electronics
  P.O. Box 627
  Mendocino, Calif. 95460

*Autogenic Systems, Inc.
  809 Allston Way
  Berkeley, Calif. 94710

Bio Behavioral Instruments
  P.O. Box 631
  Claremont, Calif. 91711

*Bio-Dyne Corporation
  154 E. Erie
  Chicago, Ill. 60611

Biofeedback
  255 West 98th Street
  New York, N.Y. 10025

Biofeedback Electronics, Inc.
P.O. Box 1491
Monterey, Calif. 93940

Biofeedback Instruments
223 Crestcent Street
Waltham, Mass. 02154

Biofeedback Research Institute
6233 Wilshire Blvd.
Los Angeles, Calif. 90048

*Biofeedback Systems, Inc.
2736 47th Street
Boulder, Colo. 80301

*Bio-feedback Technology, Inc.
10612A Trask Avenue
Garden Grove, Calif. 92643

BioMonitoring Applications
270 Madison Avenue, Suite 1506
New York, N.Y. 10016

BioScan Corporation
P. O. Box 14168
Houston, Tex. 77021

Coulbourn Instruments, Inc.
P.O. Box 2551
Lehigh Valley, Pa. 18100

*Cyborg Corporation
342 Western Ave.
Boston, Mass. 02135

Edmund Scientific Co.
EDSCORP Bldg.
Barrington, N.J. 08007

*Electro Labs
P.O. Box 2386
Pomona, Calif. 91766

Electronic Developments
37 E. Platts Eyot
Lower Sunbury Rd.
Hampton, Middlesex TW12 2HF
England

Extended Digital Concepts
P.O. Box 9161
Berkeley, Calif. 94709

*Huma Tech Industries
1725 Rogers Ave.
San Jose, Calif. 95112

Inner Space Electronics
P.O. Box 308
Berkeley, Calif. 94701

J & J Enterprises
Rt. 8, P.O. Box 8102
Bainbridge Island, Wash. 98110

Lawson Electronics
P.O. Box 711
Poteet, Tex. 78065

M.O.E.
Dept. 6, P.O. Box 2693
Santa Cruz, Calif. 95063

Marietta Apparatus Co.
118 Maple Street
Marietta, Ohio 45740

Med Associates, Inc.
P.O. Box 47
East Fairfield, Vt. 05448

Medical Device Corporation
P.O. Box 217
Clayton, Indiana 46118

Medlab
P.O. Box 31035
San Francisco, Calif. 94131

*Narco Bio-Systems, Inc.
7651 Airport Blvd.
P.O. Box 12511
Houston, Tex. 77017

Neuronics, Inc.
3021 John Hancock Center
875 No. Michigan Ave.
Chicago, Ill. 60611

Ortech, Inc.
100 Midland Road
Oak Ridge, Tenn. 37830

Phenomenological Systems, Inc.
72 Otis Street
San Francisco, Calif. 94103

Quartec
1662 Doone Road
Columbus, Ohio 43221

Radioshack
2017 West 7th Street
Fort Worth, Tex. 76107

RB Biofeedback Research
  Associates
  Layton Park Plaza, Suite 3
  Layton, Utah 84041

Royer-Anderson
  763 LaPara Ave.
  Palo Alto, Calif. 94306

Self Control Systems
  P.O. Box 6462
  San Diego, Calif. 92106

Stoelting Co.
  1350 So. Kostner Ave.
  Chicago, Ill. 60623

Stress Transformation Centers, Ltd.
  405 North Saint Andrews Place
  Los Angeles, Calif. 90004

Systec, Inc.
  500 Locust Street
  Lawrence, Kan. 66044

Terrasyn, Inc.
  P.O. Box 975
  Longmont, Colo. 80501

Uniquity
  P.O. Box 990
  Venice, Calif. 90291

# ASSESSMENT DEVICES IN BIOFEEDBACK TREATMENT PROGRAMS

This list of references and tests is suggested as potentially valuable for use in the various facets of biofeedback treatment programs. The person needing other and more detailed information on assessment devices will find the following bibliography of maximum help.

## Bibliography

Anastasi, Anne. *Introduction to Psychological Testing,* 4th ed. 1976.
A very readable introduction to the individual searching for basic information on test and measurements.

Buros, Oscar K. *Seventh Mental Measurements Yearbook.* The Gryphon Press, 1972.
This reference provides excellent information on the nature of most psychological tests, including a description, critical reviews, publishers, price, etc. Information on vintage tests may be cited in the Seventh Yearbook and reader referred to one of the previous yearbooks for the extensive review of the tests. Subject-matter indexing provides speedy access to specific areas.
Buros also has a volume titled *Tests in Print* that may be valuable in locating particular tests.

Buros, Oscar. *Personality Tests and Reviews.* The Gryphon Press, 1970.
Similar in style to his Mental Measurements Yearbook(s) but much more comprehensive in its treatment of personality assessment devices.

Cronbach, Lee J. *Essentials of Psychological Testing,* 3rd ed. Harper & Row, 1970.
A very complete textbook and reference on the test-

ing field. Particularly excellent section on basic concepts such as reliability and validity with appropriate statistical formuli and logic. A good balance of theory and research in substantive material.

Lanyon and Goodstein. *Personality Assessment*. Wiley, 1971.

A good introduction to the various personality tests and to the theory behind the different approaches to personal assessment. Solid information on the major tests including comments on interpretation in clinical use.

## Tests

1. *Tests of Personality: Directed toward the measurement of relatively enduring characteristics of the person*
   a. Inventories focusing on "normal" traits and dimensions
      California Q—Set
      California Psychological Inventory
      Edwards Personal Preference Schedule
      Omnibus Personality Inventory
      Sixteen Personality Factor Questionnaire
      Thurstone Temperament Schedule
   b. Inventories focusing on "pathological" traits and dimensions
      Eysenck Personality Inventory
      Minnesota Multiphasic Personality Inventory
      Thirty-two Personality Factor Questionnaire
   c. Miscellaneous Personality Devices focussing on specific dimensions of behavior
      Firo-B and Firo-F (Interpersonal relations orientation-behavior and feeling)
      Holtzman Inkblot Technique
      Rotter Internal-External Scale (locus of control)
      Thematic Apperception Test

2. *Perceptual Tests*
      Bender Gestalt Test
      Benton Visual—Motor
      Pursuit Rotor
      Embedded Figures Test
      Rod and Frame Test

3. *Anxiety Tests*
    Cattell's IPAT Anxiety Scale Questionnaire
    Fenz-Epstein Anxiety Scale
    Life Change Inventory
    State-Trait Anxiety Inventory
    Taylor Manifest Anxiety Inventory

4. *Physically Related Tests of Stress*
    Cold Pressor Test
    Bicycle Ergometer
    Harrower Stress Tolerance Test
    Sustained Handgrip
    Treadmill and Step-Stress Tests

5. *General Complaint Inventories (Physical and Psychological) adjective check list*
    Cornell Medical Index
    Mooney Problem Check List
    Seriousness of Illness Rating Scale

# IN DEFENSE OF ALPHA

In the early days of biofeedback, the promise of being able to control brain waves, and so to control consciousness or emotion or the movement of thought or how the central nervous system regulates body functions engendered a controversy about the practical merits of alpha that still sputters in the halls of academia. Psychotherapists and researchers of states of consciousness have argued for the potency of brain wave control as the genesis and elixir of subjective life, and just as firmly, a handful of vociferous experimental psychophysiologists have argued that alpha is merely the mechanical byproduct of brain activity that has virtually nothing to do with those higher cerebral functions underlying the complexities of mental life.

While there is a great deal of outspoken discussion by these psychophysiologists concerned with the experimental mechanics of alpha, and because in science it is faddish to claim that fads are pointless, at first glance it would seem that the scientific attitude about the clinical usefulness of alpha has been muddied. A very large part of the confusion exists for the simple reason that the reductionist theoretical approaches used by laboratory scientists for their experiments fail utterly to account for either the positive, surprisingly broad clinical applications of alpha biofeedback, or for the impressive modulations of mind and consciousness that alpha training may produce.

If one attempts to reconcile experimental with clinical outcomes of alpha training, it becomes obvious that the EEG biofeedback art is in a shocking state of disarray. The crux of the alpha biofeedback problem is that alpha (including its many variants,[1] such as slow alpha, the

---

1. There is suggestive, although not conclusive, neurophysiological evidence that the brain electrical activity recorded at the scalp as the

alpha-theta range, fast alpha of 12 to 16 Hz, temporal alpha, mu rhythm, etc.) firstly is importantly related to complex subjective states and activities which have been poorly characterized, if at all. Subjective experience is notoriously difficult to quantify by the scientific method; it is ephemeral, elusive, variable, dynamic, and capable of description mainly by analogy. With such imprecision of measurement, there are obvious difficulties in relating subjective experience to the elusive, dynamic, and variable EEG. And secondly, learned control over alpha (or any of its variants) alters perception of internal events, that is, it alters the perception of the unmeasurable relationships among sensations, images, perceptual or experiential memories, motivation, evaluation, judgments, and other mental activities. The inherent difficulties in establishing a correspondence between EEG alpha (or any other component or pattern) and mind and consciousness are compounded by an inexplicable lack of consolidation of information available about alpha.

There have been no comprehensive reviews of alpha, and indeed, there has been no attempt on the part of either the laboratory researcher or the clinical investigator to develop any unifying concepts of alpha that pull together the many factors and influences which can all significantly affect its occurrence or nonoccurrence, or its relationships to emotion and behavior. For the most part psychophysiological researchers have confined their work to

---

EEG is rhythmic at different frequencies, such as alpha, theta, etc., because there are generators of rhythmic activities, or neuronal structures that perform timing functions, of a particular frequency. This dominant cyclic activity is presumably influenced by the electrical activity of the hundreds of related brain structures, such that the fundamental frequency is modulated and appears as subharmonics or harmonics of the fundamental frequency, and seen in the EEG, for example, as 5 Hz theta or 10 Hz alpha or 20 Hz rhythm; or more likely the multiple influences can become sufficiently great as to dissipate the rhythmic activity where it is recorded, and the recorded EEG is seen as nonrhythmic. This is often labelled as mixed frequency, but computer analysis can uncode all of the specific frequencies involved. Gaarder and Speck's study of the quasi-harmonic relations of alpha and beta was interpreted as representing fundamental timing properties of the nervous system. Finding a synchrony of neuronal firing with a power spectrum peak near 20 cps would mean that alpha occurs when every other cycle is suppressed. According to this theory, a lack of alpha or beta would indicate a desynchronization (no rhythmic activity) that might accompany data processing in the brain.

exploring the role of alpha in (a) arousal responses, (b) visual mechanisms, (c) conditioned learning, and (d) experimental anxiety. The techniques and methods used for these kinds of investigations are invariably inappropriate to an examination of alpha activity as it occurs within the normal range of behavior. With diametrically opposing objectives, the clinician employs procedures relevant to the patient's psychological status, and is relatively unconcerned by mechanical, reflex, or theoretical influences.

However much confusion a few laboratory studies may interject against the potential clinical usefulness of alpha training, the present situation is simply that there are some forty or more research reports which indicate a role of alpha activity in states of emotion or consciousness characterized as relatively tranquil, nonanxious, or inwardly directed. Moreover, *all* clinical reports to date, including extended studies, note remarkable shifts in behavior, emotions, and attitudes following alpha biofeedback and the majority of treated patients who improved significantly were those who had failed to respond to conventional treatments. There are no more than three research reports that suggest the opposite.

Despite the relative unanimity of clinical data and research studies of the effectiveness of alpha, there are numerous research reports still quibbling over the concept of control of alpha. It is not the purpose of this book to make a critical analysis of research studies on alpha; however, it is extremely important that the practitioner of biofeedback not be misled by the laboratory, experimental study of alpha. The following subsections are designed specifically to note areas of alpha research that are the cause for considerable misunderstanding and misuse of EEG alpha and alpha biofeedback.

*1. The Concept of Control.* Of crucial importance in documenting the efficacy of alpha biofeedback is quantification of the degree of control over alpha achieved by the patient. The question is: has the patient learned to *control* his EEG (alpha or other) activity, or, has he been trained to perform by changing his EEG *in response to a signal*? There is a world of difference between these two concepts of control.

The term "control" can have different meanings in psychology and in biofeedback. In the idiom of experimental psychology, it is used chiefly in the context of experimental learning situations, and generally means that a response occurs or is elicited by conditions controlled by the experimenter. Take away the external controller and learning usually decays rapidly. In the context of voluntary control the concept of control indicates action directed and regulated by the individual.

The majority of psychologists working with alpha use the experimental designs of conditioned learning in which the alpha biofeedback signal is given as a reinforcement. Since this is to reinforce acceptable performance, it means that the reinforcing signal is given *after* the performance. Say that an individual produces the amount of alpha the experimenter has decided upon as indicative of a meaningful change. The instrument calculates the amount over the chosen time period, then gives a signal that the alpha performance *has been* satisfactory. This "feedback" signal is often also supplemented by the reinforcement of verbal encouragement. The signals indicating satisfactory performance are post facto (almost posthumous) . . . after the fact. Given the ephemeral, dynamic movement of the EEG, it bends the imagination to believe that a significant association between brain electrical activity and subjective state could be readily established. This is not to say that such associations will not occur, but they will be established only if ample time is allowed. Unfortunately most *research* alpha studies are conducted in a single session!

In this kind of procedure, where the reinforcement follows the performance, the emphasis of the learning situation is on an association between having performed and the reinforcing signal. Most researchers fail to recognize the importance of the association made between the reinforcing signal and the physiologic (and psychologic) state of having completed the performance. This physiologic state is quite different from that occurring while performing or learning to perform. Whatever "control" develops is, to varying degrees, dependent upon the presence of the reinforcing signal.

Almost everyone in biofeedback talks about control and voluntary control. The confusion lies in the researcher considering the control to be a response to a stimulus, while voluntary control is universally considered to be a self-generated and directed activity. In terms of alpha control, the difference is simply whether in the one case a consistent change (increase) in alpha occurs to the reinforcement, or, in the other case, whether the individual develops the ability to produce alpha at will, without the need of a signal.

The biofeedback process may be a cerebral process quite different from those cerebral processes generally conceptualized as important to learning. The evidence that control, *voluntary* control, over brain wave activity can be developed is unequivocal. The intriguing aspect of learned control over alpha, or any physiologic activity, is that it cannot be proven to be a response to any specific situation or condition, but is a change in physiologic activity following upon the integration of information relevant to the system and the objective. The more accurate and relevant and complete the information, the more rapid and complete the learning. Nor is it trial-and-error learning in the sense that there is conscious direction of the physiology or mental processing, as there is in learning either a physical or mental skill.

Clinically effective alpha biofeedback, as assessed by significant clinical improvement, regularly has used the biofeedback signal in a continuously available form. When used in this way, the biofeedback signal provides a one-to-one tracking of the EEG fluctuations and can, depending upon the accuracy and versatility of the instrumentation, reflect a reasonable approximation of the activity of specific EEG components, such as alpha. The biofeedback signal thus contains directly relevant information about the physiological processes that are intimately associated with, if not a direct cause of, the very subjective experience related to its appearance. If associations are to be made between EEG (alpha) and subjective experience, then the more directly and immediately accessible the information, the more immediate and direct are the associations. Many of the researchers treat alpha as a brain electrical activity that is independent of subjective experience.

The presence of a continuous monitor of physiologic activity provides information for the ongoing learning process and is integral to it. In the case of alpha training, for example, the presence of alpha not only signals the existence of a particular physiological state, but *also* signals information about the objective to be achieved, and both types of information are used to consolidate and shape the learning process. The continuous signal contains additional information by its moment-to-moment reinforcement. If we view learning as an information-processing phenomenon, then the continuous physiological monitor supplies at least the three "bits" (actually five) of information noted above in contrast to when the signal is used to reinforce performance, which contains only one "bit" of information. As a matter of fact, the continuously available monitor also supplies two additional bits of information: information to make comparisons, i.e., when the signal stops, it signifies that the physiologic state has disappeared or fallen below threshold, and this information is used to compare which strategies are effective and which are not. Particularly in the case of brain waves, with their constantly changing activity, the temporal aspects of learning and associations about the validity and reliability of the information, along with the relative importance of external versus internal dependence, become crucial to the learning and control processes.

Voluntary control over anything evolves from the experiential equally as much as from rewards or reinforcements. Vast stores of experiential data are judged and evaluated for appropriateness to situations for exerting voluntary control, and in a great sense, it is the mind looking at its own repertoire of activities and selecting the responses that are appropriate or useful or both.

If control over physiological activities is selected, activated, directed, and modulated, consciously or unconsciously, as it is in voluntary control, then the likelihood is that the controlling mechanism cannot be that physiologic activity being selected, activated, and directed, but is some other force or mechanism, even though that other factor can be one aspect of the totality of the neuronal organization integral to implementing the control.

There is considerable neurophysiological bias against labelling any physiologic structure or system as a control device, since the evidence indicates that no single structure is capable of the entire range of events necessary to control a physiologic activity. It is the entire system's activities which implement control. Physiologic systems, of course, *do* control themselves, but only to a limited extent, such as in reflex actions, but this is not intentional, voluntary control. Reflex control is the ability to return toward a stable state *after* a system has been disturbed.

The force or system or mechanism that directs selected activity toward a projected goal (the ability to project goals is a complex mental construct in itself), and which qualifies as voluntary, does so in such a way that the action is (a) appropriate to the situation, (b) compatible with the most parsimonious use of the physiologic mechanisms, and (c) precisely compatible with the projected, predetermined concept of the goal.

Certainly heuristically, postulating the existence of some controlling mechanisms or system is equally as valid as assuming transfers of associations in other learning theory. These other concepts have validity because some apparently related (correlative) behavior has been measured. The reason that a theory of a "supersystem" of voluntary control has not been seriously considered is probably because of the difficulty in measuring subjective activities. This difficulty is now being surmounted, both by improved techniques for testing and as a result of biofeedback. I cannot state too frequently the importance of EEG biofeedback in making possible relatively steady states of brain electrical activity. Once the brain electrical activity is reasonably steady, the subjective experiences which accompany it can be much more accurately identified.

Voluntary control, in contrast to the "stimulus control" of experimental psychology in which physiologic action is response to stimulus, implies that a particular physiologic activity or action can be evoked by intention of the individual.

What is enormously misleading in current biofeedback research, and especially in alpha biofeedback, is the failure of the researcher to document control. Most psychophysiologists assume that a statistically significant change in alpha activity in a group of subjects constitutes control. What this means to them is that the stimulus (the biofeedback signal) consistently elicits a response of certain magnitude of alpha change *on the average*. This is an erroneous interpretation on two counts: first, there is a great deal of variation in alpha activity and its reactivity both in individuals and from individual to individual. If this variation is not controlled for over appropriately long periods, particularly with respect to habituation to the experimental situation, no discrimination can be made between spontaneously occurring alpha and alpha occurring in response to a signal. That is, under situations where alpha comprises say more than 35 percent of the EEG pattern, as in relaxed conditions or with the eyes closed (which are the usual experimental conditions), the seemingly random, spontaneous appearance of alpha can frequently coincide with the alpha appearing in response to the signal. Special statistical treatment, using data from control studies, is required to eliminate the significant influence of coincidentally occuring spontaneous, cyclical alpha. If, as is usually done, the alpha responses are averaged among subjects in such an experiment, the spontaneous alpha is averaged in along with the response alpha, with the statistical result of a significant change. The resulting value does not, however, represent only the response alpha and is therefore misleading.

The vast majority of alpha biofeedback studies have been interpreted as showing that individuals have learned how to control their alpha activity. Except for my own publication, there has not been a single instance in which data has been provided that demonstrates subjects have learned to control alpha *without* the biofeedback signal, i.e., that they can consistently produce alpha upon demand, by intention. If biofeedback learning indeed is the learning of voluntary control over physiologic functions, then it should be an absolute requirement that the control can be demonstrated in the absence of the biofeedback monitor. Otherwise, the effect of alpha biofeedback cannot be distinguished from responses to a stimulus or habituation or the influence of its own inherent cyclic nature.

Numerous, in fact the majority of, recent biofeedback publications have seriously misused the concept of control. Almost unbelievably, some researchers have used an alpha training period of ten or fewer minutes, even breaking this short learning time into "trials," then have used extraordinarily inappropriate and weak statistics to "prove" that their subjects had learned how to control alpha activity. In addition to the failure to control for spontaneously occurring alpha, these studies are generally compounded by other quite gross errors, such as a few seconds of habituation time, no EEG records, poor instrumentation, no tests for alpha reactivity, etc. The tragedy of such papers appearing in specialty journals is that the rest of the scientific community tends to trust at least the editorial advisors that the studies published are reliable and representative of proper application of scientific methodology and logic. The fact that poor quality papers are flooding the psychology and medical journals is simply testimony to the scientific isolationism that has prevailed for so long between psychology and medical physiology.

2. *Concepts of Alpha.* There is a prevailing tendency for psychophysiologists to treat alpha as an entity or variable that can be manipulated with the simplicity that one manipulates a body chemical or a fundamental component of physiologic activity, and that as a specific element, it relates more or less precisely to specific, definable subjective or behavioral states. This is a grossly erroneous concept. It cannot be stated too emphatically that *alpha activity is a complex of EEG components,* that alpha activity is a fairly general index of the activity of the *whole* brain, that its appearance and form and characteristics are dependent upon numerous interacting brain activities (cortical, integrative, reticular, limbic, visual, etc.), and that, in fact, alpha activity is only a relatively small part of the brain's electrical components manifest in the EEG pattern.

There are two extremely important elements in the consideration of alpha activity. The first is that whatever alpha is, it is *not* necessarily or generally the most abundant or important component of the EEG pattern, and second, that alpha itself is a complex sign or phenomenon with many different features, each of which can reflect important influences. Alpha researchers consistently isolate alpha from the rest of the EEG pattern in a way that is quantifiably disproportionate to its actual prevalence. The average human being exhibits alpha activity only between one and perhaps 20 percent of the time when the eyes are open, and anywhere from 35 to 75 percent of the time when the eyes are closed. These values are obtained from recording devices which filter out higher frequency components long before the recording result is obtained, and as such, represent values valid only *after* prior electronic manipulation of the actual EEG. Frequently higher frequency EEG components "ride on top" of alpha waves; thus measurements of the abundance of alpha activity are almost always misleading and artificial. Even so, the usual values indicate that alpha rarely occupies more than 50 percent of the total EEG activity. When subjective or behavioral correlations are made to these values, the remainder of the EEG activity is ignored. If alpha is a valid index of any brain activity, it is most likely that it is an index of changing direction of the EEG pattern. With alpha as only one of hundreds of brain electrical activities occurring almost continuously and simultaneously, and the ease of rough measurement of alpha, its importance may have been either markedly overemphasized or over-generalized.

The neurophysiological literature, in contrast to the psychophysiological literature, reveals the complex nature of alpha and the importance of its various aspects or characteristics. Of greatest significance is that *each* of the aspects of alpha activity can be predisposing to specific effects and behavioral correlations. It is not merely the amount of alpha that is important, it is the specific nature of each of its characteristics. There are at least *eleven* quite different elements of alpha that have been demonstrated to be of individual and significant specific importance to specific and significant subjective or behavioral characteristics. These are: abundance, specific frequency, amplitude, topographical location, phase (propagation time), synchrony, variability, reactivity, and the burst characteristics of rate of onset, duration, and frequency of occurrence.

For example, higher than average I.Q.s have been correlated with fast alpha (11 to 13 Hz), a more reactive alpha, and with a hemispheric asymmetry of alpha, while different cognitive styles have been related to differences in alpha dominance in the two hemispheres. Different amplitudes of alpha, low and high, not only relate to different states of consciousness, but also relate to different abilities for learning control over alpha production. Slow, regular, abundant alpha has been related to passive personality and underachieving, as well as to related behavioral problems.

The reactivity of alpha is also an important consideration. As noted before, many individuals innately respond to an alerting stimulus, not by a disappearance of alpha, but with the appearance or *increase* of alpha. Compensated neurotics may show resting high amplitude abundant alpha, but react with a striking alpha blocking response to even a mild sensory stimulus. Other personality types may react to the same stimuli by a brief flood of alpha. The rate of the habituation of the alpha blocking response serves as an index to distinguish neurotic and psychotic from normal behavior.

These are only a few of the relationships established between specific features of alpha activity and specific characteristics of subjective and behavioral activity. It is obvious, then, that generalizations on correlations between "alpha" and any specific behavior can be distorted either in a positive or negative direction by the make-up of the subject population. This is much less true of a patient population in which the disease process has influenced EEG activity in a direction peculiar to that pathology.

The same general principle appears to hold for alpha biofeedback training. The biofeedback signal monitoring the alpha tends to elicit responses of alpha appropriate to the particular situation, that is, whether the situation is relaxing, sensory limited, or does or does not contain stimuli evoking reactions. The clinical effectiveness of alpha biofeedback may bear little resemblance to effects of alpha training obtained experimentally in which almost ghoulish tests are carried out to prove one or another theoretical points (such as rolling the eyes, confined in total darkness, using conditioning signals that have alerting qualities such as tones, lights, using electric shocks, etc.).

The tendency for non-neurophysiologist researchers to treat alpha as a single experimental variable with special properties and precise relationships to behavior has led to the extraordinary misconception that the disappearance of alpha from the EEG pattern represents an arousal response. For example, in a survey of all research papers to date dealing with alpha activity that have appeared in psychology specialty journals, the disappearance of alpha from the EEG pattern has been equated with arousal in at least 85 percent of the articles. One reason for the emphasis on arousal is that arousal theory constitutes the major and easiest experimental psychophysiological approach to the study of behavior. The no-alpha arousal interpretation is based upon EEG research of more than twenty-five years ago and ignores research published in neurophysiological journals in which quantifications of basal EEG alpha activity, stimulus strength, and temporal aspects reveals that (a) an arousal stimulus elicits alpha *production* in 50 percent of the normally distributed population, and (b) whether alpha appears or disappears in an alerting situation is dependent upon a variety of factors, such as inherent EEG pattern, personality, strength of stimulus, and significance of the stimulus.

While the ideal of physiological arousal occupies the psychology researcher, it is a selected aspect of altering (or arousal) that has the most critical relevance to clinical problems. When the psychologic researcher speaks of arousal and arousal theory, he is speaking of the generalized physiological response of any organism, which includes "arousal" of the autonomic nervous system, the skeletal muscles, and the central nervous system. This concept is fully discussed in Chapter 2. It is generally assumed that attention is part of arousal, and that directing or focussing one's attention involves physiologic activity similar to that in arousal, but in attenuated form. More recent research and particularly that excited by both biofeedback and by effects of yogic and Zen meditation indicates that different *types* of attention are accompanied by different EEG patterns. A good bit of research evidence suggests that reasonably persistent alpha (or theta, or probably the persistence of any EEG pattern) is a characteristic of a particular type of attention, i.e., those kinds of attention that are directed toward internal events. There seems to be some justification for the concept that certain EEG beta patterns, or no-alpha patterns, accompany different kinds or degrees of attention to *external* stimuli or events, while certain types of alpha EEG patterns accompany different degrees and kinds of attention to *internal* stimuli or events.

Evidence that different kinds of alpha activities in fact do occur when the attention is directly inwardly come from meditation, biofeedback, autogenic training, and hypnosis studies. For example, most studies of Zen meditation report a dominant EEG pattern of slow alpha frequency, often in the range of 6 to 8 Hz, whereas it has been reported that autogenic training can result in an increase in alpha frequency of about one Hz. In an extensive study of the EEG activity of advanced yogic practitioners, Das and Gastaut (1957) found that the more profound the meditation, the faster the EEG waves. In the early stages of the yogic meditation, alpha frequency increased remarkably, and, in fact, would not be ordinarily called alpha.[2] I have personally recorded EEGs from two Indian swamis advanced in yogic meditation in my laboratory and found exactly the same kinds of EEG patterns as Das and Gastaut. In contrast, Green, working with Swami Rama, found slow alpha wave activity.

Finally, I have always been fascinated with one particular aspect of alpha biofeedback. As I reported in 1970, almost immediately after an individual begins the biofeedback experience, the frequency of his alpha reduces by a full cycle per second. This has been reported more recently by other investigators. One of the theories of the neurophysiological significance of alpha is that it serves some kind of timing or pacing function. Investigations into the origin of alpha indicate that there are at least three "generators" responsible for the fundamental alpha frequency in different brain areas. If there is a fundamental alpha frequency which is often masked when alpha is recorded at the scalp by all of the brain electrical activities that influence it, then whatever brain perceptual mechanisms are triggered by the biofeedback signal may feed back in such a way as to modulate and slow the alpha frequency. This effect may be due in part, or possibly in its entirety, to a mechanical artifact contributed by the filters used in EEG biofeedback as discussed below under instrumentation. This biofeedback as discussed below under instrumentation. This biofeedback effect is reminiscent of the effects of repetitive visual or auditory stimuli in the alpha frequency range. At certain intensity levels, the electrical activity of the visual or auditory cortex produces alpha-like waves which follow the stimulus frequency, while at slightly higher stimulus intensity levels the stimuli actually drive the cortex in the sense that more and more brain areas respond with alpha-like waves. It may be possible that, depending upon the locus of the internal events, the brain electrical activities contributing to both the events and the attention to the events can modulate alpha frequency in either direction.

3. *Methodology.* One serious difficulty in trying to compare laboratory with clinical effects of alpha biofeedback is the difference in procedures used. Researchers have a

---

2. See Figure 11.

number of favorite gambits they use in an attempt to uncover mechanisms or influences involved or to test theories,
and many of these can in themselves affect the course of
alpha activity. On the other hand, the practitioner is interested solely in the effect of the learning to control alpha
on the course of an illness, and intervenes in the training
only with measures supportive to the objective of the
training.

Unhappily, because the clinician has come to rely upon the experimental work done to establish new drugs, he
frequently follows the experimental techniques as a means
of replicating effects. This is good procedure when it
comes to using drugs, but research and clinical studies are
vastly different when it comes to biofeedback. For example, a large majority of research studies with alpha use
the experimental prototype of operant conditioning designed to demonstrate that two opposing directions of a
response can be elicited or conditioned by the same reinforcement. This is the alpha experiment in which short
periods, no more than 90 seconds, are alternated between reinforcing production and then reinforcing the
suppression of alpha activity. Because the underlying
neurological mechanisms of these two states of alpha are
both different from each other and complex, this amounts
to the individual having to learn two quite different
physiological activities almost simultaneously. Just as soon
as he begins to get a clue how to accomplish one objective, the learning trial is switched to the opposite.

In the clinical situation, where the objective is to increase the production of alpha activity, it is obviously
most disruptive to learning to be faced with alternating
between two objectives, one of which is the antithesis of
the therapeutic objective. Yet time after time, the clinical
investigator, unfamiliar with either the neurophysiology
of alpha or with the flow of procedures from laboratory
to clinic, faithfully alternates training trials designed to
increase and then suppress alpha activity. A look at the
successful therapeutic applications of alpha training shows
that the clinical investigators used single objective training, with sessions of adequate length and with adequate
numbers of training sessions. (It is, however, true that to
demonstrate control, the individual needs to learn how to
suppress alpha activity equally as well as produce it, but
these two learning tasks are best tackled separately.)

The relationship between alpha activity and visual mechanisms is important to the alpha biofeedback learning process, and is important to recognize in the selection of procedure.

Ever since the discovery of the alpha rhythm, investigations of the role of visual mechanisms in the appearance and disappearance of alpha in the EEG pattern have been a large part of the research effort. The relationships between EEG alpha and visual phenomena are complex because they involve both direct and indirect neuronal connections between the eye muscles and brain as well as effects deriving from the significance and implications of the visual material. Eye movements and eye tremors, which are common, can, under fairly ordinary circumstances, affect, actually evoke, alpha or alpha-like activity; similarly, the meaning of the visual information can result in feelings of relaxation or apprehension. Some neurophysiological studies have indicated that the primary effect on alpha is the visual input, and other studies have shown that the greater the complexity of the visual input, the stronger is the alpha blocking response. This relationship may, however, be more complicated in view of research showing that the alpha blocking response is generally found only in individuals whose alpha activity is in the middle alpha frequency range (8.5 to 10.5 Hz). This finding suggests that it is the state of the underlying brain electrical activity that determines how visual information is processed, i.e., according to how its significance is interpreted. Nor does this need to be consciously appreciated, since, for example, Dixon has shown that individuals also respond differently in their alpha reactivity to subliminal stimuli. Approximately 50 percent *produce* alpha activity in response to threatening subliminal stimuli, while the other 50 percent respond by a decrease in alpha activity.

These kinds of research studies mean that such things as "arousal" or "alerting" stimuli can have different effects in different people, as has been demonstrated in other neurophysiological studies.

Some people, in whom eye muscle-visual cortex neuronal connections play a dominant role, readily learn to control alpha by means of unconscious eye movements. A good example of this, although on a conscious level, is the trick Dewan used. He showed people how to send Morse code by producing different durations of alpha bursts simply by moving their eyes upward for different lengths of time.

The important issue is the problem of procedure; the simple choice between learning situations with the eyes open or the eyes closed, or a judicious sequence of these sensory conditions. It is a simple fact that alpha becomes maximal in amount when the eyes are closed. Since the objective of alpha training is to increase the amount of alpha, and particularly to acquire the ability to carry over the learning and the subjective accompaniments to real-life situations, then the training conditions should be those which can ensure the greatest and most effective amount of learning. When the eyes are closed, and after an adaptation period, let's say the alpha content of the EEG is around 70 percent, actually an average figure. Since the maximal amount of alpha normally possible in the EEG is about 90 percent (owing to its cyclic appearance in bursts), then the greatest change possible from alpha training would be about 20 percent. On the other hand, while the average amount of alpha in the eyes-open EEG pattern may reach 10 to 20 percent, if the individual is relaxed, the maximum possible amount is still some 90 percent. This means that the maximal change can extend to 75 or 80 percent, which is a good deal more "learning room." Even more relevant is the fact that real-life situations are generally those where the eyes are open (and absorbing the significance of the visual scene). No studies have been reported that learned biofeedback-increased alpha in the eyes-closed condition carries over to the eyes-open state; on the contrary, Travis and colleagues in a careful study found *no* relationship between alpha learning performance with the eyes closed and with the eyes open.

The major justification for alpha training with the eyes closed would be to induce an initial stage of relaxation conducive to further learning.

Oftentimes research methodological errors are undetected in the discussion, interpretation, or in the publicity of dramatic results, either positive or negative. One group of investigators published a paper that received media coverage largely because they claimed their studies demonstrated alpha has little to do with relief from apprehension, arousal, or anxiety. The crux of their argument was that when people were trained with alpha biofeedback in total darkness, and with their eyes closed, their EEGs failed to respond to a noxious stimulus, an electric shock (painful but noninjuring!). The relationship between anticipation of, or apprehension about, a forthcoming painful electric shock to clinical anxiety is about the same as the relationship between riding a benign hobby horse and a bucking bronco. While it is generally (but not always) true that anxious people are hyperactive to unexpected stimuli, they may not be to anticipated stimuli, and it has never been demonstrated that the apprehension in an electric shock experiment is related to either the psychologic or physiologic conditions of nonspecific apprehension and anxiety. More serious deficiencies in the study were that the investigators made no attempt to demonstrate that the EEG response, i.e., the disappearance of alpha, to anticipation actually does occur in the habituated, eyes-closed alpha state, nor was any data provided to indicate whether the reported changes of alpha abundance were due to the presence of the conditioning, reinforcing signal or due to a learned change in alpha. In fact, the figures provided indicate that no real change in alpha abundance occurred that was different from that in control conditions! The primary evidence cited for the conclusion that alpha was unrelated to relief from anxiety was that the volunteer subjects reported (a highly subjective evaluation, subject to numerous influences) being apprehensive while waiting for the electric shock, whereas no change in alpha occurred at the moment of shock although there was a change in skin electrical activity, the indicator that was used to establish anxiety and apprehension. The investigators concluded that alpha training is useless for anxiety, that training to produce alpha simply may assist subjects in learning how to ignore otherwise distracting influences which would account for the reports that increased alpha activity is accompanied by calm, tranquil, and peaceful states. Which, of course, is one chief objective of alpha training; by learning to turn the attention inwardly, you naturally decrease the visual input of anxiety-related information.

The point here is that the study did indeed reveal a highly significant relationship between alpha *reactivity* and the anticipation of or apprehension about a potential noxious stimulus. If the physiological indices such as skin electrical activity, or possibly heart rate (which changed marginally), did reflect body responses, then a more reasonable interpretation of these results would be (a) that the more primitive arousal mechanisms have a much lower threshold for responsiveness than do the cerebral mechanisms, or (b) that the cerebral mechanisms concerned with alpha activity can be readily dissociated from the autonomic arousal mechanisms (a dissociation which has been demonstrated repeatedly in pharmacological experiments), or (c) that the mechanisms that subserve alpha are related to those which foster an internal focus of attention, such as cerebral mechanisms involved in the appreciation and evaluation of the significance of stimuli; hence augmented alpha production would decrease attention to the external environment and increase attention paid to internal or interior events, or (d) that cerebral and autonomic arousal are mediated by two different processes of the central nervous system.

There is little justification for deducing much of anything about alpha activity in the eyes-closed, total darkness condition. The bulk of neurophysiological evidence about alpha shows an intimate relationship with visual mechanisms. Nor is the relationship a simple one, as noted above. Over and above the effects from eye movement activity, there is the influence of the cognitive recognition of the significance of the visual stimuli as well as the influence of a correlate of visual dependence, that experiential significance of visual stimuli which establishes patterns and habits for focussing attention. Just ask someone to remember some obscure event, and his eyes will roll in various habitual directions, patterns so firm that psychologists have now defined right and left eye movers.

*4. Role of Information.* If biofeedback is considered as an information-processing phenomenon, a good bit of insight about the best ways to use biofeedback training can be gained. The first consideration is the fidelity of the physiological information as provided by the biofeedback instrument; this is discussed in the following section. For now, assuming a fairly high fidelity of biofeedback information (e.g., reasonably accurate indicators of alpha abundance or amplitude or symmetry), the first procedural problem lies in conveying the *significance* of the indicator to the patient. It is generally found that cognitively useful information about what the brain waves represent, how they are recorded and analyzed, what they relate to with respect to subjective states, how the biofeedback instrument works, etc., helps to bridge the relationship between the patient and the instrumentation and procedure. The patient uses this information both directly and indirectly to understand his role and the objective of the training.

The second procedural problem is that the patient probably hasn't the faintest idea of what to do to produce more alpha, or any other EEG component. This is remedied by providing strategy information, much as in the EMG biofeedback procedures. Concepts such as turning the attention inwardly, relaxing physically, not trying, emptying the mind, encouraging the patient to invent mental strategies, are all useful strategies.

As described in Chapter 2, a third kind of information is supportive, reinforcing, and motivating. For some people, and especially patients, the first few alpha biofeedback training sessions may be the equivalent of cultural shock. The person as patient is used to the tradition of being controlled, by drugs, or advice, or by the authority of the therapist. His first insights into biofeedback, and especially when the procedure involves something as unknown as tampering with brain waves, is often the awareness that he actually has to learn to do something new and unknown to assist his recovery, and that external dependence is no longer there for support. This recognition, in the face of the traditional dependencies, can create considerable emotional confusion for the patient, making him unsure of his role and status. It is in this period that supportive measures can be important for his learning.

In sum, the type, quality, quantity, significance, and relevance of all varieties of information relevant to the learning process are important adjuncts to the alpha biofeedback learning process. It is not like giving a youngster a bicycle and letting him learn for himself; it is more like suddenly being faced with learning how to pilot a space ship without ever having flown.

*5. Instrumentation.* Nowhere in the instrumentation of physiologic activities is the design and accuracy of the device more important than in EEG work. While many people new to EEG biofeedback are familiar with the

concept of electronic filtering to isolate particular EEG
components of interest, such as alpha, most are not
familiar with the conventional design of signal amplifiers
in the ordinary EEG machine. For the most part, the
electrical activity detected by the scalp electrodes is composed of many different frequencies of rhythmic and nonrhythmic waves ranging between 0.2 and several hundred
Hertz. The conventional EEG amplifier, however, in order
to reduce electrical noise and interference, employs filters
which reduce the amplitude of the EEG by some 50 to
80 percent at EEG frequencies of one Hz and below and
similarly reduce the amplitude of EEG components which
have a frequency of 30 Hz and above. The significance of
this is that traditional EEG studies and literature are really concerned only with EEG frequencies between one and
about 30 Hz.

Many people working with EEG biofeedback are not
familiar with the characteristics of the electronic filters
used in their instruments, yet the filter is one of the three
critical elements of the instrument. Active, analogue
filters that are generally used are characterized in terms of
roll-off, i.e., the amplitude and frequency characteristics
of the edges of the filter. This means that EEG signals
of a specific amplitude and at the designated edge frequencies do not pass through the filter. This does *not*
mean, however, that EEG frequencies near the filter
limits will not pass if their amplitudes are high enough.
Suppose, for example, that a filter is designed for an
"alpha" range of 7 to 13 Hz (which is unusually wide);
then waves of 6.5 or 6 Hz will not pass through the
filter *only if* their amplitudes do not exceed the set limits.
Unfortunately these limits are rather small, meaning that
slower waves of 6 or 5 or 4 Hz can pass through the filter
because the amplitudes of these lower frequencies are
generally quite large. Waves of frequencies higher than
the upper filter limits are generally not of large amplitude
and so are not a major problem.

Many operators of biofeedback instruments misuse the
instruments by setting either the EEG amplifier gain too
high or setting the threshold for filter action too high.
These manipulations overdrive the filters such that a wide
range of frequencies pass through the filters, not just
those designated as characteristic of the filter action. This
amounts to nothing more than using the instrument to

discriminate between very low and somewhat higher amplitude EEG activity regardless of frequency.

Another question about instrumentaton is: should the feedback signal be analogue or digital? When alpha or theta or any specific EEG component is used for the biofeedback signal, the signal generally represents either the amplitude or the abundance of the EEG component, or an integration of the total voltage of the filtered waves over a convenient time period, such as 0.5, 1, 2, 5, or 10 seconds. In each case the feedback signal is activated by a voltage, and the analogue form simply means that the intensity of the display signal varies directly with the voltage. When *amplitude* of the alpha activity is used for the feedback signal, the analogue display, either auditory or visual, actually provides two "bits" of information because it signals both the presence of alpha and the amplitude. When the biofeedback signal is a measure of the *amount* of alpha present in the EEG, there are also two "bits" of information: the length of time alpha is present as well as how much is present. The integrated signal (sum of the voltages over time) also gives only two "bits" of information, the presence and the relative amount of alpha in terms of combined amplitude *and* frequency. None of the currently used EEG biofeedback instruments gives information about the frequency of alpha.

A digital signal simply divides the voltages into convenient parts. If the digital signal gives information about the amplitude of alpha, or any of the parameters used for analogue displays, the number of bits of information is actually the same as for analogue signalling.

It is when the feedback signal is used as a reinforcement, after the fact, that less information is conveyed. When the signal simply indicates that some criterion has been reached, such as producing X amount of alpha, the amount of information is solely that the criterion has been met. Further, the confirming signal does not necessarily coincide with the physiologic event, and information indicating ongoing activity and changes is lost. Most research studies purporting to investigate the mechanisms of alpha biofeedback use the biofeedback signal as reinforcement. Essentially, the individual is "rewarded" by the reinforcement for performance of a particular activity. In the clinical use of biofeedback, where the feedback signal is given as a continuing monitor of the physiological activity, the signal does have a certain reinforcing value, but its primary effect is as a conveyor of information about the process. Moreover, as learning progresses, the value of the information changes. The information conveyed by an occasional burst of alpha is quite different from the information conveyed by frequently occurring bursts; the first is an indication of direction, a guide, and the second is largely confirmatory that the strategies are being successful.

A potentially embarrassing instrumental problem for alpha biofeedback, particularly for research studies, may lie in the contribution of the physical characteristics of filters to the alpha biofeedback effect. This is the characteristic of all filters for averaging random activity toward the midpoint of the filter. If, for example, an alpha filter has a band pass of 8 to 12 Hz, the midpoint of the filter is 10 Hz; if the filter range is from 9 to 13 Hz, the midpoint will be 11 Hz, but if the range is from 7 to 13, the midpoint will be 10 Hz. The nature of EEG recording, with its difficulties in amplifying its very low voltages and the electrical interference, is such that there frequently can be significant amounts of random electrical activity that influence the filter and result in an instrumental, non-EEG, increase of filtered activity around the frequency midpoint of the filter. The poorer the technique of electrode attachment, and the poorer the instrument, the greater this effect is.

This action of the filter may account for the persistently occurring, puzzling result of most alpha biofeedback studies which have used the continuous feedback signal. Average alpha frequencies are generally reported as 10 Hz or slower. This would not be an unexpected result in certain psychoses, drug abuse problems, or social behavioral problems, since the average alpha frequency is generally on the low side in such patients. It will be of interest when clinical investigators begin to use training for these kinds of patients which will increase alpha frequency.

# EXAMPLES OF NORMAL
# EEG PATTERNS AND EEG ACTIVITY
# DURING THETA BIOFEEDBACK

Brain wave (EEG) biofeedback is rapidly increasing in appeal to the biofeedback practitioner because of its surprising range of effects and its apparent effectiveness and efficiency in the treatment of disorders discussed in Chapter 7.

There is, however, no existing guide which defines the kinds of EEG patterns which can be found in a cross-section of the population. Moreover, no illustrative material exists on the course of events occurring during EEG biofeedback training. The examples of EEG records selected for this Appendix were chosen mainly to illustrate different kinds of normal EEG patterns and the way in which EEG patterns change with biofeedback training. Some records also demonstrate the use of procedural parameters helpful to establishing the validity and accuracy of EEG recording.

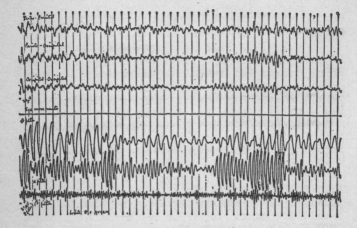

Fig. 12. Record from a normal individual showing a frequently occurring EEG pattern. On the left hand side there is very
poorly formed irregular theta (large, irregular waves) which is
picked up by the theta filter (fifth line) that reads theta only
when amplitude increases and rhythmicity occurs. Theta activity can be seen in all three of the EEG leads: when theta
disappears, very slow irregularly formed alpha-theta activity
can be seen in the occipital region (third line) and very irregular activity in the other two areas. Presently alpha appears
in the parietal-occipital and occipital leads and this is picked
up and shown in the alpha filter (sixth line).

Fig. 13. An EEG record illustrating the various ways alpha can appear in the EEG pattern.

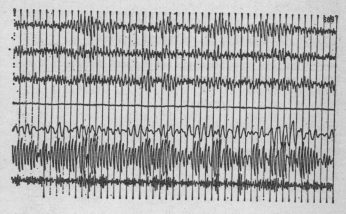

Fig. 13A.

Fig. 13A. Reading top to bottom, the records are (1) right temporal-parietal; (2) right parietal-occipital; (3) right occipital-occipital; (4) eye movements: (5) filtered theta; (6) filtered alpha; (7) filtered beta 13–28 Hz.

The subject's eyes are closed and the EEG record illustrates both how alpha activity can appear to be the only component present in the EEG yet vary in its characteristics. Throughout the record alpha cyclically waxes and wanes in amplitude. These changes are typical alpha bursts despite the fact that the background EEG is also mainly alpha, but of a smaller amplitude. Variations in alpha frequency can also be seen by noting differences in breadth of individual waves.

The tracing also shows the difference in clarity in alpha bursting among different leads and indicates that alpha bursts may occur independently in the frontal (temporal) areas as indicated by a large slowish alpha burst in the first lead on the left hand side, not accompanied by a very pronounced alpha burst in the third lead, but soon an alpha burst occurs in the third lead but none in lead 1 but almost immediately thereafter all leads show a burst of alpha. Subsequently there are well-defined alpha bursts in the top lead and poorly defined if any alpha activity in the occipital-occipital lead. The record of the filtered information in the last three leads is from the second recording, the parietal-occipital lead.

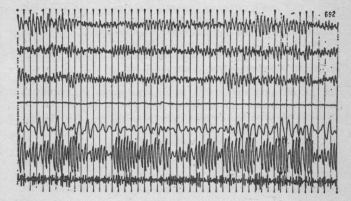

Fig. 13B.

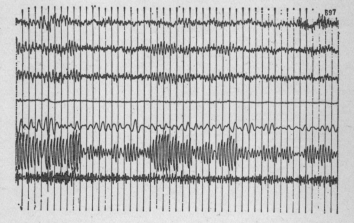

Fig. 13C.

Figs. 13B and C. Clearer discrimination in alpha activity can be seen among three leads and between small, medium-size, and large-amplitude alpha activity. The subject opens his eyes. There is an immediate desynchronization (loss of rhythmic activity and decrease in amplitude) of the EEG pattern but within two seconds alpha bursting occurs in the parietal and occipital regions, followed by fast EEG activity and low amplitude occipital alpha. This is in sharp contrast to the dominance of activity with the eyes closed in this individual who showed his dominant alpha activity in the temporal regions with the eyes closed.

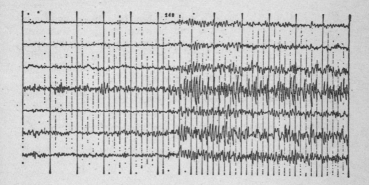

Fig. 14. This record shows the effect of adequate amplification on EEG recording. In the first portion the amplification of the EEG machine was that used for diagnostic EEG recording. In the second half the amplification was increased some 2 to 3 times in order to make the various EEG components more visible. The record is totally free of electrical interference and a wide variety of frequencies can be seen. A second item of interest is that the leads 1, 2, and 3 are from the left hemisphere and leads 4, 5, and 6 are from the right hemisphere, respectively, of the temporal, parietal, and occipital regions. The seventh lead is a pairing between right and left occipital areas.

A comparison of the kinds of activity from right to left hemisphere shows a considerable difference in the activity of the two hemispheres. The differences are mainly in amplitude, although some differences in frequencies can be seen. The alpha is rather high frequency and shows many irregular components.

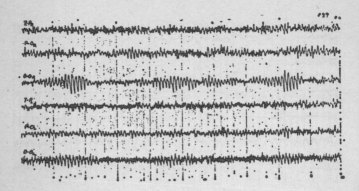

Fig. 15. From a normal subject showing both alpha activity and high frequency rhythmic activity. The high frequency activity is predominant in the right and left temporal areas although occasionally they contain a few alpha waves. On the whole the EEG is high frequency, very rhythmic, and rather high amplitude activity for this kind of fast EEG activity. The two occipital leads and particularly the one on the right side show alpha activity. The right occipital shows considerable alpha activity with the typical bursting characteristics. The left occipital lead is contaminated by noise and the fast EEG activity cannot be seen.

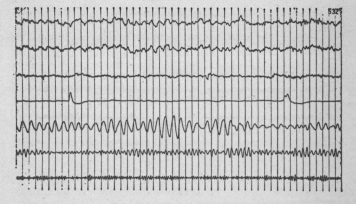

Fig. 16. The same lead configuration is followed. The record shows an extremely alerted EEG pattern. The background EEG activity is very low amplitude. The second lead from the top is the one which has been used for the filter activity. The filtered theta record (fifth trace) shows considerable theta activity although it is poorly defined in the original EEG. This is a typical orienting kind of EEG.

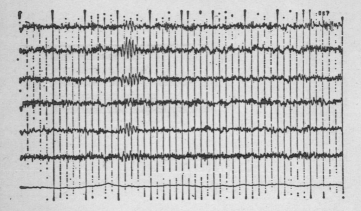

Fig. 17. EEG leads are the same as described for the other figures from the left and right hemispheres with the bottom trace being eye movements. The record is interesting because it shows a very high frequency rhythmic activity, particularly in the right and left temporal areas. The large bursting activity, about one third of the way through the record, is alpha and it occurs in all but the left temporal and left occipital region. The alpha looks like any alpha, it is high amplitude and well defined, but it occurs very rarely in this subject, who was a heavy smoker. Some of the EEG leads contain high frequency muscle artifacts and when these are irregular they cannot be discriminated from irregular high frequency EEG activity. High frequency muscle artifacts are frequent in anxious individuals.

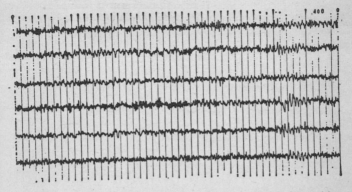

Fig. 18. This is a record from another heavy smoker subject and shows very much the same kind of activity as that in Figure 17. The subject's eyes wer closed and the record shows very high frequency rhythmic activity (beta) with only occasional very low voltage alpha activity in the right parietal and occipital leads.

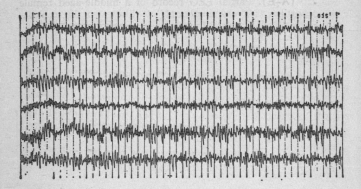

Fig. 19. A record from another heavy smoker subject showing, again, very high frequency, very rhythmic EEG activity. It is exceptional because the amplitude of the high frequency activity is very large. Toward the left hand side one burst of alpha activity can be seen.

Fig. 20 (A–E). Partial EEG record of a middle-aged female self-reporting as "very emotional." It illustrates the remarkable range of EEG activity that can be seen in the space of one hour of recording. The subject is participating in a theta biofeedback training experiment. The three EEG activity tracings are (1) temporo-parietal, (2) parietal-occipital, and (3) occipital-occipital. Skipping the straight line, the next record is of horizontal eye movements.

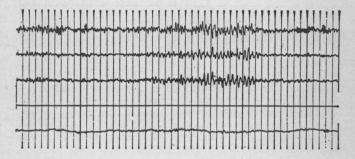

Fig. 20A. Excerpt from the early part of the recording session. EEG shows an alert pattern and occasional bursts of very high frequency rhythmic activity in lead 1 (temporo-parietal). The higher amplitude activity in the middle of the record is an interesting development of alpha, since it begins with a marked increase in amplitude and either fast activity (temporal region) or irregularly formed waves, and finally slows to a more or less conventional run of alpha activity.

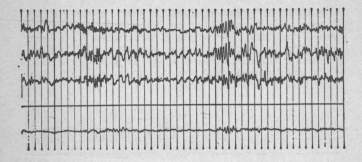

Fig. 20B. Although eyes are open and subject is receiving biofeedback of theta activity, the amplitude of the EEG has increased and is alternating between fast rhythmic activity and large slow waves. Midway through the tracing poorly defined theta waves can be seen in the parietal-occipital and occipital tracings, followed by a short burst of large amplitude alpha.

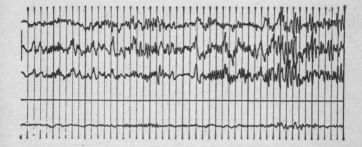

Fig. 20C. Shift from mixed slow wave and fast rhythmic activity toward bursts of high amplitude alpha activity. The subject here reported being very relaxed but not drowsy.

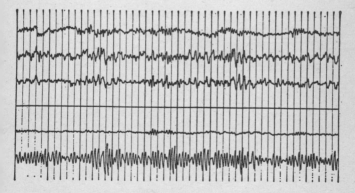

Fig. 20D. Record of filtered alpha added as the last recording channel. The patient is toward the end of the theta biofeedback session and shows a tendency toward stabilizing her theta at a frequency of about 6 Hz.

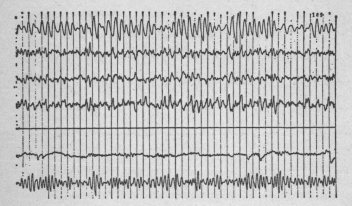

Fig. 20E. Record of filtered theta added as the first tracing. The subject's EEG pattern is now consistently slow and high amplitude.

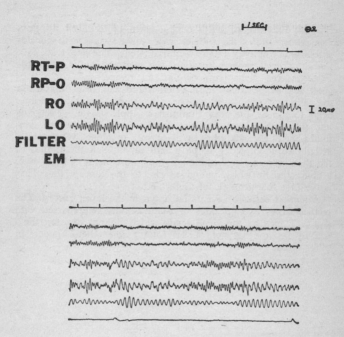

Fig. 21.

Fig. 21. Example of EEG during theta biofeedback training. Top record shows the subject in a relaxed state with considerable alpha activity in the occipital areas. The first trace is a time marker, 1 second duration, the second trace is a recording from the right temporal-parietal region and contains a great deal of electrical noise, often found with recordings from the temporal region. It can be seen that when alpha waves begin to appear, the noise diminishes. Approximately 2 seconds into this record, theta activity begins very abruptly and continues for 5 seconds when it gives way to alpha. When alpha activity recurs it looks to be a half alpha, half theta, that is, the theta waves look as though they were being split in two, a characteristic which has given rise to the concept that theta is the first subharmonic of alpha activity.

A similar series of events is shown in the lower record. The record shows two episodes of theta activity interspersed with alpha. Typically, the EEG leads which do not develop theta activity become desynchronized (alert) when theta appears in other areas.

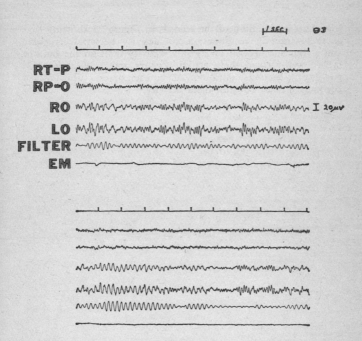

Fig. 22.

Fig. 22. Continuation of the records in Figure 21 showing that as theta training continues, alpha activity becomes irregular and at times is broken up by slow activity until on the bottom record well-formed theta activity occurs and is of at least 3, possibly 5, seconds' duration. As before, other cortical areas become "alerted" during theta activity.

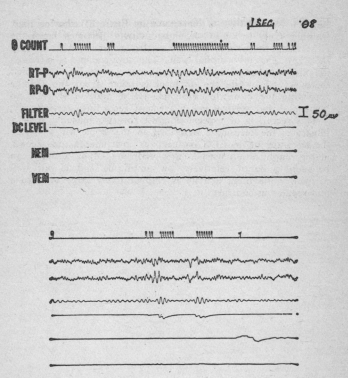

Fig. 23.

Fig. 23. Record from a subject during EEG theta biofeedback training. Only two EEG leads are shown: RT-P is from the right temporal-parietal pair of electrodes and RP-O is from the right parietal-occipital pair. The top tracing is a rough index of number of theta waves; filter is a recording of filtered theta activity, while the dc level is taken from the voltage activating the biofeedback signal. HEM and VEM refer to horizontal and vertical eye movement recordings respectively.

This record is of especial interest for two reasons: first, it illustrates the technique described in the book for verifying the accuracy of an EEG biofeedback instrument; and second, at the amplification used in this recording, alpha activity can be seen to be of relatively low amplitude and is not well formed, while theta activity is comparatively large amplitude and regular in contrast.

Fig. 24. (A–G). First session of a subject beginning theta biofeedback training.

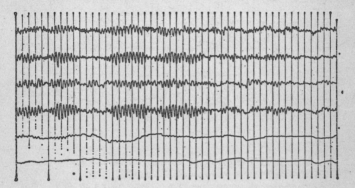

Fig. 24A. Top to bottom tracings: (1) EEG lead 1 temporo-parietal electrode pairing; (2) EEG lead 2, parietal-occipital; (3) EEG lead 3, occipital-occipital; (4) same as EEG lead 2; (5) horizontal eye movements; (6) vertical eye movements. All EEG leads are from the left hemisphere. In general, alpha tends to appear in all leads at the same time, which is somewhat unusual. Alpha typically appears in "bursts"; those on the left side are very rhythmic and show the typical waxing and waning, then suddenly the amplitude decreases and rhythmicity diminishes. Even though the eyes are closed there is considerable eye movement activity both horizontally and vertically.

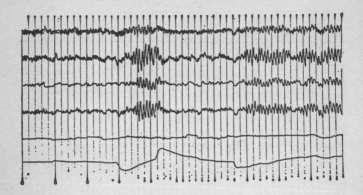

Fig. 24B. EEG events upon closing the eyes. The EEG is intensely alert. Eyes were open. A typical, large vertical eye movement occurs when the eyes close. Although one alpha burst appears immediately with closing the eyes, alpha does not become sustained for 3 seconds, EEG lead 1 has developed considerable electrical "noise" in the record, which is prominent with the eyes open but later becomes masked by the alpha when the eyes are closed. (The leads involved were subsequently changed to eliminate the noise.)

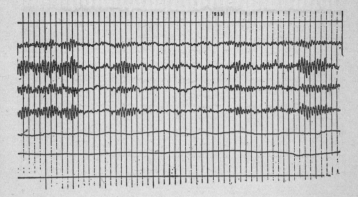

Fig. 24C. Change in EEG activity occurring with shift in mental attention in the eyes-closed condition. Because the subject has had his eyes closed for some time, alpha activity is near maximal with respect to abundance and amplitude. Alpha is completely lost as the subject's attention shifts then soon returns maximally.

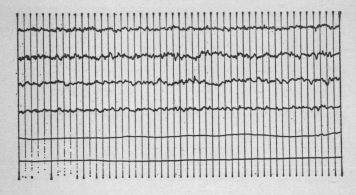

Fig. 24D. Tracing from start of theta biofeedback training. Subject shows a very alert type of EEG pattern, but the experienced eye can detect signs of theta activity although it is very poorly defined.

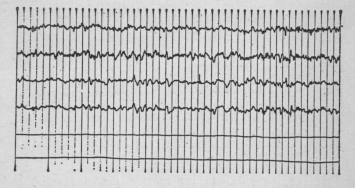

Fig. 24E. Ten minutes later the amplitude of the EEG slow waves increased and theta activity appears to be forming.

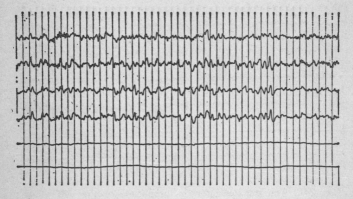

Fig. 24F. Minutes later the amplitude of the slow waves increased considerably and theta activity can be seen in leads 2, 3, and 4.

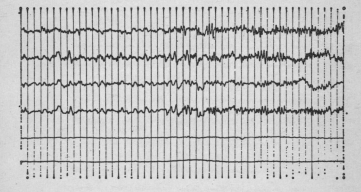

Fig. 24G. Two minutes later, subject no longer sustains slow wave activity and the amplitude of the EEG first decreases and then reverts to fast rhythmic activity in the upper range of alpha activity.

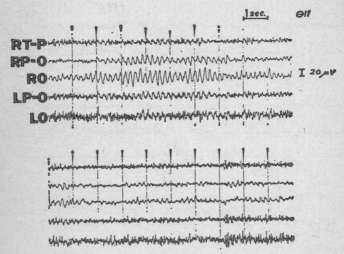

Fig. 25. This individual is *not* receiving theta biofeedback. He was a very nervous individual. The middle of the top record indicates the kind of activity this individual showed consistently throughout his EEG recording, i.e., remarkable theta activity. It is predominant in the right occipital area. The other leads have so much electrical noise and muscle artifact that other activity cannot be precisely determined; nonetheless, when slow wave activity occurs it tends to "override" the electrical interference. The lower tracing shows his normal EEG pattern when it does not contain well-defined theta activity: very low voltage pattern, with very irregular waves and marked muscle electrical interference.

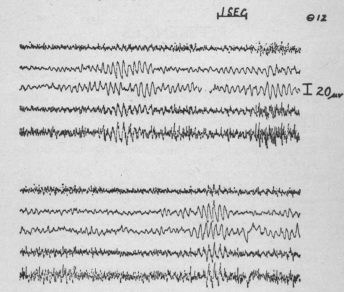

Fig. 26. This record is a continuation of the spontaneous normal EEG tracing shown in Figure 25. The theta activity was a consistent feature of his record, but in this record the theta is better formed now in the left hemisphere. In both the upper and lower tracings the difference in amplitude of theta activity can be easily seen, e.g., in the upper record in the third EEG lead, there is a quantity of approximately 15–20 µV theta which suddenly increases in bursts to somewhere between 20 and 30 microvolts.

# REFERENCES

## Chapters 2 and 3. EMG Biofeedback

Aarons, L.: Subvocalization: Aural and EMG feedback in reading. *Percept Mot Skills,* 1971, *33:*271.

Aarons, L.: Diurnal variations of muscle action potentials and word associations related to psychological orientation. *Psychophysiology,* 1968, *5:*77–91.

Agras, S. W.; Leitenberg, H.; Barlow, D. H.; Curtis, N.; Edwards, J.; and Wright, D.: Relaxation in systematic desensitization, *Arch Gen Psychiat,* 1971, *25:*511.

Alexander, A. B.; French, C. A.; and Goodman, N. J.: A comparison of auditory and visual feedback in biofeedback assisted muscular relaxation training. *Psychophysiology,* 1975, *12:*119–123.

Alexander, A. B.: An experimental test of assumptions relating to the use of electromyographic biofeedback as a general relaxation training technique. *Psychophysiology,* 1975, *12:*656–662.

Badri, M. B.: A new technique for the systematic desensitization of pervasive anxiety and phobic reactions. *J Psychol,* 1967, *65:*201–208.

Bakal, D. A.: Headache: A biopsychological perspective. *Psycho Bull,* 1975, *82:*369–382.

Benson, H.; Klemchuk, H. P.; and Graham, J. R.: The usefulness of the relaxation response in the therapy of headache. *Headache,* 1974, *13:*49–52.

Berkovec, T. D. and Fowles, D. C.: Controlled investigation of the effects of progressive and hypnotic relaxation on insomnia. *J Abnorm Psychol,* 1973, *82:*153–158.

Berkovec, T. D.; Steinmark, S. W.; and Nau, S. D.: Relaxation training and single-item desensitization in the group treatment of insomnia. *Behav Ther Exp Psychiat,* 1973, *5:*401–403.

Braud, Lendell W.: The effects of EMG biofeedback and progressive relaxation upon hyperactivity and its behavioral concomitants. *Dissertation, Univ. of Houston, 1974.*

Braud, Lendell W.; Lupin, Mimi N.; and Braud, W. G.: The use of electromyographic biofeedback in the control of hyperactivity. *J Learning Disabilities,* 1975, *8:*21–26.

Budzynski, T.: Biofeedback procedures in the clinic. *Sem Psychiat*, 1973, *5*:537–547.

Budzynski, T.; Stoyva, J.; Adler, C. S.; and Mullaney, D. J.: EMG biofeedback and tension headache: A controlled outcome study. *Psychosom Med*, 1973, *35*:484–496.

Budzynski, T. and Stoyva, J.: An electromyographic feedback technique for teaching voluntary relaxation of the masseter muscle. *J Dent Res*, 1973, *52*:116.

Budzynski, T.; Stoyva, J.; and Adler, C.: Feedback-induced muscle relaxation: Application to tension headache. *J Behav Ther Exp Psychiat*, 1970, *1*:205.

Connor, W. H.: Effects of brief relaxation training on autonomic response to anxiety-evoking stimuli. *Psychophysiology*, 1974, *11*:591–599.

Coursey, R. D.: Electromyograph feedback as a relaxation technique. *J Consult Clin Psychol*, 1975, *43*:825–834.

Cox, D. J.; Freundlich, A.; and Meyer, R. G.: Differential effectiveness of electromyograph feedback, verbal relaxation instructions, and medication placebo with tension headaches. *J Consult Clin Psychol*, 1975, *43*:892–898.

Davis, M. H.; Saunders, D. R.; Creer, T. L.; and Chai, A.: Relaxation training facilitated by biofeedback apparatus as a supplemental treatment in bronchial asthma. *J Psychosom Res*, 1973, *17*:121–128.

Fowler, R. and Kraft, G.: Tension perception in patients having pain associated with chronic muscle tension. *Arch Phys Med*, 1974, *55*:28–30.

Good, R.: Frontalis muscle tension and sleep latency. *Psychophysiology*, 1975, *12*:465–467.

Green, E.; Green, A.; and Walters, D.: Voluntary control of internal states: Psychological and physiological. *J Transpersonal Psychol*, 1970, *11*:1–26.

Green, E.; Walter, E. D.; Green, A.; and Murphy, G.: Feedback technique for deep relaxation. *Psychophysiology*, 1969, *6*:371.

Grim, P. F.: Psychotherapy by somatic alteration. *Ment Hyg*, 1969, *53*:451–458.

Grossan, M.: A brief introduction to biofeedback for otolaryngologists. *O R L Digest*, 1975, 15–19.

Hardyck, C.; Petrinovich, L.; and Ellsworth, D. W.: Feedback of speech muscle activity during silent reading: Rapid extinction, *Science*, 1966, *154*:1467–1468.

Haynes, S. N.; Griffin, P.; Mooney, D.; and Parise, M.: Electromyographic biofeedback and relaxation instructions in the treatment of muscle contraction headaches. *Behav Ther*, 1975, *6*:672–678.

Hefferline, R. F.: The role of proprioception in the control of behavior. *Trans. NY Acad. Sci.*, 1958, *20*:739–764.

Hefferline, R. F.; Keenan, B.; and Harford, R. A.: Escape and

avoidance conditioning in human subjects without their observation of the response. *Science*, 1959, *130*:1338–1339.

Hefferline, R. F. and Perera, T. B.: Proprioceptive discrimination of a covert operant without its observation by the subject.
*Science*, 1959, *139*:834–835.

Hutchings, D. F. and Reinking, R. H.: Tension headaches:
What form of therapy is most effective. *J Biofeedback and
Self-Control* (accepted April 1975).

Jacobson, E.: *Progressive Relaxation*. Chicago: University of
Chicago Press, 1958.

Jacobson, E., ed.: *Tension in Medicine*. Springfield, Ill.: Charles
C. Thomas, 1967.

Johnson, D. and Spielberger, C.: The effects of relaxation training and the passage of time on measures of state- and trait-
anxiety. *J Clin Psychol*, 1968, *24*:20–23.

Kahn, M.; Baker, B. L.; and Weiss, J. M.: Treatment of insomnia by relaxation training. *J Abnorm Psychol*, 1968, *73*:556–
568.

Kinsman, R.; O'Banion, K.; Robinson, S.; and Staudenmayer,
H.: Continuous biofeedback and discrete post-trial verbal feedback in frontalis muscle relaxation training. *Psychophysiology*
1975, *12*:30–35.

Kondas, O.: Reduction of examination anxiety and "stage-fright"
by group desensitization and relaxation. *Behav Res Ther*, 1967
5:275.

Krahne, W. and Taneli, B.: EEG and transcendental meditation.
*Pfluger Arch*, 1975, *359(S)*:R95.

Lader, M. H. and Mathews, A.: A physiological model of phobic
anxiety and desensitization. *Behav Res Ther*, 1968, *6*:411–421.

Lehrer, P.: A laboratory analog of "systematic desensitization":
Psychophysiological effects of relaxation. *Psychophysiology*,
1969, *6*:634 (abstract).

Lomont, J. and Edwards, J.: The role of relaxation in systematic desensitization. *Behav Res Ther*, 1967, *5*:11.

Luthe, W.: Autogenic training: Method, research and application
in medicine. *Am J Psychother*, 1963, *17*:174–195.

Lutker, E.: Treatment of migraine headache by conditioned relaxation: A case study. *Behav Ther*, 1971, *2*:592–593.

Mathews, A. M. and Gelder, M. G.: Psychophysiological investigations of brief relaxation training. *J Psychosom Res*, 1969,
*13*:1–12.

McGlynn, F. Dudley; Reynolds, E. Joyce; and Linder, Lowell
H.: Systematic desensitization with pre-treatment and intra-
treatment therapeutic instructions. *Behav Res & Ther*, 1971,
*9*:57–63.

Mitchell, K. R. and Mitchell, D. M.: Migraine: An exploratory
treatment application of programmed behavior therapy techniques. *J Psychosom Res*, 1971, *15*:137–157.

Moustgaard, I. K.: Perception and tonus. *Scand J Psychol*, 1975, *16*:55–64.

Noble, P. J. and Lader, M.: An EMG study of depressed patients. *J Psychosom Res*, 1971, *15*:233–239.

Otis, L. S.: TM and sleep. *APA Proc*, New Orleans, 1974.

Paul, G.: Extraversion, emotionality, and physiological response to relaxation training and hypnotic suggestion. *Int J Clin Exp Hypn*, 1969, *17*:89–98.

Paul, G.: Psychological effects of relaxation training and hypnotic suggestion. *J Abnorm Psychol*, 1969, *74*:425.

Paul, G.: Inhibition of physiological response to stressful imagery by relaxation training and hypnotically suggested relaxation. *Behav Res Ther*, 1969, *7*:249–256.

Paul, G. and Trimble, R.: Recorded vs. "live" relaxation training and hyponotic suggestion: Comparative effectiveness for reducing physiological arousal and inhibiting stress response. *Behav Ther*, 1970, *1*:285–302.

Phillips, R.; Johnson, G.; and Geyer, A.: Self-administered systematic desensitization. *Behav Res Ther*, 1972, *10*:93–96.

Rachman, S.: The role of muscular relaxation in desensitization therapy. *Behav Res Ther*, 1968, *6*:159.

Rachman, S.: Studies in desensitization—I: The separate effects of relaxation and desensitization. *Behav Res Ther*, 1965, *3*:245.

Raskin, M.; Johnson, G.; and Rondestvedt, J.: Chronic anxiety treated by feedback-induced muscle relaxation. *Arch Gen Psychiat*, 1973, *23*:263–267.

Reeves, J. and Mealiea, W.: Biofeedback-assisted cue-controlled relaxation for the treatment of flight phobias. *J Exp Psychol Behav Ther* (in press).

Rugh, J. and Solberg, W.: Electromyographic studies of bruxist behavior before and during treatment. *J Dent Res*, 1975, *54*: L141 (abstract).

Sargent, J.; Green, E.; and Walters, E.: The use of autogenic feedback training in a pilot study of migraine and tension headaches. *Headache*, 1972, *12*:120.

Simard, T. G. and Basmajian, J.V.: Methods in training the conscious control of motor units. *Arch Phys Med*, 1967, *48*:12–19.

Smith, R.: Frontalis muscle tension and personality. *Psychophysiology*, 1973, *10*:311–312.

Spoerri, Th.: Autogenic training and psychosomatic disorders. *Psychother Psychosom*, 1969, *17*:354–364.

Steffen, J.: Electromyographically induced relaxation in the treatment of chronic alcohol abuse. *J Consult Clin Psychol*, 1975, *43*:275.

Stoudenmire, J.: Effects of muscle relaxation training on state and trait anxiety in introverts and extraverts. *J Personality Soc Psychol*, 1972, 273–275.

Tasto, D. and Hinkle, J.: Muscle relaxation treatment for tension headaches. *Behav Res Ther,* 1973, *11*:347–349.

Taub, E. and Berman, A. J.: Movement and learning in the absence of sensory feedback. In:*The Neuropsychology of Spatially Oriented Behavior,* S. J. Freedman (ed.), Dorsey Press, Homewood, Ill., 1968.

Townsend, R. E.; House, J. F.; and Addario, D.: A comparison of biofeedback-mediated relaxation and group therapy in the treatment of chronic anxiety. *Am J Psychiat,* 1975, *132*:598–601.

Wallace, R. K.: Neurophysiology of enlightenment: Scientific Research on transcendental meditation. 26th International Congress of Physiological Sciences, New Delhi, October 1974.

Whatmore, G. B. and Kohli, D. R.: Dysponesis: A neurophysiologic factor in functional disorders. *Behav Sci,* 1968, *13*:102.

Wickramasekera, I.: The application of verbal instructions and EMG feedback training to the management of tension headache-preliminary observations. *Headache,* 1973, *13*:74–76.

Wickramasekera, I.: Effects of electromyographic feedback on hypnotic susceptibility: More preliminary data. *J Abnorm Psychol,* 1973, *82*:74–77.

Wickramasekera, I.: Electromyographic feedback training and tension headache: preliminary observations. *Am J Clin Hypn,* 1972, *15*:83.

Wickramasekera, I.: Instructions and EMG feedback in systematic desensitization: A case report. *Behav Ther,* 1972, *3*:460–465.

Wickramasekera, I.: Effects of EMG feedback training on susceptibility to hypnosis: Preliminary observations. *Proc 79th Annual Conv Am Psychol Assoc,* 1971, *6*:783–784.

Wilson, A. and Wilson, A. S.: Psychophysiological and learning correlates of anxiety and induced muscle relaxation. *Psychophysiology,* 1970, *6*:740–748.

Yemm, R.: Variations in the electrical activity of the human masseter muscle occurring in association with emotional stress. *Arch Oral Biol,* 1969, *14*:874.


*References in Biofeedback Research Society Meeting Abstracts; Colorado Springs, 1974.*

Alexander, A. and Hanson, D.: An experimental test of assumptions relating to the use of EMG biofeedback as a general relaxation training technique.

Clayman, K. and Simkins, L.: The relationship between EMG and mood correlates of the menstrual cycle.

Coursey, R. and Frankel, B.: EMG feedback as a relaxation technique.

Fowler, J. and Budzynski, T.: The effects of an EMG biofeedback relaxation program on the control of diabetes in one patient.

Haynes, S.: Assessment of the comparative effectiveness of electromyographic biofeedback and relaxation training in laboratory and clinical settings.

Le Boeuf, A.: The importance of individual differences in the treatment of chronic anxiety by EMG feedback technique.

Love, W. A., Jr.; Montgomery, D.; and Moeller, T.: A post hoc analysis of correlates of blood pressure reduction.

Montgomery, D. and Besner, H.: Effects of electromyographic relaxation training on self reported sleep patterns in insomniacs.

Montgomery, D.; Love, W. A., Jr.; and Moeller, T.: Effects of electromyographic feedback and relaxation training on blood pressure in essential hypertensives.

Otis, L. S.; McCormick, N. L.; and Lucas, J. S.: Voluntary control of tension headaches.

Rugh, J. D. and Solberg, W. K.: The identification of stressful stimuli in natural environments using a portable feedback unit.

*References in Biofeedback Research Society Meeting Abstracts; Monterey, 1975.*

Austad, R. G.: WIN biofeedback research study.

Breeden, S.; Bean, J. A.; Scandrett, S.; and Kondo, C.: EMG levels as indicators of "relaxation."

Diamond, S. and Franklin, M.: Intensive biofeedback therapy in the treatment of headache.

Disraeli, R. and Perlis, D.: Dental applications of biofeedback.

Freedman, R. and Papsdorf, J.: Biofeedback and progressive relaxation treatment of sleep onset insomnia: A controlled, all night investigation.

Gibb, J.; Stephan, E.; and Rohm, D. E.: Belief in biofeedback: A tentative method for the control of short term stress.

Hutchings, D.; Reinking, R.; Morgret, M.: Tension headaches: What type of therapy is most effective?

Jacobs, D. and Smith, G.: Personality changes as a function of EMG training in a group of marijuana users.

Jordon, C. and Schallow, J.: The role of locus of control in electromyographic feedback and brief progressive relaxation.

Kohli, D. R.: The physiopathology of fatigue and the necessity for thorough neuromuscular biofeedback training.

Kondo, C.; Canter, A.; and Knott, J.: Relaxation training as a method of reducing anxiety associated with depression.

Mehearg, L. E. and Eschette, N.: EMG measures and subjective reports of tension in feedback and no-feedback groups.

Montgomery, D. and Besner, H.: Reduction of chronic onset insomnia through electromyographic relaxation training.

Otis, L. D. and Turner, A.: EMG training and headache reduction: Some methodological issues.

Pagano, R.; Rose, R.; Stivers, R. M.; and Warrenburg, W. S.: Occurrence of sleep in transcendental meditation.

Reeves, J. L.: EMG-biofeedback reduction of tension headache: A cognitive skills training approach.

Simkins, L. and Clayman, K.: EMG biofeedback: Control of menstrual distress.

Staples, R. and Coursey, R.: Comparison of EMG feedback with two other relaxation techniques.

Staudenmayer, H.: Awareness: Of signal or process?

Townsend, R. and Addario, D.: Treatment of chronic anxiety with biofeedback-mediated electromyographic relaxation: A comparison study.

Travis, T. A.; Kondo, C. Y.; and Knott, J. R.: Heart rate, muscle tension, and alpha production of transcendental mediators and controls.


*References in Biofeedback Research Society Meeting Abstracts; Colorado Springs, 1976.*

Diamond, S. and Franklin, M.: Biofeedback—choice of treatment in childhood migraine.

Engelhardt, L.: The application of biofeedback techniques within a public school setting.

Freedman, R.: Generalization of frontalis EMG biofeedback training to other muscles.

Gregg, R.; Frazier, L.; and Nesbit, R. A.: Effects of techniques of biofeedback on relaxation during childbirth.

Haight, M.; Irvine, A.; and Jampolsky, G.: Response of hyperkinesis to EMG biofeedback.

Hauri, P.; Phelps, P.; and Jordan, J.: Biofeedback as a treatment for insomnia.

Kleinman, K.M.: Use of EMG feedback to inhibit flexor spasticity and increase active extension in stroke patients.

Kleinman, Kenneth M.; Keister, Michael E.; Riggin, Carole S.; Goldman, H.; and Korol, Bernard: Use of EMG feedback to inhibit flexor spasticity and increase active extension in stroke patients.

Miller, M.; Murphy, P.; Miller, T.; and Smouse, A.: The effects of EMG feedback and progressive relaxation training on stress reactions in dental patients.

Montgomery, P. S.: A basis for individualizing biofeedback.

Otis, L. S. and Low, D.: The use of timers to reduce tension headache frequency: Failure to replicate.

Sheridan, C.L.; Boehm, M. B.; Ward, L. B.; and Justesen, D. R.; Autogenic-biofeedback, autogenic phrases, and biofeedback compared.

Strauss, N.: Electromyographic biofeedback versus suggestion in inducing muscle relaxation—A test for placebo effects.

Weinstock, S. A.: The reestablishment of intestinal control in functional colitis.

## Chapter 4. Neuromuscular Re-education

Andrews, J. M.: Neuromuscular re-education of the hemiplegic with the aid of the electromyograph. *Arch Phys Med Rehab*, 1964, *45*:530–533.

Basmajian, J. V. and Newton, W. J.: Feedback training of parts of buccinator muscle in man. *Psychophysiology*, 1974, *11*:92.

Basmajian, J. V.; Kukulka, C. G.; Narayan, M. G.; and Takebe, K.: Biofeedback treatment of foot-drop after stroke compared with standard rehabilitation technique: Effects on voluntary control and strength. *Arch Phys Med*, 1975, *56*:231–236.

Boman, K.: Effect of emotional stress on spasticity and rigidity. *J Psychosom Res*, 1971, *15*:107–112.

Booker, H.; Rubow, R. T.; and Coleman, P. J.: Simplified feedback in neuromuscular retraining: An automated approach using electromyographic signals. *Arch Phys Med*, 1969, *50*: 621–625.

Brudny, J.; Grynbaum, B. B.; and Korein, J.: Spasmodic torticollis: Treatment by feedback display of the EMG. *Arch Phy Med*, 1974, *55*:403–408.

Brudny, J.; Korein, J.; Levidow, L.; Grynbaum, B. B.; Lieberm A.; and Friedmann, L. W.: Sensory feedback therapy as a modality of treatment in central nervous system disorders of voluntary movement. *Neurology*, 1974, *24*:925–932.

Engel, W. K.: Brief, small, abundant motor-unit action potentials. *Neurology*, 1975, *25*:173–176.

Gavin, J.: Techniques and strategies for neuromuscular re-education. *Am. Psychol. Assoc. Abstr.*, 1976.

Harrison, A. and Connolly, K.: The conscious control of fine levels of neuromuscular firing in spastic and normal subjects. *Develop Med Child Neurol*, 1971, *13*:762–771.

Hart, J.: Solid state electronic behavior in biological systems. *Insulation Circuits*, 1975, 27–29.

Jacobs, A. and Felton, G.: Visual feedback of myoelectric output to facilitate muscle relaxation in normal persons and patients with neck injuries. *Arch Phys Med*, 1969, *50*:34–39.

Johnson, H. and Garton, W.: Muscle re-education in hemiplegia by use of electromyographic device. *Arch Phys Med*, 1973, *54*:320–322.

Lloyd, A. and Leibrecht, B.: Conditioning of a single motor unit. *J Exp Psychol*, 1971, *88*:391–395.

Marinacci, A. and Horande, M.: Electromyogram in neuromuscular re-education. *Bull LA Neurol Soc*. 1960, *25*:57–71.

Martin, J. and Sachs, D.: The effects of visual feedback on the fine motor behavior of a deaf cerebral palsied child. *J Nerv Ment Dis*, 1973, *157*:59–62.

Petajan, J.: Clinical electromyographic studies of diseases of the motor unit. *Electroenceph Clin Neurophysiol*, 1974, *36*:395–401.

Swann, D.; van Wieringen, P.; and Fikkema, S.: Auditory electromyographic feedback therapy to inhibit undesired motor activity. *Arch Phys Med*, 1974, *55*:251–254.

Vodovnik, L and Rebersek, S.: Information content of myo-control signals for orthotic and prosthetic system. *Arch Phys Med*, 1974, *55*:52–56.

Wagman, I.; Pierce, D.; and Burger, R.: Proprioceptive influence in volitional control of individual motor units. *Nature*, 1965, *207*:957–958.


*References in Biofeedback Research Society Meeting Abstracts; Colorado Springs, 1974.*

Gessel, A. and Harrison, S.: Case report: Bilateral EMG feedback in the treatment of chronic dislocation.


*References in Biofeedback Research Society Meeting Abstracts; Monterey, 1975.*

Finley, W. and Niman, C.: EMG biofeedback and cerebral palsy.

Russ, K. L.: EMG biofeedback of spasmodic torticollis: A case presentation.

Taylor, L. P.: Muscle reeducation of the post CVA victim using the electromyometer with audio feedback.


*References in Biofeedback Research Society Meeting Abstracts; Colorado Springs, 1976.*

Finley, W. W.; Niman, C.; Standley, J.; and Phifer, R.: Frontalis EMG biofeedback training of cerebral palsy children.

Gavin, J. and Stephen, K.: Biofeedback Muscle Re-education: A Review of Ten Clinical Cases.

# Chapter 5. Cardiovascular Biofeedback

## HEART RATE

Bell, I. R. and Schwartz, G. E.: Voluntary control and reactivity of human heart rate. *Psychophysiology*, 1975, *12*:339–348.

Blanchard, E. B.; Scott, R. W.; Young, L. D.; and Edmunson, E. D.: Effect of knowledge of response on the self-control of heart rate. *Psychophysiology*, 1974, *11*:251–264.

Blankstein, K. R.: Note on relation of autonomic perception to voluntary control of heart rate. *Percept Motor Skills*, 1975, *40*:533–534.

Bleecker, E. R. and Engel, B. T.: Learned control of ventricular rate in patients with atrial fibrillation. *Sem Psychiat*, 1973, *5*:461–474.

Bleecker, E. R. and Engel, B. T.: Learned control of cardiac rate and cardiac conduction in the Wolff-Parkinson-White syndrome. *New Engl J Med*, 1973, *288*:560–562.

Brener, J. and Kleinman, R. A.: Learned control of decreases in systolic blood pressure. *Nature*, 1970, *226*:1063–1064.

Cerny, M. and Dolezalo, V.: Biofeedback voluntary and hypnotic control of autonomic functions. *Activ Nerv Sup (Praha)*, 1975, *17*:37–38.

Di Cara, L. V. and Miller, N. E.: Heart-rate learning in the noncurarized state, transfer to the curarized state, and subsequent retraining in the noncurarized state. *Psychol Behav*, 1969, *4*:621–624.

Engel, B. T.: Clinical applications of operant conditioning techniques in the control of the cardiac arrhythmias, *Sem Psychiat*, 1973, *5*:433–438.

Engel, T. and Melmon, L.: Operant conditioning of heart rate in patients with cardiac arrhythmias. *Cond Reflex*, 1968, *3*:130.

Gatchel, R. J.: Change over training sessions of relationships between locus of control and voluntary heart rate control. *Percept Motor Skills*, 1975, *40*:424–426.

Green, E. E.; Green, A. M.; and Walters, E. D.: Voluntary control of internal states: Psychological and physiological. *J Transpers Psychol*, 1970, *2*:1–26.

Hirschman, R.: Cross-modal effects of anticipatory bogus heart rate feedback in a negative emotional context. *J Personality Soc Psychol*, 1975, *31*:13–19.

Katkin, E. S. and Murray, E. N.: Instrumental conditioning of automatically mediated behavior: Theoretical and methodological issues. *Psychol Bull*, 1968, *70*:52–68.

Lang, P. J. and Twentyman, C. T.: Learning to control heart rate: binary vs analogue feedback. *Psychophysiology*, 1974, *11*:616–629.

McCanne, T. R. and Sandman, C. A.: Determinants of human operant heart rate conditioning: A systematic investigation of several methodological issues. *J Comp Physiol Psychol*, 1975, *88*:609–618.

McCanne, T. R. and Sandman, C. A.: Instrumental heart rate responses and visual perception: A preliminary study. *Psychophysiology*, 1974, *11*:283–287.

McFarland, R. A. and Herrmann, J. A.: Precise voluntary heart control in humans. *Psychol Rep*. 1974, *35*:925–926.

McFarland, R. A. and Coombs, R.: Anxiety and feedback as factors in operant heart rate control. *Psychophysiology*, 1974, *11*:53–57.

McFarland, R. A.: Heart rate perception and heart rate control. *Psychophysiology*, 1975, *12*:402–405.

Manuck, S. B.; Levenson, R. W.; Hinrichsen, J. J.; and Gryll, S. L.: Role of feedback in voluntary control of heart rate. *Percept Motor Skills*, 1975, *40*:747–752.

Obrist, P. A.; Galosy, R. A.; Lawler, J. E.; Gaebelein, C. J.; Howard, J. L.; and Shanks, E. M.: Operant conditioning of heart rate: Somatic correlates. *Psychophysiology*, 1975, *12*: 445–455.

Prigatano, G. P. and Johnson, H. J.: Biofeedback control of heart rate variability to phobic stimuli: A new approach to treating spider phobia. *Proc APA Convention*, 1972, *80*:403–404.

Ray, W. J.: The relationship of locus of control, self-report measures, and feedback to the voluntary control of heart rate. *Psychophysiology*, 1974, *11*:527–534.

Scott, R. W.; Blanchard, E. B.; Edmunson, E. D.; and Young, L. D.: A shaping procedure for heart rate control in chronic tachycardia. *Percept Motor Skills*, 1973, *37*:327–338.

Scott, R. W.; Peters, R. D.; Gillespie, W. J.; Blanchard, E. B.; Edmunson, E. D.; and Young, L. D.: The use of shaping and reinforcement in the operant acceleration and deceleration of heart rate. *Behav Res Ther*, 1973, *11*:179–185.

Sirota, A.; Schwartz, G.; and Shapiro, D.: Voluntary control of human heart rate: Effect on reaction to aversive stimulation. *J Abnorm Psychol*, 1974, *83*:261–267.

Sovak, M.; Fronek, A.; Helland, D. R.; and Doyle, R.: Effects of vasomotor changes in the upper extremities on the hemodynamics of the carotid arterial beds: a possible mechanism of biofeedback therapy of migraine. (A preliminary report) *Proc. San Diego Biomed. Symp.*, 1976, *15*:363–367.

Stephens, J. H.; Harris, A. H.; Brady, J. V.; and Shaffer, J. W.: Psychological and physiological variables associated with large magnitude voluntary heart rate changes. *Psychophysiology*, 1975, *12*:381–387.

Suppan, P.: Feedback monitoring in anaesthesia II: Pulse rate control of halothane administration. *Brit J Anaesth*, 1972, *44*:1263–1270.

Troyer, W. G.; Twentyman, C. T.; Gatchel, R. J.; and Lang, P. J.: Learned heart rate control in patients with ischemic heart disease. *Psychophysiology*, 1973, *10*:213.

Weiss, T. and Engel, B. T.: Evaluation of an intra-cardiac limit of learned heart rate control. *Psychophysiology*, 1975, *12*:310–312.

Wickramasekera, I.: Heart rate feedback and the management of cardiac neurosis. *J Abnorm Psychol*, 1974, *83*:578–580.

Williams, J. L. and Adkins, J. R.: Voluntary control of heart rate during anxiety and oxygen deprivation. *Psychol Rec*, 1974, *24*:3–16.

*References in Biofeedback Research Society Meeting
Abstracts; Colorado Springs, 1974.*

Blankstein, K.; Egner, K.; and Tafts, J.: Individual differences in the self-control of heart rate: Locus of control.

Blankstein, K.; Tafts, J.; and D'Ambrosia, D.: Psychopathy and the voluntary control of heart rate: Implications for lie detection.

Brener, J. M. and Shanks, E. M.: The interaction between instructions and augmented sensory feedback in the training of cardiovascular control.

Murphy, P. and Smith, B.: Cognitive and respiratory mediation and tonic heart level in operant cardiac conditioning.

Tafts, J. C. and Blankstein, K.: Volunteer effects on the feedback control of heart rate: Achieving tendency.

*References in Biofeedback Research Society Meeting
Abstracts; Monterey, 1975.*

Blankstein, K. R.: Test-retest consistency and stability of subject differences in bidirectional cardiac control: A one year follow-up of good versus poor controllers.

Dale, A. and Anderson, D.: Feedback variables (field dependence, heart rate perception, shock sensitivity, and analog biofeedback) in the experimental control of human heart rate.

Davidson, R. J. and Schwartz, G. E.: Sex differences in cerebral lateralization during cardiac self-regulation versus affect self generation.

Rayter, B. and Sandler, L: The effect of cardiac variability and cardiac awareness upon heart rate conditionability.

Schneider, R.; Darte, E.; and Blankstein, K.: Learning to control heart rate: Continuous trial vs. discrete post-trial feedback.

Sirota, A.; Shapiro, D.; and Schwartz, G; Self regulation of heart rate and perception of a noxious stimulus.

Surwit, Richard S. and Shapiro, David: Digital temperature autoregulation and associated cardiovascular changes.

*Reference in Biofeedback Research Society Meeting
Abstracts; Colorado Springs, 1976.*

Zimmerman, J. and Blankstein, K.: Sex and tonic heart rate differences in the ability to control heart rate.

## BLOOD PRESSURE

Akagi, M.; Yoshimura, M.; and Ohno, Y.: Clinical applications of biofeedback techniques. Symposium *Biofeedback Conditioning,* 3rd Congress of International College of Psychosomatic Medicine, Rome, 1975.

Benson, H.; Shapiro, D.; Tursky, B.; and Schwartz, G.: Decreased systolic blood pressure through operant conditioning techniques in patients with essential hypertension. *Science,* 1971, *173:*740–742.

Brener, J. and Kleinman, R. A.: Learned control of decreases in systolic blood pressure. *Nature,* 1970, *226:*1063–1064.

Elder, S. T.; Ruiz, Z. R.; Deabler, H. L.; and Dillenkoffer, R. L.: Instrumental conditioning of diastolic blood pressure in essential hypertensive patients. *J Appl Behav Anal,* 1973, *6:*377–382.

Ternstedt, G. C. and Newcomer, J. P.: Blood pressure and pulse wave velocity measurement for operant conditioning of autonomic responding. *Behav Res Methods Instr,* 1974, *6:* 393–397.

Kleinman, K. M.; Goldman, Herbert; Snow, Murial Y.; and Korol, Bernard: Effects of stress and motivation on effectiveness of biofeedback training in essential hypertensives.

Kristt, D. A. and Engel, B. T.: Learned control of blood pressure in patients with high blood pressure. *Circulation,* 1975, *51:*370–378.

Moeller, T. A.: Reduction of arterial blood pressure through relaxation training and correlates of personality in hypertensives. Doctoral Dissertation, Nova University, 1973.

Patel, C.: 12-month follow-up of yoga and biofeedback in the management of hypertension. *Lancet,* 1975, ii, 62.

Patel, C.: Yoga and biofeedback in the management of "stress" in hypertensive patients. *Clin Sci Molecular Med,* 1975, *48:* 171s–174s.

Patel, C.: Randomised controlled trial of yoga and biofeedback in management of hypertension. *Lancet,* 1975, ii, 93.

Patel, C.: Yoga and biofeedback in the management of hypertension. *Lancet,* 1973, ii, 1053.

Schwartz, G. E. and Shapiro, D.: Biofeedback and essential hypertension: Current findings and theoretical concerns. *Sem Psychiat,* 1973, *5:*491–503.

Schwartz, G. E.: Voluntary control of human cardiovascular integration and differentiation through feedback and reward. *Science,* 1972, *175:*90–93.

Schwartz, G. E.; Shapiro, D.; and Tursky, B.: Learned control of cardiovascular integration in man through operant conditioning. *Psychosom Med,* 1971, *33:*57.

Schwartz, G. E.: Operant conditioning of human cardiovascular integration and differentiation. *Psychophysiology,* 1971, *8:*245.

Shapiro, D.; Tursky, B.; Gershon, E.; and Stern, M.: Effects of feedback and reinforcement on the control of human systolic blood pressure. *Science,* 1969, *163:*588.

Shapiro, D.; Tursky, B.; and Schwartz, G. E.: Differentiation of heart rate and systolic blood pressure in man by operant conditioning. *Psychosom Med,* 1970, *32:*417.

Shapiro, D.; Tursky, B.; and Schwartz, G. E.: Control of blood pressure in man by operant conditioning. Suppl I to *Circ Res,* 1970, *26 & 27:* 1–27.

Shapiro, D.; Schwartz, G. E.; and Tursky, B.: Control of diastolic blood pressure in man by feedback and reinforcement. *Psychophysiology,* 1972, *9:*296.

*References in Biofeedback Research Society Meeting Abstracts; Colorado Springs, 1974.*

Love, W. A.; Jr.; Montgomery, D. D.; and Moeller, T. A.: Working Paper Number 1. Nova University Biofeedback Laboratory.

Montgomery, D. D.; Love, W. A., Jr.; and Moeller, T. A.: Working Paper Number 2. Nova University Biofeedback Laboratory.

Patel, C. and Datey, K. K.: Relaxation and biofeedback technique in the management of hypertension.

Russ, K. L.: Effect of two different feedback paradigms on blood pressure levels of patients with essential hypertension.

*References in Biofeedback Research Society Meeting Abstracts; Monterey, 1975.*

Datey, K. K.; Deshmukh, S. N.; Dalvi, C. P.; and Vinekar, S. L.: Effect of relaxation using biofeedback instruments in systematic hypertension.

Love, W. A., Jr.; Montgomery, D. D.; and Weston, A. A.: The treatment of essential hypertension with EMG feedback and blood pressure feedback.

McGrady, A.; Mitch, P. S.; Iannone, A.; and Marks, R.: Effect of direct biofeedback of systolic blood pressure on systolic and diastolic blood pressure of essential hyptertensives.

Patel, C.: Yoga and biofeedback in the management of stress in hypertensive patients.

Weston, A.; Love, W. A., Jr.; and Montgomery, D. D.: Combining feedback methods for blood pressure reduction.

*References in Biofeedback Research Society Meeting Abstracts; Colorado Springs, 1976.*

Sedlacek, K.: A combination of EMG, GSR and peripheral temperature training for treatment of hypertension.

Walsh, P.; Dale, A.; Brethauer, L.; Eagan, R.; Frick, J.; Ostrowski, N.; Walberg, M.; and Weiss, S.: A comparison of pulse wave velocity feedback coupled with verbal sphygmomanometric feedback versus deep relaxation treatments in drug controlled and non-drugged essential hypertensives.

## VASOCONSTRICTION

Koppman, J. W.; McDonald, R. D.; and Kunzel, M. G.: Voluntary regulation of temporal artery diameter by migraine patients. *Headache*, 1974, *14*:133.

Machac, M.: Vasomotor response to intentional autoregulative operations of the relaxation activation method. *Activ Nerv Sup (Paraha)*, 1969, *11*:42.

Shean, G. D.: Vasomotor conditioning and awareness. *Psychophysiology*, 1968, *5*:22.

Snyder, C. and Noble, M.: Operant conditioning of vasoconstriction. *J Exp Psychol*, 1968, *77*:263.

Stern, R. M. and Pavloski, R. P.: Operant conditioning of vasoconstriction: a verification. *J Exp Psychol*, 1974, *102*:330–332.

Volow, M. R. and Hein, P. L.: Bidirectional operant conditioning of peripheral vasomotor responses with augmented feedback and prolonged training. *Psychophysiology*, 1972, *9*:271.

Zamani, R.: Treatment of migraine headache: Biofeedback versus deep muscle relaxation (unpublished manuscript, University of Minnesota).

*References from Biofeedback Research Society Meeting Abstracts; Monterey, 1975.*

Savill, G. E. and Koppman, J. W.: Voluntary temporal artery regulation compared with finger blood volume and temperature.

## SKIN TEMPERATURE BIOFEEDBACK

Bakal, D. A.: Headache: A biophysiological perspective. *Psychol Bull*, 1975, *82*:369–382.

French, D. J.; Leeb, C. S.; and Boerner, G. L.: Theoretical applications of biofeedback hand temperature training to prepared (Lamaze) childbirth training. *Percept Mot Skills*, 1973, *37*:326.

Grabowska, M. J.: Changes of skin temperature during hypnotic suggestion. *Pol Tyg Lek*, 1970, *25*:328.

Jacobson, A. M.; Hackett, T. P.; Surman, O. S.; and Silverberg, E. L.: Raynaud phenomenon. Treatment with hypnotic and operant technique. *JAMA*, 1973, *225*:739.

McDonagh, J. M. and McGinnis, M.: Skin temperature increases as a function of base-line temperature, autogenic suggestion, and biofeedback. *Proc 81st Ann Conv APA*, 1973, 547–548.

Maslach, C.; Marshall, G.; and Zimbardo, P. G.: Hypnotic control of peripheral skin temperature: A case report. *Psychophysiology*, 1972, *9*:600.

Newman, R. W.: Autoregulation of finger temperature. *Am J Physical Anthrop*, 1975, *42*, 320 (abstract).

Sargent, J. D.; Walters, E. D.; and Green, E. E.: Psychosomatic self-regulation of migraine headaches. *Sem Psychiat*, 1973, *5*:415–427.

Sargent, J. D.; Green, E. E.; and Walters, E. D.: The use of autogenic feedback training in a pilot study of migraine and tension headaches. *Headache*, 1972, *12*:120–124.

Surwit, R. S.: Biofeedback: A possible treatment for Raynaud's disease. *Sem Psychiat*, 1973, *5*:483–490.

Wickramasekera, I.: Temperature feedback for the control of migraine. *J Behav Ther Exp Psychiat*, 1973, *4*:343–345.


*References in Biofeedback Research Society Meeting Abstracts; Colorado Springs, 1974.*

Bertelson, A. and Klein, M.: The effects of autogenic and anti-autogenic phrases on ability to increase and decrease hand temperature.

Diamond, S. and Franklin, M.: Indications and contraindications for the use of biofeedback therapy in headache patients.

Engel, R. R. and Schaefer, S.: Operant control of forehead skin temperature.

Keefe, F. J.: The effect of instructions upon the conditioning of changes in absolute skin temperature.

Leeb, C.; French, D.; Fahrion, S.; and DeJoseph, F.: Voluntary control of hand temperature: Increase and decrease.

Leeb, C.; Fahrion, S.; and French, D.: The effect of instructional set on autogenic biofeedback hand temperature training.

Peper, E. and Grossman, E. R.: Preliminary observation of thermal biofeedback training in children with migraine.

Roberts, A. H.; Schuler, J.; Bacon, J.; and Zimmerman, R. L.: Individual differences and autonomic control: Absorption, hypnotic susceptibility and the unilateral control of skin temperature.

Russell, H. L.; Hunter, S. H.; and Russell, E. D.: The ability of elementary school children to learn autoregulation of fingertip skin temperature: preliminary results.

Surwit, R. S. and Shapiro, D.: Skin temperature feedback and concomitant cardiovascular changes.

Taub, E.; Emurian, C.; and Howell, P.: Further progress in training self-regulation of skin temperature.


*References in Biofeedback Research Society Meeting Abstracts; Monterey, 1975.*

Clayman, K. K. and Simkins, L.: The relationship of temperature control to menstrual distress.

Drury, R. L.; DeRisi, W.; and Liberman, R.: Temperature

feedback treatment for migraine headache: A controlled study.

Eversaul, G. A.: The treatment of arthritis and other functional disorders resulting from circulatory dysponesis, by feedback thermometer training and nutrition.

French, D. J.; Leeb, C. S.; and Fahrion, S.: Biofeedback hand temperature training in the mentally retarded.

Mitch, P. S.; McGrady, A.; and Iannone, A.: Autogenic feedback training in treatment of migraine: A clinical report.

Pearse, B. A.; Walters, E. D.; Sargent, J. D.; and Meers, M.: Exploratory observations of the use of an intensive autogenic biofeedback training (IAFT) procedure in a follow-up study of out-of-town patients having migraine and/or tension headaches.

Surwit, R. S. and Shapiro, D.: Digital temperature autoregulation and associated cardiovascular changes.

Turin, A.: Biofeedback for migraines.

*References in Biofeedback Research Society Meeting Abstracts; Colorado Springs, 1976.*

Datey, K. K.: Temperature regulation in the management of hyptertension.

May, D. S. and Weber, C. A.: Temperature feedback training for symptom reduction in Raynaud's disease: A controlled study.

Stephenson, N. L.: Two cases of successful treatment of Raynaud's disease with relaxation and biofeedback training and supportive psychotherapy.

# Chapter 6. Gastrointestinal Biofeedback

Engel, B. T.; Nikoomanesh, P; and Schuster, M. M.: Operant conditioning of recto-sphinctric responses in the treatment of fecal incontinence. *New Eng J Med*, 1974, *290*:646–649.

Furman, S.: Intestinal biofeedback in functional diarrhea: A preliminary report. *J Behav Ther Exp Psychiat*, 1973, *4*:317–321.

Gray, E. R.: Conscious control of motor units in a tonic muscle. *Am J Phys Med*, *50*:34–40.

Kohlenberg, R. J.: Operant conditioning of human anal sphincter pressure. *J Appl Behav Anal*, 1973, *6*:201–208.

Moore, J. G. and Schenkenberg, T.: Psychic control of gastric acid: response to anticipated feeding and biofeedback training in a man. *Gastroenterology*, 1974, *66*:954–959.

Schuster, M. M.: Operant conditioning in gastrointestinal dysfunctions. *Hospital Practice*, 1974, 135–143.

Welgan, P.: Learned control of gastric acid secretion in ulcer patients. *Psychosom Med*, 1974, *36*:411–419.

Whitehead, W. E.; Renault, P. F.; and Goldiamond, I.: Modification of human gastric acid secretion with operant-conditioning procedures. *J Appl Behav Anal*, 1975, 8:147–156.

*Reference in Biofeedback Research Society Meeting Abstracts; Monterey, 1975.*

Gorman, P.: Biofeedback and the regulation of human gastric acid.

*Reference in Biofeedback Research Society Meeting Abstracts; Colorado Springs, 1976.*

Beaty, E. T.: Feedback-assisted relaxation training as a treatment for gastric ulcers.

## Chapter 7. Brain Wave Biofeedback

Baron, J.: An EEG correlate of autonomic discrimination. *Psychon Sci*, 1966, 4:255.

Beatty, J.: Similar effects of feedback signals and instructional information on EEG activity. *Physiol Behav*, 1972, 9:151.

Brown, B. B.: Recognition of aspects of consciousness through association with EEG alpha activity represented by a light signal. *Psychophysiology*, 1970, 6:442.

Brown, B. B.: Awareness of EEG-subjective activity relationships detected within a closed feedback system. *Psychophysiology*, 1971, 7:451.

Cazard, P.: Synchronie interhemispherique des rhythmes alpha parieto-occipitaux attention et experience consciente. *Annee Psychol*, 1974, 74:7–22.

Coger, R. and Werbach, M.: Attention, anxiety, and the effects of learned enhancement of EEG alpha in chronic pain: A pilot study in biofeedback. In B. L. Drue, Jr. (ed.) *Pain Research and Treatment.* New York, N.Y., Academic Press, 1975.

Das, N. N. and Gastaut, H.: Variations de l'activite electrique du cerveau, du coeur et des muscles squelettiques au cours de la meditation et de l'extase yogique. *Electroenceph Clin Neurophysiol (Suppl)*, 1955, 6:211.

Dimond, Stuart J. and Beaumont, J. Graham: "Experimental Studies of Hemisphere Function in the Human Brain" in *Hemisphere Function in the Human Brain,* Dimond and Beaumont, eds. A Halstead Press Book, John Wiley & Sons, N.Y., 1974.

Doyle, J. C.; Ornstein,; R. and Galin, D.: Lateral specialization of cognitive mode: II. EEG frequency analysis. *Psychophysiology*, 1974, 11:567–578.

Dumas, R. and Morgan. A.: EEG asymmetry as a function of occupation, task, and task difficulty. *Neuropsychologia*, 1975, 13:219–228.

Fenwick, P. B. C.; Donaldson, S.; Bushman, J.; Gillis, L.; and Fenton, G. W.: EEG and metabolic changes during transcendental meditation. *Electroenceph Clin Neurophysiol,* 1975, *39:*220–221.

Finley, W. and Smith, H.: Sensorimotor EEG biofeedback training of epileptics: A replication study. *Electroenceph Clin Neurophysiol,* 1975, *38:*336 (abstract).

Gannon, L. and Sternbach, R.: Alpha enhancement as a treatment for pain: A case study. *J Behav Ther Exp Psychiat,* 1971, *2:*209–213.

Goesling, W.; May, C.; Lavond, D.; and Barnes, T.: Relationship between internal and external locus of control and the operant conditioning of alpha through biofeedback training. *Percept Motor Skills,* 1974, *39:*1339–1343.

Hardt, J. V.: Alpha EEG responses of low and high anxiety males to respiration and relaxation training and to auditory feedback of occipital alpha. *Dis Abstr Int,* 1974, *35.*

Hoffman, E. and Willanger, R.: Low arousal induced by EMG and EEG feedback in various patient groups: description of the methodology in a pilot study. *Electroenceph Clin Neurophysiol,* 1975, *39:*557.

Hord, D.; Naitoh, P.; and Johnson, L.: Intensity and coherence contours during self-regulated high alpha activity. *Electroenceph Clin Neurophysiol,* 1972, *32:*429.

Johnson, R. and Meyer, R.: The locus of control construct in EEG alpha rhythm feedback, *J Consult Clin Psychol,* 1974, *42:*913.

Johnson, R. and Meyer, R.: Phased biofeedback approach for epileptic seizure control. *J Behav Ther Exp Psychiat,* 1974, *5:*185–187.

Kirschbaum, J. and Gistle, E.: EEG-alpha-prozent, alpha-feedback, angst und entspannung bei klinisch unauffalligen studenten. *Arch Psychol,* 1973, *125:*263–273.

Kondo, C. Y.; Travis, T. A.; and Knott, J. R.: The effects of changes in motivation on alpha enhancement. *Psychophysiology,* 1975, *12:*388–389.

Korein, J.; Maccario, M.; Carmona, A.; Randt, C. T.: and Miller, N.: Operant conditioning techniques in normal and abnormal EEG states. *Neurology,* 1971, *21:*395 (abstract).

Kuhlman, W. N. and Klieger, D. M.: Alpha enhancement: Effectiveness of two feedback contingencies relative to a resting baseline. *Psychophysiology,* 1975, *12:*456–460.

McKenzie, R.; Ehrisman, W.; Montgomery, P. S.; and Barnes, R. H.: The treatment of headache by means of electroencephalographic biofeedback. *Headache,* 1974, *13:*164–172.

Martindale, C. and Armstrong, J.: The relationship of creativity to cortical activation and its operant control. *J Genet Psychol,* 1974, *124:*311–320.

Melzack, R. and Perry, C.: Self-regulation of pain: the use of alpha feedback and hypnotic training for the control of chronic pain. *Exp Neurol*, 1975, *46*:452-469.

Mills, G. K. and Solyom, L.: Biofeedback of EEG alpha in the treatment of obsessive ruminations: An exploration. *J Behav Ther Exp Psychiat*, 1974, *5*:37-41.

Morgan, A. H.; Macdonald, H.; and Hilgard, E.: EEG alpha: Lateral asymmetry related to task, and hypnotizability. *Psychophysiology*, 1974, *11*:275-282.

Nowlis, D. and Wortz, E.: Control of the ratio of midline parietal to midline frontal EEG alpha rhythms through auditory feedback. *Percept Motor Skills*, 1973, *37*:815-824.

Nunn, C. M. H. and Osselton, J. W.: The influence of the EEG alpha rhythm on the perception of visual stimuli. *Psychophysiology*, 1974, *11*:294-303.

O'Malley, J. E. and Comers, C. K.: The effect of unilateral alpha training on visual-evoked response in a dyslexic adolescent. *Psychophysiology*, 1972, *9*:467.

Sheer, D.: Biofeedback training of 40 Hz EEG and behavior. In N. Burch and H. Altschuler (eds.) *Behavior and Brain Electrical Activity*, New York, N.Y., Plenum Press, 1975.

Sterman, M. B.: Neurophysiologic and clinical studies of sensorimotor EEG biofeedback training: Some effects on epilepsy. *Seminars Psychiat*, 1973, *5*:507-525.

Sterman, M. B. and Friar, L.: Suppression of seizures in an epileptic following sensorimotor EEG feedback training. *Electroenceph Clin Neurophysiol*, 1972, *33*:89-95.

Sterman, M. B.; Macdonald, L. R.; and Stone, R.: Biofeedback training of the sensorimotor EEG rhythm in man: Effects on epilepsy. *Epilepsia*, 1974, *15*:385-416.

Stigsby, B.; Risberg, J.; and Ingvar, D. H.: EEG changes in the dominant hemisphere during memorizing and reasoning in normal subjects. *Electroenceph Clin Neurophysiol*, 1975, *38*:214.

Travis, T. A.; Kondo, C. Y.; and Knott, J. R.: Parameters of eyes-closed alpha enhancement. *Psychophysiology*, 1974, *11*:674-681.

Valle, R. S. and Levine, J. M.: Expectation effects in alpha wave control. *Psychophysiology*, 1975, *12*:306-309.

Verbaten, M.; Beaujon, J.; and Sjouw, W.: EEG alpha rhythm, ocular activity and basal skin resistance. *Acta Psychol (Amst)*, *39*:153-160.

Walsh, D. H.: Interactive effects of alpha feedback and instructional set on subjective state. *Psychophysiology*, 1974, *11*:428-435.

Wenger, M. A.; Bagchi, B. K.; and Anand, B. K.: Experiments in India on "voluntary" control of the heart and pulse. *Circulation*, 1971, *24*:1319-1327.

Werbach, M. R.: Psychiatric applications of biofeedback. *Psychiatry Digest*, 1974, April: 23-27.

Werbach, M. R.: General clinical experience with biofeedback. UCLA Seminar on New Therapeutic Approaches with Biofeedback, 1975, Asilomar, Calif.

Yamaguchi, Y.; Niwa, K.; and Negi, T.: Feedback of midfrontal theta activity during mental work and its voluntary control. *Electroenceph Clin Neurophysiol*, 1973, *34*:704–705.

*References in Biofeedback Research Society Meeting Abstracts; Colorado Springs, 1974.*

Andreychuk, T. and Skriver, C.: Hypnosis and biofeedback in the treatment of migraine headache.

Brown, B. B. and Klug, J. W.: Exploration of EEG alpha biofeedback as a technique to enhance rapport.

Feinstein, B. and Sterman, M. B.: Effects of sensorimotor rhythm biofeedback training on insomnia.

Finley, W. W.: Reduction of seizures and normalization of the EEG in a severe epileptic following sensorimotor biofeedback training.

Kaplan, B. J.: EEG biofeedback and epilepsy.

Klug, J. W. and Brown, B. B.: Learned control of EEG theta activity.

Kondo, C.; Knott, J. R.; and Travis, T. A.: The effects of varying levels of motivation on performance in alpha enhancement training.

Kuhlman, W. N.: Topography and long term feedback training of sensorimotor area EEG activity in normal human subjects.

Pelletier, K. R.: Neurological, psychophysiological, and clinical parameters of alpha, theta, and the voluntary control of bleeding and pain.

Rouse, L.; Peterson, J.; and Shapiro, G.: EEG alpha entrainment reaction to the biofeedback setting and some possible effects on epilepsy.

Selzer, F. A. and Fehmi, L. G.: Auto-regulation of EEG alpha wave production as a function of the direction of conjugate lateral eye movements.

Sterman, M. B.: Somatic and cognitive correlates of the sensorimotor rhythm in man.

Stoyva, J.; Budzynski, T.; Sittenfeld, P.; and Yaroush, R.: A two-step EMG-theta feedback training in sleep onset insomnia: Preliminary results.

Travis, T. A.; Kondo, C.; and Knott, J. R.: Subjective reports following feedback training of the occipital alpha rhythm.

Weber, E. S. and Fehmi, L. G.: The therapeutic use of EEG biofeedback.

*References in Biofeedback Research Society Meeting
Abstracts; Monterey, 1975.*

Ancoli, S.: Authoritarianism, introspection, and alpha wave biofeedback conditioning.

Bean, J. A.; Kondo, C. Y.; Travis, T. A.; and Knott, J. R.: Changes in heart rate associated with increases in occipital alpha.

Birbaumer, N. and Lutzenberger, W.: An experiment on the feedback of the theta activity of the human EEG.

Brolund, J. W. and Schallow, J. R.: The effects of feedback, reward, and locus of control on occipital alpha enhancement.

Childers, C. A.: Modification of social behavior problems by alpha biofeedback training.

Chisholm, R. C.; Valle, R. S.; Adams, A. S.; and DeGood, D. E.: Effects of occipital alpha training on EEG response to a laboratory stressor.

Don, N. S.: Cortical activity changes during a psychotherapeutic procedure: Implications for EEG biofeedback training.

Finley, W. W.: Seven weeks noncontingent feedback after one year of SMR BFT in a severe epileptic: Follow-up study.

Hardt, J. V.: Relaxation during breathing feedback, yogic breathing, and alpha feedback: Effects on alpha EEG activity in low and high anxiety males.

Legewie, H.: Subjective correlates of EEG feedback: Discrimination learning or superstition.

Lubar, J. F. and Seifert, A. R.: Patient control of the sensorimotor rhythm in the management of epilepsy.

Moore, R. T.: Alpha training, instructional set and hypnotic susceptibility.

Newton, F. A.; Bird, B. L.; and Sheer, D. E.: Conditioning and suppression of 40 Hz EEG activity in humans: Analysis of voluntary control and subjective states.

Poirier, Fernand: Traitement de l'epilepsie par retroaction.

Twemlow, S. W.; Bowen, W. T.; and Wilson, T.: Personality and functional change in alcoholics following alpha-theta biofeedback.

Valle, R. S.; Chisholm, R. C.; and DeGood, D. E.: The relationship of state and trait personality factors to alpha-controlling ability.


*References in Biofeedback Research Society Meeting
Abstracts; Colorado Springs, 1976.*

Benjamins, J. K.: The effectiveness of alpha feedback training and muscle relaxation procedures in systematic desensitization.

Graham, C.; Fotopoulos, S.; Cohen, H.; and Cook, M.: The use of biofeedback during acute opiate withdrawal.

Kuhlman, W. M.: EEG feedback training in epileptic patients: Clinical and neurophysiological analysis.

Lubar, J. F.: Maintenance of seizure control in epileptics during long term sensorimotor rhythm (SMR) training and post training follow-up.

Shouse, M. N. and Lubar, J. F.: Management of the hyperkinetic syndrome in children concurrent with sensorimotor rhythm (SMR) biofeedback training.

Sterman, M. B.; Macdonald, L. R.; Lucia, M.; and Walsh, G.: Effects of operant conditioning of central cortical EEG patterns on epilepsy.

# ADDITIONAL READING

Related adventures in reading. Some books are directly related to biofeedback, stress, or relaxation.

Alland, A. *The Human Imperative.* New York: Columbia University Press, 1972.

Assagioli, R. *The Act of Will.* Baltimore: Penguin Books, 1974.

Basmajian, J. V. *Muscles Alive,* Baltimore: Williams and Wilkins, 1967.

Bateson, G. *Steps to an Ecology of Mind.* New York: Ballantine Books, 1973.

Beech, H. R. *Changing Man's Behavior.* Baltimore: Penguin Books, 1969.

Benson, H. *The Relaxation Response.* New York: William Morrow, 1975.

Bernstein, D. and Borkovec, T. D.: *Progressive Relaxation Training: A Manual for the Helping Professions.* Champaign, Ill.: Research Press, 1973.

*Biofeedback and Self-Control.* An Aldine Annual on the Regulation of Bodily Processes and Consciousness. Chicago: Aldine, 1970, 1971, 1972, 1973, 1974, 1975/76.

Borger R. and Seaborne, A. E. M. *The Psychology of Learning.* Baltimore: Penguin Books, 1966.

Brown, B. B. *The Biofeedback Syllabus.* Springfield, Ill. Charles C. Thomas, 1975.

———. *New Mind, New Body.* New York: Harper & Row, 1974.

———. and Klug, J. W. *The Alpha Syllabus.* Springfield, Ill.: Charles C. Thomas, 1974.

Calder, N. *The Mind of Man.* New York: Viking Press, 1970.

Dixon, N. F. *Subliminal Perception: The Nature of a Controversy.* New York: McGraw-Hill, 1971.

Dodwell, P. C., ed. *New Horizons in Psychology 2.* Baltimore: Penguin Books, 1972.

Elliott, H. C. *The Shape of Intelligence.* New York: Charles Scribner & Sons, 1969.

Eysenck, H. J. *Sense and Nonsense in Psychology.* Baltimore: Penguin Books, 1957.

Faraday, A. *Dream Power*. New York: Berkeley, 1973.

Feldenkrais, M. *Awareness Through Movement*. New York: Harper & Row, 1972.

Ferguson, M. *The Brain Revolution*. New York: Taplinger, 1973.

Fink, D. H. *Release from Nervous Tension*. New York: Simon & Schuster, 1965.

Freedman, S. *The Neuropsychology of Spatially Oriented Behavior*. Homewood, Ill.: Dorsey Press, 1968.

Freese, A. S. *Pain*. New York: Penguin Books, 1975.

Friedman, M. and Rosenman, R. H. *Type A Behavior and Your Heart*. Greenwich, Conn.: Fawcett, 1974.

Gregory, R. L. *The Intelligent Eye*. London: Weidenfeld & Nicolson, 1970.

Hangen, G.; Dixon, H.; Dickel, H. *A Therapy for Anxiety Tension Reactions*. New York: The Macmillan Co., 1959.

Hess, H. *The Human Animal*. New York: G. P. Putnam's Sons, 1970.

Jacobson, E. *Tension Control for Businessmen*. New York: McGraw-Hill, 1968.

———. *You Must Relax*. New York: McGraw-Hill, 1962.

Janis, I. L. *Stress and Frustration*. New York: Harcourt Brace Jovanovich, 1969.

Jonas, G. *Visceral Learning: Toward a Science of Self-Control*. New York: Cornerstone Library, 1974.

Key, W. B. *Subliminal Seduction*. New York: Signet, 1974.

Krishna, G. *The Awakening of Kundalini*. New York: E. P. Dutton, 1975.

*Kriya*. Monghyr (Bihar): Bihar School of Yoga, 1974.

Leonard, G. B. *The Transformation*. New York: Delacorte Press, 1972.

Le Shan, L. *How to Meditate*. Boston: Little Brown, 1974.

Lilly, J. C. *The Center of the Cyclone*. New York: Julian Press, 1972.

———. *The Human Biocomputer*. New York: Bantam Books, 1974.

———. *Simulations of God*. New York: Simon & Schuster, 1956.

Luce, G. G. *Body Time*. New York: Pantheon Books, 1971.

McCartney, J. *Yoga: The Key to Life*. London: Rider & Co., 1972.

McKellar, P. *Experience and Behavior*. Baltimore: Penguin Books, 1968.

McQuade, W. and Aikman, A. *Stress*. New York: Bantam Books, 1974.

Masters, R. and Houston, J. *Mind Games*. New York: Viking Press, 1972.

Meerlov, J. A. M. *The Rape of the Mind*. New York: Universal Library, 1961.

Mines, S. *The Conquest of Pain.* New York: Grosset & Dunlap, 1974.

Montagu, A. *Touching: The Human Significance of the Skin.* New York: Columbia University Press, 1971.

Morgan, C. T. *Physiological Psychology.* New York: McGraw-Hill, 1965.

Murphy, G. *Outgrowing Self-Deception.* New York: Basic Books, 1975.

Naranjo, C. and Ornstein, R. *On the Psychology of Meditation.* New York: Viking Press, 1971.

Nathan, P. *The Nervous System.* Philadelphia: J. B. Lippincott, 1969.

Obrist, P. A.; Black, A. H. et al., eds. *Cardiovascular Psychophysiology.* Chicago: Aldine, 1974.

Ornstein, R., ed. *The Nature of Human Consciousness.* San Francisco: W. H. Freeman, 1973.

———. *The Psychology of Consciousness.* New York: Viking Press, 1972.

Osmond, H.; Osmundsen, J.; Agel, J. *Understanding Understanding.* New York: Harper & Row, 1974.

Parsegian, V. L. *This Cybernetic World of Men, Machines, and Earth Systems.* New York: Anchor Books, 1973.

Pearce, J. C. *The Crack in the Cosmic Egg.* New York: Julian Press, 1971.

Penfield, W. *The Mystery of the Mind.* Princeton: Princeton University Press, 1975.

Porter, A. *Cybernetics Simplified.* New York: Barnes & Noble, 1970.

Progoff, I. *Jung, Synchronicity, and Human Destiny.* New York: Julian Press, 1973.

———. *The Symbolic and the Real.* New York: Julian Press, 1963.

Rose, S. *The Conscious Brain.* New York: Alfred A. Knopf, 1973.

Rosenfeld, A. *The Second Genesis: The Coming Control of Life.* New York: Arena Books, 1972.

Saraswati, P. S. *Tantra of Kundalini Yoga.* Monghyr (Bihar), 1971.

———. *Yogasanas Pranayama Mudra Bandah.* Monghyr (Bihar): Bihar School of Yoga, 1971.

Selye, H. *The Stress of Life.* New York: McGraw-Hill, 1956.

———. *Stress Without Distress.* Philadelphia: J. B. Lippincott, 1974.

Skinner, B. F. *Beyond Freedom and Dignity.* New York: Alfred A. Knopf, 1971.

Stevens, L. A. *Explorers of the Brain.* New York: Alfred A. Knopf, 1971.

Strongman, K. T. *The Psychology of Emotion.* New York: John Wiley & Sons, 1973.

Taylor, J. G. *The Shape of Minds to Come.* Baltimore: Penguin Books, 1974.

Thompson, W. I. *Passages About Earth.* New York: Harper & Row, 1973.

Thomson, R. *The Psychology of Thinking.* Baltimore: Penguin Books, 1959.

Vernon, M. D. *Human Motivation.* New York: Cambridge University Press, 1972.

————. *The Psychology of Perception.* Baltimore: Penguin Books, 1962.

Weil, A. *The Natural Mind.* Boston: Houghton Mifflin, 1972.

Weil, J. L. *A Neurophysiological Model of Emotional and Intentional Behavior.* Springfield, Ill.: Charles C. Thomas, 1974.

Whatmore, G. and Kohli, D. R. *The Physiopathology and Treatment of Functional Disorders.* New York: Grune & Stratton, 1974.

Wickramasekera, I., ed. *Biofeedback, Behavior Therapy and Hypnosis.* Chicago: Nelson-Hall, 1976.

Wilentz, J. S. *The Senses of Man.* New York: Thomas Y. Crowell, 1968.

Wright. D. *The Psychology of Moral Behavior.* Baltimore: Penguin Books, 1971.

*Yoga-Mimamsa:* A Quarterly Journal Devoted to Scientific and Philosophic-Literary Research in Yoga. Kaivalyadhama, Lonavla (Maharashtra-India), 1973.

# INDEX

## ABOUT THE AUTHOR

BARBARA B. BROWN is an expert in psychiatry, pharmacology and cardiovascular physiology. She is associated with the Sepulveda Veterans Hospital and with the UCLA Medical School. Recognized as a creative researcher, and in wide demand as a lecturer, she was one of the pioneers in the work that resulted in the development of the stress-reducing techniques of biofeedback. Dr. Brown has edited two reference books, *The Bio-Feedback Syllabus* and *The Alpha Syllabus,* the latter with J. Klug. She is the author of the first comprehensive book on biofeedback, *New Mind, New Body.*

# Bantam Book Catalog

Here's your up-to-the-minute listing of every book currently available from Bantam.

This easy-to-use catalog is divided into categories and contains over 1400 titles by your favorite authors.

So don't delay—take advantage of this special opportunity to increase your reading pleasure.

Just send us your name and address and 25¢ (to help defray postage and handling costs).

---

**BANTAM BOOKS, INC.**
Dept. FC, 414 East Golf Road, Des Plaines, Ill. 60016

Mr./Mrs./Miss_____
(please print)

Address_____

City_____State_____Zip_____

Do you know someone who enjoys books? Just give us their names and addresses and we'll send them a catalog too!

Mr./Mrs./Miss_____

Address_____

City_____State_____Zip_____

Mr./Mrs./Miss_____

Address_____

City_____State_____Zip_____

FC—6/77

# Bantam
## On Psychology